RUNNING THE RAPIDS

K. Dobbs Esquire
Scribbler

R. Searle 58
sketcher

RUNNING
THE RAPIDS
A WRITER'S LIFE

Kildare Dobbs

Dundurn Press
Toronto

Library and Archives Canada Cataloguing in Publication

Dobbs, Kildare, 1923–
    Running the rapids: a writer's life / Kildare Dobbs.

ISBN-10: 1-55002-594-5
ISBN-13: 978-1-55002-594-1

    1. Dobbs, Kildare, 1923– 2. Authors, Canadian (English)—20th century—Biography. I. Title.

PS8507.O35Z472 2005   C818'.5409   C2005-903979-5

1   2   3   4   5   09   08   07   06   05

Conseil des Arts du Canada   Canada Council for the Arts   Canadä   ONTARIO ARTS COUNCIL CONSEIL DES ARTS DE L'ONTARIO

We acknowledge the support of the Canada Council for the Arts and the Ontario Arts Council for our publishing program. We also acknowledge the financial support of the Government of Canada through the Book Publishing Industry Development Program and The Association for the Export of Canadian Books, and the Government of Ontario through the Ontario Book Publishers Tax Credit program, and the Ontario Media Development Corporation.

Printed and bound in the United Kingdom by MPG Books.

www.dundurn.com

Dundurn Press
3 Church Street, Suite 500
Toronto, Ontario, Canada
M5E 1M2

Dundurn Press
2250 Military Road
Tonawanda NY
U.S.A. 14150

Co-published in Ireland with The Lilliput Press, Dublin

for Bryan Montgomery & Gunnar Stromshbolm
semper aliquid novi

Preface

I do not admire my own past or earlier selves. When I pass a mirror I do not pause to adjust my necktie, if any, or gaze long and pensively at dear me. Nor is looking back on earlier days my favourite occupation. So why do I think it worthwhile to tell this story of my life?

I have my reasons. My life has been interesting and I've enjoyed most of it. My story is that of a man raised in an already obsolete tradition, and educated for a role that no longer existed, who nevertheless managed to become a different sort of person, better adapted to the tempestuous times in which he found himself. The change was achieved with some pain. I had to go through a time of promise, only to be publicly shamed and disgraced, and then, from the depths of disillusion, to find my way into a more worthwhile life. No recovery would have been possible without the support of family and friends. In different ways, this is a progress many people make in the quest for their true vocation, for the work they are meant to be doing.

When I was born in India, the British empire dominated the world. In Ireland, though, where I grew up, British authority had been overthrown. My countrymen, who had done so much to conquer and hold the territories and dominions of the British Crown, and were so active in ruling and administering the empire, had abandoned it in disgust. 'When we got out,' a Dublin workman recently said to me, 'the whole shebang collapsed. And a good job too.' The Irish had also begun to rewrite their history, and to celebrate a new

7

national myth. Those decried as seditious malcontents were now revered as heroes and martyrs.

Although I first became conscious in the 1920s, a time of modernization in many other places, my little world in rural Ireland was socially backward, still Victorian. Brought up in a country house with servants, I lived in a large family without wireless, telephone, electricity or labour-saving machines. We had many books, which we read by candlelight, and made our own music and entertainment. Protestants in an overwhelmingly Catholic population, we received a quite erroneous idea of ourselves as different from our neighbours and of finer quality. Rather than muck in with the barefoot children in the national school, my siblings and I began our education at home with governesses. My brother Bernard and I went on to a small private boarding school lit by gaslight where, with the help of canes, blazers and bibles, we began what was essentially training for imperial responsibility. The social model was the gentleman, the paragon of courtesy and of competence without visible striving.

Meanwhile the call was to serve. In the fullness of time Bernard, after war service in the Rifle Brigade and Gurkhas, and some years as an East India merchant, became the last British ambassador to Laos. I myself was for a short while a district officer in East Africa, after wartime service at sea and in Combined Operations with the Royal Navy. More than a year as an ordinary seaman had corrected my ideas about being different or superior; all that mattered was whether or not your shipmates could rely on you. By the time I left Africa, the empire was at its last gasp. Exhausted by war and hard-won victory, the metropolis no longer believed its own myth. Its illusions had withered after the loss of Singapore.

Ours was a childhood of privilege, though the modest family income was steadily eroded by inflation between the world wars. My father was never without a servant, though at the time of his death there was only one left. Privilege came with public duty. Ancestors and kinsfolk had served the empire. Grandfather Bernard, a divine, was also a privy councillor; his father had died building the Bengal railway. Cousin Vivian Bernard was an admiral; two great-grandfathers were inspectors general of Fleet Hospitals. Great-uncle Herbie had commanded his regiment in India. Aunt Alice worked in the Foreign Office; Great-aunt Eva was matron of the Royal Naval Hospital at Portsmouth; Father was one of the men who ruled India. In the Great War two uncles, a great-uncle and an uncle by marriage, all regular officers, were killed in action. We remembered them in the two minutes silence on Armistice Day, though my brother and I had never known them. In World War II the Irish Free State was neutral, while hundreds of thousands of Irish volunteers, including three of our six sisters and us boys, joined the British forces. Others worked in large numbers in British war industries.

Travel overseas was in ships. Not until the fifties did air-travel become the rule. Postal service was swift, efficient and cheap; long-distance telephone unreliable. Telegrams were delivered by bicycle from the post office. Television had been invented in the thirties, though it was not generally available until twenty years later. In medicine, antibiotics were discovered, penicillin coming into use during World War II.

After the war, technology began to flourish, with new inventions appearing at ever-shorter intervals. Domestic servants were replaced with labour-saving appliances and products. Motorways were constructed to allow faster, safer travel by car. Feminism enfranchised women. Supermarkets rationalized distribution of consumer goods, driven by television advertising and marketing. From the late seventies the world became dominated by the computer revolution. The information-highway may have helped to bring down the Soviet tyranny.

Rudyard Kipling had addressed a prophetic poem to Theodore Roosevelt, 'Take up the White Man's burden'. The United States took over the imperial mission with ever-increasing military power to enforce it. After World War II the world entered the long freeze known as the Cold War. For years the Soviet Union and the US faced each other down with nuclear deterrents. When the Soviet empire collapsed from within, the US claimed victory and, ludicrously, 'the end of history'.

I not only witnessed these events, I took part in them. Leaving Ireland at eighteen to join the British navy, I moved about in the world. No longer a gentleman, entitled to respect, I was now a working stiff living by his wits. I was going straight.

After personal disaster in Africa, where the imperial nannies were deserting their charges, I migrated to Canada to begin a new life. The African experience had given me ambition. I was not pursuing a distant goal – I made up my life as I went along. Times were changing too fast for anyone to set and pursue an objective. Like people in a canoe running the rapids, our whole concern is to keep off the rocks.

Writing memoirs is like looking at a beach where the tides have thrown up litter, kelp, seashells. Trying to make sense of the flotsam and jetsam of memory, I began to travel extensively in the eighties, which opened new perspectives. No longer believing in a fixed point of view, I saw myself as a mind on the move, open to change.

I married three times, first when I was just twenty-one during World War II, committing to life at a time when foresight was impossible. Two sons were born to us before we parted after ten years. The second marriage lasted thirteen years, with two daughters. The third marriage will last my time.

Throughout these changes, I never lost the ambition to be a writer, and to be a poet, even though I did other things. My interest in narrative was not so much in fiction; it came from a desire to show the world as I saw it. I explored places for the same reason that the poet Rimbaud took drugs: for alienation, for the estrangement that clears the eyes and permits vision. I took up the ancient literary form – older than the novel – of travel-narrative, reaching a climax over the millennium, when I spent four months voyaging around the earth, traversing oceans and straits, recording a weekly column for CBC News on Line, sent by satellite from the ship.

When inspiration deserted me, poetry was the thread that ran through all my days. I had no specific goal. The reader who expects a Horatio Alger story, a success tale, progressing from rags to riches or from innocence to wisdom, will be disappointed.

A more apt image of the life that invents itself as it goes along is the medieval wheel of Fortune, now up, now down. It's not a funeral march, like Samuel Beckett's *Worstward Ho!* I do not invite misery by thinking about the end at the beginning, and complaining because the end is always lamentably the same. I am so far from being a planner that I have tried to free my thoughts from foresight. A saying of Jesus, preserved in the Muslim tradition and written over the great gate of the deserted city of Fatehpur Sikri, strikes me with the force of revelation, 'Life is a bridge; build no houses but pass over.'

And so, as Aristotle had it, let us observe the natural order, and begin at the beginning.

$$One$$

Early in 1923 Maudie Dobbs was pregnant again and this time her five daughters were told to pray for a brother. Joan and Nancy, the two eldest, were living at the Provost's House at Trinity College, Dublin, with Grandpa and Granny Bernard; Kitty, Mary and Lucinda were with Maudie in India at Commissioner's House, Meerut, where her husband Evelyn was acting commissioner. The little girls in India took their instruction seriously, to the point of preparing a crib for the baby in one of the empty rooms of the immense house. They had seen little naked Indian boys in the bazaars and knew what they looked like. So, to back up their prayers, they sewed little cloth tubes into the groins of their rag dolls. And they prayed earnestly that this time the baby be sent to the children instead of the grown-ups.

On 10 October their prayers were answered, but only in part. At an early hour that day a brother was born, but not to the children. Kitty lost her faith. Mary decided to bide her time and kill him. Lucinda thought, I will love my little brother. Evelyn recorded in his journal the birth of an ugly baby boy. I was yellow and jaundiced, though not in any danger. The Commissioner Sahib was not really disappointed. He took extraordinary measures to celebrate the nativity of an heir, ordering fireworks with a setpiece of burning letters spelling out the legend 'GOD BLESS W.E.J. DOBBS ESQ.', his own name.

Over the great pile of Commissioner's House, the Union Jack

of empire flaunted its red, white and blue in the bright sunlight of India's cold weather. Despite cracks in the fabric after four years of devastating war, the empire was still the most powerful the world had seen, with dominions, colonies, protectorates and territories from the Arctic tundra to the Indies and South Seas. India was the most cherished possession, its teeming millions ruled by a few hundred white officials, my father among them. 'The British Empire', said Tim Healy, an Irish Nationalist MP, 'is a vast outdoor relief scheme for the better classes.'

I was named Kildare, after my great-grandfather (1800–68), under-agent of the vast Wandesforde estate in Castlecomer, Ireland; Robert, after Maudie's brother Lieutenant Robert Bernard of the Royal Dublin Fusiliers, killed at Gallipoli, 1915; and Eric, after Evelyn's brother Lieutenant Colonel Eric Dobbs of the Royal Engineers, killed in Flanders, 1917.

The next year, as the hot weather approached, Mama took us four children home to Dublin, renting a house at 43 Fitzwilliam Place, where we were together with our sisters.

Everything I have said to this point is hearsay. Memories begin in St Stephen's Green in Dublin with a nurse I disliked, my sister Lucinda whom I loved, and my new brother, Bernard, in his pram. While the nurse chatted with friends, Lucinda and I played on the walks, kept off the grass by Crosspatch, a red-faced keeper with a spiked stick to collect litter.

These memories are vignettes, like magic lantern slides.

We loved to visit Grandpa Bernard in the Provost's House. He had resigned the archbishopric of Dublin in 1919 to become provost at the urging of Lloyd George, who thought that in revolutionary times the college needed strong leadership. The change was unpopular; legend has it that undergraduates threw pennies at Grandpa as he took up his new appointment, implying that he did it for money. He became a stern, conservative provost, though very kind to us children. He liked to take us in a horse-drawn cab to the zoo. We also rode in his big Fiat saloon car. A window shut us off from the chauffeur, but we talked to him through a voice pipe.

Lucinda and I were in St Stephen's Green one morning when the nurse seized our hands and dragged us to the railings. A funeral was passing, on its way to St Patrick's Cathedral, led by a glass hearse drawn by black horses with sable plumes. Onlookers parted to let us through. There were respectful murmurs, 'It's their grand-daddy, the poor little dotes.'

Grandpa was a Victorian polymath, who won his fellowship as a mathematician, translated Immanuel Kant, edited texts in Latin and Greek, became lecturer in divinity and left a lasting monument in his critical *Commentary on St John's Gospel*. He also wrote charming travel essays. On his death, Granny Bernard moved to England, where the king gave her an apartment in Hampton Court Palace.

After that, I remember the voyage back to India in 1927, with Mama, two-year-old Bernard and the nurse. We were aboard the P&O liner *China*, fogbound in the river Mersey. Before we got under way on 6 October 1927, Mama wrote to Granny Bernard from the ship: 'Nurse is being very absurd and refusing to go to din-ner in the 2nd class because it is too grand! She says she couldn't eat where there are ladies and gentlemen! She'll have to get over that feeling, I'm afraid, or she won't get enough to eat.'

Daddy met us at the gangway in Bombay. I knew him right away. Mama reported, 'He was so pleased to see Evelyn and tried to copy him reading the newspaper!' and said it was such a blessing to have another man in the house. We travelled to Delhi by train, Daddy repelling the beggars, saints and vendors who assailed pas-sengers at every station. At last we arrived at Budaun in the United Provinces, where Daddy was now Collector, governing a large dis-trict by the Ganges. Mama was a reluctant memsahib, resisting the stiff protocol of government wives.

Memories of this time are especially radiant, probably because I kept them to offset the miseries of boarding school and Irish weather. There was a garden full of flowers behind the big, pillared house. In one memory, seen from the veranda in clear sunlight, the compound was teeming with monkeys, the beautiful langurs who fought for the god Rama in Hindu scripture. A bearer came out on the veranda with a shotgun. He fired into the air. All the monkeys took off like scalded cats, leaving the garden to the weaver birds and bee-eaters.

In Daddy's office there was red sealing wax and a candle to melt it. He used his gold signet ring with the unicorn head to make seals. There was always a stack of files tied with pink ribbon, the famous red tape that prevented corrupt action, or indeed any action at all. On a leather chair were 12-bore cartridges, red or green ones, and a few that were yellow – don't touch! A silver tortoise crouched on the desk; if its head was pressed a bell rang summoning a turbaned messenger immediately.

The household employed about thirty servants. The *kitmagar*, or butler, was a venerable man with a white beard named Supan. He had been with my father for twenty years, with an interlude when he was briefly dismissed by Mama in a vain attempt to gain control of the house. As his name sounded like soup-on, I remember him bringing soup to the table. There were several bearers, there was the cook and his helpers, fiercely whiskered *chokidars* and *chuprassies* or armed guards, *dhobis* (launderers), a *darzee* (tailor), *saises* to look after the horses, a *bhisti* to carry water, a barber, valets, gardeners, orderlies, sweepers and hangers-on. And always there was the nurse with her hairbrush, castor oil and nursery sayings.

How old was she? 'As old as my tongue and a wee bit older than my teeth!' 'Don't care was made to care.' 'Handsome is as handsome does.' 'Why? *That's* the why!' 'Curiosity killed the cat.' 'Ask no questions, ye'll be told no lies, inquisitive people never grow wise.' 'Pride comes before a fall.' 'Little pitchers have big ears.' 'It's a pity about ye!' 'Don't make a face! If the wind changes that's the face ye'll have for ever!'

On the whitewashed walls, pale geckoes waited to snap up flies and other insects. How did they run up walls and across ceilings? Ask no questions. We slept under mosquito nets. Some nights we could hear hyenas roar and chuckle. Out there, too, were leopards and tigers.

Bernard and I were treated like little princes. All this was part of the imperial con-game. The Indian rulers kept splendid state. His Majesty's servants could not be less splendid. For them, however, the grandeur was tempered with irony. The Collector Sahib knew that he would soon retire to modest comfort, perhaps in a suburb.

Every day we were taken for a ride on a government elephant assigned for our use. Our own elephant! For children it was the summit of happiness. When we left India, we missed our elephant more than anything. It was not full grown; the young mahout had to squat on its shoulders. When he hit its trunk with a heavy cane, it cried like a baby.

We did not go to the circus. It came to us in the compound, with acrobats and dancing bears. In one glowing memory Mama, Bernard and I sit in a gilded *howdah* on a caparisoned elephant escorted by turbaned spearmen. Daddy leads the procession on a bigger elephant, a couple more elephants behind carrying garlanded *nawabs* and officials. All around us an immense silent crowd of Indian men in white turbans and *dhotis* stare and whisper. There were times in later life when I doubted this memory – until I found a tattered photograph that proved it true.

The best times were in camp, when we lived in tents. The evil-tempered camels that carried our baggage, snarling as they were loaded, scared me. Once we rode elephants on our way to Narora, on the Ganges Canal, where there was a dam and power station (today a nuclear generator). At the start of this trip, the nurse and we boys were roped onto a huge black bull elephant, with Mama on a smaller female. Our elephant began to trumpet, toss his head and act up – he was in *musth,* a state that resembles madness. The mahout cursed and beat him on the head with his iron *ankus.* We held tight to the ropes. The nurse screamed 'I'm getting off!' Mama now showed her steely nerve, yelling at the nurse to stay put and hold onto the children. Had the woman jumped off, the bull would almost certainly have trampled her to death.

The mahout brought the beast under control. We were taken off and remounted on a safe cow-elephant. Crossing wide sands, we came to the bungalow where we were to stay.

One of the bearers was my dear friend. He carried me on his bicycle to watch the Delhi Express roar by. He caught turtles and at night stuck lighted candles with wax on their shells. We watched them amble toward the Ganges and saw their lights extinguished as they sank into the black stream. The bearer never let me near the bank, which was infested with muggers, big crocodiles that Daddy sometimes shot. In his office there was a little gold bracelet taken from a mugger's stomach.

One morning Daddy took me with him to inspect the jail. He said this was where bad men were shut up until they learned to be good. Everything – walls, steps, buildings – was white. Prisoners wore white cotton. In the heat of the shadeless yard, they hung around the water pump taking turns to drink. The cooks were Brahmins, so that other castes could eat without being polluted. The bad men smiled when they saw me and put their palms together in greeting.

My religion was Mama's care. The nurse was Roman Catholic. She was not supposed to impose her religion, although naturally could not help crossing herself at moments of panic. Where did God live? Above the blue sky, where there was a home for little children. That meant the sky was the floor of Heaven, so there must be another sky above it where another God lived, and another above that, and another and another. Like the thought of eternity, it was too much. But I did want to be good and not get sent to jail.

Meanwhile I was growing into my family, a numerous race with many stories.

Two

Mama's maiden name was Bernard, a Norman family from Kerry. She was the eldest child of Archbishop Bernard and his cousin Nannie Bernard, who grew up in Caen, Normandy. Mama's sister Alice was in the British Foreign Office. Her brother Robbie, a lieutenant in the Royal Dublin Fusiliers, was killed at Gallipoli. Her brother Sidney served in the British navy and went to South America with the consular service.

Mama was the one who taught us nursery rhymes and read stories and poems to us. She found children amusing. An Edwardian lady, she employed nursemaids and governesses to deal with the boring parts of raising a family, but she also knew how to comfort and reassure us when we were scared by a thunderstorm or loud fireworks. And she insisted on peace among warring siblings. 'Let not the sun go down upon your wrath' was the slogan.

Maudie had met Evelyn Dobbs and his equally tall, blond brothers at a house party. Eric, gallant soldier and athlete, was the lady's man – Maudie found him tiresome. She thought Evelyn, shy though he was, the best of the lot. Besides, as the daughter of a scholar, she had a prejudice in favour of intellect. Evelyn had graduated from Trinity College, Cambridge, with a double first in law and classics. Against him was his domicile in India, not that the place was outlandish. Her father had been born in India, where her grandfather, a civil engineer, had died of sunstroke while building the Bengal railway. Her brother Robbie had also served in India. Uncle Herbie

Bernard had been colonel of the Rattray's Sikhs until his retirement in 1914, when he came home to command a battalion of Royal Irish Rifles. A full colonel, he was killed leading them at the Somme.

Evelyn came from a large clan of whiskery, sporting Dobbses who flourished in Castlecomer, County Kilkenny, at the end of the nineteenth century and before the Great War. Great-grandfather Kildare Dobbs had been agent for the 200,000-acre Wandesforde estate. He was succeeded by his eldest son William. His younger son Joseph was Evelyn's father, who leased the anthracite mines on the estate and made a fortune, supporting a bevy of female relations, which gave them the right to nag and bully him. Willie and Joseph Dobbs, with brother-in-law Willie Edge and short-lived nephew Dicky Swan, comprised the Castlecomer polo team, champions of All Ireland in 1878 and 1879, beating all-comers including the rich British cavalry regiments.

Evelyn and Maudie had been married in St Patrick's Cathedral on 4 June 1914. Grandpa, Bishop of Ossory since 1911, performed the ceremony. Cousin Herbert Grierson gave away the bride. The reception in the Deanery may have been the last function at which so many magnates of mid-Leinster were assembled. In July 1914, an assassin's bullet in Sarajevo blew away their comfortable world, as the Great War with Germany and the Central Powers broke out, and so many young soldiers marched away to die.

At intervals during four years of war, dreadful news reached India in cables and telegrams from the War Office and Whitehall: Robbie and Herbert Bernard and Eric Dobbs killed, John Dobbs a prisoner, brother-in-law Barry Hartwell killed, Robert Grove White wounded. Such was the carnage that the bereaved felt they had little time for private sorrow. Worst of all from the imperialist viewpoint, Ireland rose in rebellion in 1916. Soon the peaceful country houses of Maudie's youth were in flames and their owners leaving Ireland forever.

We children could have been a sort of consolation. But Evelyn, though genial in manner, was a pessimist, all set to be disappointed in us, especially the girls. If Maudie was an Edwardian,

Evelyn was a Victorian through and through, gloomy, sentimental, given to hero-worship.

One could accuse the Castlecomer Dobbses of bad timing. They had risen into the gentry just in time for their decline and fall. Evelyn himself joined the Indian Civil Service at exactly the wrong moment. Something like affirmative action was beginning, Indians being promoted over the heads of more senior, sometimes better-qualified men. The intention was admirable, since it allowed the British to leave India with a sound administration, but it was often unjust to individual officers, including Evelyn.

Mama took us boys with her on her last voyage home, leaving Daddy to his last tour of duty. I remember our ship anchoring off Port Sudan in East Africa. Bernard and I were in our best sailor-suits, Mama very smart in a big hat. Standing at the ship's rail we were watching a white launch. A bluejacket stood at its bow, boathook at the ready. I imagined it was coming to take our captain ashore. The launch glided up to our ship's ladder. 'Come along,' Mama said, 'This is the governor's launch. It's for us.' Passengers lined the rail to watch us board. And away we went to take tea with the British governor, a family friend, in his residence. On his hands and knees the governor chased me under the table, growling.

Retired at fifty, Daddy sailed home to join us. He had ruled Indians; now he had no one to rule but us. As he and Mama roamed the Irish Free State looking for a country seat (there was no question of settling in Ulster), we wandered in a wilderness of lodgings. And now I encountered a strange contradiction in Daddy's misogyny, his reverence for dear old hags, some related to us, some not.

Chief of the dear old hags was Granny Dobbs, an invalid – for idle women the role could be a relief. She lay in a dim room called the lounge in her big, *art nouveau* mansion on Temple Road in Rathmines. Joseph Dobbs had died here; in the fullness of time Evelyn too would breathe his last in the house.

Granny was attended by three maids and Nora the cook. Every Sunday she would go for an excursion in her car, driven by Mickey

McDonald. Mickey took his meals at the kitchen table, served by Nora. They had not spoken for twelve years.

Then there was Annie Harte, known to Daddy as plain 'Auntie', one of Granny Dobbs' formidable maiden sisters. She lived in the Mageough Home for 'the habitation, support and clothing of aged Protestant females'. Auntie was an original, a crank, agnostic, vegetarian, anti-vivisectionist and dead set against the taking of life.

Another maiden sister of Granny's, Eva Harte, had followed the lamp of Florence Nightingale to become a naval nurse, retiring as matron of the Royal Naval Hospital at Portsmouth.

At last we settled at Viewmount, near Gowran in County Kilkenny, a Victorian mansion with walled gardens and fine trees. It was not far from Castlecomer, where Father had grown up, and about eleven miles from Kilkenny, where Grandpa had been bishop from 1911 to 1915. While the house was being done up, we waited as paying guests in Brandondale, near Graiguenamanagh. Other paying guests included mad Miss Boskin and a retired colonial planter. The widow Burchaell had managed to retain her house by taking in lodgers like ourselves.

Intoxicated by spring wildflowers, I filled my bedroom with fragrant primroses in jam-jars. Mrs Burchaell looked in. 'Ah, the darling things!' she said.

Here began our experience with a governess, my first formal education. Miss Leeper came from Surrey to find herself in the wild Irish countryside. Pink and moon-faced, she was shocked at my ignorance.

'Recite the Lord's Prayer,' Miss Leeper said.

I began, 'Our Father, bejart in heaven …'

'*What* was that you said? After Our Father?'

Miss Leeper taught us to place our Bibles on top of all other books. She found us delinquent in other matters. I was brushing my teeth the wrong way. She took all my primroses and threw them out. 'Most unhealthy,' she said. 'You should never sleep with flowers in the room.'

Next morning, when about to start lessons, the governess

looked out the schoolroom window and gasped in shock. Lucinda and I looked too. Miss Boskin, muttering, had found a secluded spot in the laurel bushes. She hoicked up her long skirts and petticoats, squatted down and, grunting, began to do a big job. Ooh. This was too much for Miss Leeper. She left at once, without giving notice, to return to her English certainties. Ireland was every bit as savage as she had been told, full of dangerous Roman Catholics and mad gentlefolk.

Once settled in Viewmount, neat and welcoming with new paint, rich Indian carpets and family furniture taken out of storage, we were at home again. Life resumed its rhythm, regular meals, walks, church-goings and domestic music. The tall rooms were lit by lamps and candles, heated by log fires in marble chimneypieces.

Viewmount was well named, sited in clear view of Mount Leinster. The changing light on the mountain – now purple, now blue, now brownish – was never the same from moment to moment. The mountain was framed on one side by the walled gardens with herbaceous border in front, and on the left by tall trees, including a majestic *Sequoia gigantea*.

Bernard and I shared a big bedroom with a chimneypiece of black Kilkenny marble. Daddy supplied prints of Irish role models, the Duke of Wellington and Lord Roberts. In his study, Daddy hung portraits of his own heroes – Patrick Sarsfield, Daniel O'Connell, Henry Grattan – two of them Catholics, all of them Irish patriots. Evelyn Dobbs was a man of contradictions.

Sometimes nightmares seized him and he howled in anguish in his sleep. I could not imagine what furies pursued him.

At Viewmount Lucinda and I began lessons with a new governess. Miss Caldwell was a trouper who would have taught us any subject required by the Master. Sanskrit? Certainly. Not that we tackled anything quite so recondite. We did learn to write in a neat hand in lined copybooks, each page headed with the maxim to be copied, 'Silence is golden, speech is silver', and, 'Set a stout heart to a steep hill'.

Miss Caldwell took us for long walks in all weathers and even gave piano lessons, which may be one reason why I never learned to do it right. She drilled us in table manners. In another drill, we had to form fours like soldiers, though there were only two of us. When Lucinda left for boarding school in Wales, Bernard joined the lessons.

One evil day, when our parents were away in Dublin, something snapped and we rose in revolt. After all, our country existed because of a rebellion. When Miss Caldwell tried to collar us, I whacked her on her corsetted behind with a cricket stump, a disgraceful deed, though she was well armoured. We ran out and hid in the hayloft.

It was the herdsman who betrayed us. He believed that the smell of children on hay put his cows off their feed. For some reason they were not put off by the stink of unwashed, tobacco-reeking stockmen. The good news was that the enemy would not parlay. The bad news was that Dinah, the pretty red-headed maid who often befriended us, came out to negotiate a solution – in the form of unconditional surrender. We knew we had gone too far.

When Daddy came home, he heard Miss Caldwell's case in silence. I was told to apologize, which I did with heartfelt insincerity. Then Daddy took me into his dressing room to execute his own judgment. He put me over his knee and beat me with a slipper.

I don't believe it hurt much. But hitherto I had known my father as a benign figure who read to Bernard and me in his study and sometimes showed us his favourite plants and flowers. It did not matter to me that I deserved punishment. I just could not believe that my nice, bookish Daddy, his myopic eyes enormous behind thick glasses, was doing his damnedest to inflict pain. I bawled with outrage and shock.

This horrified my father, who hated the whole business. He exclaimed with disgust, 'I'm ashamed of you! By Gad, I've watched a native being flogged, his bottom cut to ribbons, and he never made a sound. And here you – you're squalling like a stuck pig!'

It was the words that fell on me like sickening blows. The image of that flogged man attached itself to my glowing memories of India. I had to think of myself as a coward and a weakling (a word I had learned from a Charles Atlas advertisement), a disgrace to my family.

Luckily we had dogs. They would listen to our sorrows, watching us mournfully. After a course of dog-therapy, I became more detached from my father, taken as I was by the depth of his knowledge and by his love of words, which I shared.

Disappointed in me, my father also saw himself as upholding old-fashioned righteousness in a household of degenerate women. 'What's that beastly stuff you've got on your face?' he'd exclaim with disgust to a daughter wearing lipstick.

Worse than lipstick was nail varnish. Women who used such things were 'fast', persons who drank gin instead of whiskey, drove sports cars and consorted with metropolitan sophisticates called 'lounge lizards'. Over the years Father became somewhat reconciled to changing fashions, though this did not seem to soften his misogyny. When his Dublin club voted to admit women guests at luncheon, he resigned.

There was an incident that brought us together when Granny Dobbs died. For a few weeks my parents moved into the Dublin house. I came with them, along with two of my sisters. Shortly after the funeral, while no one was home, the house was broken into. Nothing was taken. Two big detectives came to investigate. They left, baffled. When they had gone, Father took me aside, his eyes big behind his glasses. 'I know what the thief was looking for. But you mustn't tell anyone. We don't want to scare them.' I promised.

While Mother and the girls were out shopping, I helped pry up a floorboard in the breakfast room. From a space underneath, Father pulled out something wrapped in oilcloth and sacking. There were two rusty rifles, both .22 calibre, a Mauser, and a lever-action Martini. 'We have to get rid of these,' Father said. The Civil War was only ten years behind us. Possessing unlicensed firearms was a serious offence. The IRA still existed and was always on the scrounge for arms. These rifles had been hidden during the Troubles. Maybe an electrician or plumber had learned about them and had passed the word.

Wrapping the guns in an old blanket, we snuck them into the Ford. Father had given Mickey the day off. Now he drove at a reckless thirty miles per hour into County Wicklow. On the road to Blessington we passed the steam tram, then almost at its last puff. I did not yet know enough about cars to be frightened by my father's driving. He kept to the wrong side of the road. 'That's my good eye,' he'd explain. 'I've become a cyclops.' Still, he could drive after a fashion. Neither of my grandfathers could; gentlemen left such things to chauffeurs and coachmen. But Grandpa Dobbs had compromised by having a horn mounted on his side, which he ponked at corners in case Mickey was slow with his own ponker.

Away out in the country, among blue hills and yellow gorse, we came to a bridge over the Liffey. It spanned a cataract at Poulaphouca. We stopped on the bridge and surveyed the road in both directions, then the river: on one side the rapids rushing over rocks, on the other the waterfall and the black pool into which it fell. (This whole scene was to disappear when the river was dammed for a reservoir and power plant.) There was no one in sight. Carrying the rifles to the rampart, we dropped them into the deep pool. Father and I were now linked in crime. I did not realize quite how extraordinary this was, Father being deeply imbued with notions of law and justice. He explained that this place belonged to the Pookah, an evil spirit. Since the eighteenth century this so-called Daemon's Hole, on the lands of the Earl of Milltown, had been a beauty spot much visited by tourists in their post-chaises. Today, somewhere in the depths, the rifles lie.

Knowing that I was now Father's accomplice in crime made me feel easier with him.

Mother's passion was music. There were evenings in the lamp-lit drawing-room when Joan played her violin, Nancy the cello, as Mother accompanied on the piano. Sometimes Father would bring sheet music and we sang songs by Stephen Foster, Percy French and others. On great occasions Mother brought toy instruments – tin trumpet, drum, nightingale, triangle – and got us going on Haydn's 'Toy Symphony'. Skill in sight-reading music ran down the family from Joan to Mary, skipped Lucinda, Bernard and me, and hit again with Sally.

Some nights I lay in bed listening to Joan playing a Scarlatti sonata on the drawing-room piano or Nancy's light touch in Debussy's 'Doctor Gradus ad Parnassum', while the grandfather clock on the front stairs ticked off the hours.

During holidays from school, where we took singing lessons, Mother persuaded me to sing Schubert lieder to her accompaniment. I taught myself to play tunes and hymns by ear on the piano, discovering harmony. And whenever I could get at an organ without an audience I attempted that too, fascinated by the names and sounds of the stops: *bourdon, hautbois, gedackt, mixture* (three ranks), *stopped diapason.*

Mary the cook taught me to play jigs and reels on the melodeon. In the kitchen the maids sat at the long harvest table reading their dreambooks by candlelight. Bernard and I learned ballads and come-all-ye's from Bill Lawlor, the carpenter who did odd jobs and sang as he worked. In the harness room where Dublin Jack and Old Carroll sheltered from rain by the turf fire, we heard many tales and *pishogues*. Dublin Jack told raunchy tales of the cattleboats and Liverpool taverns and brothels. We knew we were lucky to be immersed in such rich and diverse lore.

In 1934 Sir Alan Cobham's Air Circus came to our county, an entertainment called 'barn-storming' in America. In a farmer's field, a small flight of biplanes performed aerobatics, daredevils stood on the wings, did handstands and pretended to fall. A biplane with a hook on the end of one wing used it to pick a handkerchief off the ground. Best of all, members of the public could be taken up for a flight. Father's instructions were that the girls might fly, but the boys were not to do it. We did not see it at the time, in the bitterness of our disappointment, but this was an expression of Father's misogyny. Flying was dangerous, but girls could risk it because they were expendable.

Lucinda gave a first-hand report. It was marvellous up there, she said. Everything on the ground looked so neat and tidy! Very noisy, the engines roaring; still, it was a kind of miracle just to be above the birds and trees.

Not long after that, there was a grand wedding in our county. Groom and best man were to stay overnight at Viewmount, along with one or two other guests, including a French baron, a friend of the Loftuses. The best man, like the groom a naval officer, was to arrive in a chartered Gypsy Moth biplane. He landed near Viewmount in Paddy Mullins' forty-acre field – where the local point-to-point race-meeting was held every year. No sooner had the pilot shaken hands with the spectators than another aeroplane appeared, a Farman monoplane. This too landed and rolled to a halt near the Moth. Out stepped the French baron, a charming, rather ceremonious man who almost immediately invited Bernard and me to fly to Dublin with him the following week. He would be staying at Burton Hall in County Carlow. He put the invitation to Father in such diplomatic terms that permission was granted for one boy at a time to fly.

The following week, as Bernard and I set out with Mother in the car for Burton Hall, Father repeated his condition about one boy at a time. As it happened, the baron could not make two trips. He assured Mother that it was perfectly safe. After some hesitation, she said we could both go. We hugged her in gratitude.

It was just as Lucinda had said. We flew at about 4000 feet above the green fields and farms of Carlow and Kildare, before coming to earth at Baldonnell airport in County Dublin. He took care of some business at the airport, while we boys chatted with a couple of soldiers in green uniforms. Then up again to fly back to Burton Hall and tea and cream buns with Lady Burton, sated with adventure and ready to face down any row at home.

Father met us at the door. 'We flew! We flew to Dublin and back!' we told him. 'It was super!'

'One at a time?'

Mother said, 'That couldn't be done. To be fair, I let them both go up.'

Father gave a snort that was almost a sob. 'My wishes have been ignored!' He stormed into the house and retreated into his study.

Three

In May 1933 I left home for boarding school. Baymount was a small private school in north Dublin. My education was to be the usual brainwashing at prep school, public school and university.

At Baymount some thirty boys were locked up in a small estate where six teachers taught us Latin, French, mathematics, English, history, geography and divinity. Others came to coach us in singing, drawing, dance and physical training. The school colours were black and white: its monogram *BS* was lost on us in our innocence.

Everyone makes mistakes while learning; it's how one learns. But at our school mistakes were punished, often with the cane. As aversion therapy it sometimes worked: most of my schoolfellows distinguished themselves in later life, but among other less admirable results, it could paralyze with fear of mistakes.

I once asked a former schoolmate, the poet Richard Murphy, what he remembered of the place. 'Moral terror,' he said, 'associated with learning.' It was a fair assessment. Later, when he published his memoir, *The Kick,* I learned to my surprise that I had been his hero. He remembered my telling 'wonderful stories', for which I'd been caned.

The headmaster and owner was William Lucas Scott MA, secretly known as Bill. After my first three weeks I was sent to Bill because I kept forgetting to bring a pencil to class. He was short, his white moustache yellowed by tobacco, matching the stain at his crotch. He was waiting for me. Putting his arm around my shoulders he said softly, 'Kildare—' his first, sinister use of my Christian name, 'Kildare, this is only going to be a baby caning.' He propelled me upstairs, right to the bathroom at the top of the house. His hand smelt as sour as vomit. Pointing to a chair he said, 'Bend over.' Sick with fright, I saw him take up a heavy rattan. He felt my seat, apparently to make sure I'd not padded my trousers. I heard the evil swish of the cane and felt the explosion of pain. This time I would not make a sound. He hit me again. Later I flashed the crimson and purple weals in the dorm, which were duly admired, and from that moment I kept my distance from Bill, as I had from Father. He read books to us in the evening; I read my own books. He read *Westward Ho!* and *The White Company*. I avoided these works.

Other cruelties were the work of women – Jane, the tall, skeletal wife and Tessie, the midget scold of a matron. Every morning one of them would enquire whether our bowels had moved. If the answer was no, senna tea was administered. It gave me cramps. That, together with the repeated moments of fear, tended to result in stained underpants. The offender was made to wash his own underwear in public.

There was an underworld of *us* against *them*. The worst crime was to be a sneak. Our heroes were cricketers and footballers. My friends were Esmonde Robertson and Marcus Seigne, who liked to join me in breaking rules. Esmonde was small and incompetently attired, the bottom fly-button fastened to the top buttonhole. Without the family butler he could not dress himself. We had stayed in each other's houses, his being a castle in County Carlow. Marcus was a witty boy who loved nothing more than to walk up snipe on a bog and shoot with his 4.10 shotgun. Because it was forbidden, we often escaped at night to walk along the deserted seafront. It was best in fog, when the horns on the Bull and North Walls bellowed to each other like sea cattle, followed by the distant explosions of the Kish lightship. Later I recognized these sounds in *Finnegans Wake*.

All three of us went on from Baymount to St Columba's, a public school of the British type in the Dublin mountains. We had been children together; here we were with young men with big genitals, who shaved and put goo in their hair. We went for walks together in the hills above Dublin, to visit pubs and drink whiskey or gin and stone ginger ale. We learned the etiquette of Irish pubs, especially when we drank Guinness, the ambrosial black beer of Ireland. 'Lovely condition,' we'd tell the curate, coming on like connoisseurs. Stout and porter were shipped in wooden casks, which affected their fermentation. A countryman tasting his pint of plain would observe, 'I'd say it was a bit fresh now, Paddy.' More than once we escaped into Dublin and in the bar at the Red Bank would order mulled claret, of all things, the tipple on which his butler had reared Master Esmonde. If caught, we'd have been expelled. Bartenders asked no questions; times were hard and we were high-spirited young gentlemen, not juvenile delinquents. The American breed of teenagers did not yet exist in Ireland, or even in Britain. They would arrive in both countries with modernization.

At Baymount we'd been training for leadership in a world that was passing away; and doing it with obsolete technology. The school was lit by gaslight, an advance on Viewmount with its candles and paraffin lamps. On frosty winter mornings the school porter carried cans of steaming hot water into the dormitory and poured it into enamel basins where cold water with a skin of ice was waiting. Shivering, we left warm beds to wash faces and hands. There were two bathtubs at the top of the stairs in the room where Bill caned us. We were given one bath a week under supervision. This while we played football or cricket every day. We smelt like graveyards.

Sex loomed in our thoughts. From Lucinda I had learned with warm interest about the Facts of Life. 'It's in the Bible,' she assured me. And, by the way, the whole subject was utterly confidential; I was not to tell a soul.

'I swear!' I said.

I had been at school a year by this time. I couldn't wait to tell my friends. In the dormitory after lights-out I sprung the whole extraordinary matter on the room. Michael Yeats, the poet's son, said confidently, 'I don't believe one word of it.' Another boy exclaimed, 'So that's what my sister was doing with her fiancé!' Yeats said, 'No, it can't be true. It's ridiculous!'

'It's in the Bible,' I insisted.

If ever anyone searched the scriptures, my dormmates did it in spades the next day. Bill must have wondered what had inspired this extraordinary surge of piety, the boys' heads bowed as they frantically turned the flimsy pages, looking for the good stuff.

Baymount was a God-save-the-King sort of place. St Columba's was different. True, there was a strong element of ancien régime among the boys, who scorned the English warden's efforts to make friends with the new rulers of Ireland. But it was much more Irish than the prep school, even in the slang we used. We no longer spoke of our parents as the Pater and Mater, and we said 'fuck' quite often.

My father thought me a Bolshie. He was distressed by my apostasy from imperialism, especially since I was so rude about it. He felt it as a slur on his own life's work, though it was really the result of my struggle to think for myself. So when Bernard was ready to move on, he was sent to Shrewsbury, the great English school where Father and his brothers had been educated.

One of the oddest things the Warden did, just before World War II, was to set up exchange visits with a Nazi school for future SS officers. The German boys sang marching songs and took part in field and track sports, where they sulked if they did not win. In Germany the Irish boys were roused from bed at midnight to join a forced march. The German boys did not know that eleven alumni of Columba's were British generals, who would soon be joined by another as head of the RAF. And in the end Germany's defeat was directed by Irish generals – Alanbrooke, Alexander, Montgomery, O'Connor and others.

I could not get along with the Warden, who found me subversive. Strange how the tyrants of our childhood shrink to insignificance! The man was not formidable at all. Round-shouldered and pink-faced, he had exactly the manner of a cruise-line purser, a shop-walker's unction laced with wheelhouse gold braid. But in those days he had the power to make me suffer. He had enough sense not to trust me. Unlike my friend Peter Seale, a fine athlete and full of fun, I was never a prefect. Peter became a lifelong friend.

I never forgot one day spent with Peter Seale and his family in their house by the sea south of Dublin. It was 1938. I met a German-Jewish refugee called Hans. Mr Seale, a modest Dublin businessman, had helped him to escape from Germany. From Hans I learned about the Nazis and what they were up to. They were caging and killing Jews and other people they disliked in concentration camps. Nazis had tortured his uncle to death by putting him in a concrete-mixer. It was obvious to Hans that they meant to kill all the Jews once they'd stolen their property. Peter was not crazy about Hans, who worked for his keep in the garden. He was arrogant, shared Peter's bedroom and, 'listen to this,' said Peter, every night he pulled on a hairnet! After Hans left Dublin for Brazil, he never wrote to thank Mr Seale. Probably he could not bear to remember his tribulations. Still, we knew that his reports of the Nazi terror were true.

Back home in Kilkenny we heard plenty about Hitler from Baroness Putiany, another refugee, who was maintained in big houses around the county. She told me she did not care if the British bombed Berlin flat. 'It's so uckly,' she said. 'Just the place for Heetler. It would be a mercy to destroy it.' She would get her wish.

Never mind the British empire. Somehow the Germans had to be stopped.

During the holidays Bernard and I ran free. We were enjoying ourselves with games, nature study and scientific experiments. In winter we played with our tin soldiers in the attic, staging wars between imaginary countries. We owned an induction coil taken from a car, with which we gave shocks to unsuspecting victims, and lit up a vacuum tube. It buzzed and glowed an unearthly purple.

Our science peaked when we learned how to make gunpowder. We made spectacular fireworks. Luckily we did not go in for bangs and explosions, preferring a kind of Vesuvius effect, fiery eruptions in orange and white or, by mixing copper or iron filings with the powder, in green or crimson. After a while our chemical ventures took a commercial turn when we found that oranges and lemons contained citric acid. The chemist in Bagenalstown looked at us rather queerly when we charged this to the family account, while he muttered, 'Well, 'tis not dangerous, I hope.'

In a short time we invented 'Citrax', our brand name for a refreshing soft drink, in which two real lemons were stretched with citric acid and sugar to make about a quart of the product. It was no worse than the drinks sold today as Tom Collins mixes or wine coolers. Launching it at school, we alarmed Bill, who feared it might be poisonous. He made us withdraw it.

We were given a kid, a baby goat, who followed us everywhere. We named her Miss Barbara Hutton, housing her at night in a disused tool shed. The door needed paint, so we mixed brickdust with linseed oil and gave it a nice red coat, with a sign announcing her name. Too bad, like Paddy McGinty's goat in the song, we found she was a billy – a puckawn as the countrymen called them. The name was changed to *Mister* Barbara Hutton. Our pet was tethered on the front lawn. A guest at luncheon was the columnist Patrick Campbell, the future Lord Glenavy, his six-and-a-half feet surmounted by a long face and red head. All his life, he confessed in *The P-Penguin P-Patrick Campbell,* he had suffered an attractive impediment in his speech. Greeted by our many friendly dogs, he stammered, 'G-good lord, I've never suheen s-so many dogs in m-my life!' And just then, sighting the little goat, he cried, 'Oh Christ, there's one with horns!'

For some years I had ambitions as an equestrian. While we were small, all of us rode a Shetland pony, a donkey and an old warhorse called Tommy. The pony was an evil creature who would head straight for a tree to crush your legs against the trunk. The donkey had a mind of her own and could easily unseat a child. Tommy was best. After many falls, I developed bad riding habits, so when I took a course in equitation near Dublin in my teens, I had to begin again painfully at the beginning. I learned the forward seat.

33

In time I was ready to follow the hounds, which I did for a while with savage pleasure, riding Ginger, a smart chestnut cob who would jump anything. But she leapt like a jackknife, which made her hard to sit over fences. I preferred Gandhi, a great big bay like a brontosaur; taking a fence with him was like riding waves. I was out with the Mount Loftus Harriers many times, and at least once with the Carlow Hounds. The joke about the Carlows was that their hounds had been bred for speed, but not for voice. So they often ran away and, being silent, were lost. Master of the Carlows was Mrs Hall, a foul-mouthed old beldame who rode side-saddle without a skirt and bawled me out a couple of times.

There's no excitement to compare with the mad ride across country, through gates, over fences, hedges, banks, stone walls, following the baying hounds and the thin blasts of the horn. As a way of killing foxes, though, it is not only inefficient but ugly.

I rode in a cloth cap – no one seemed to think a hard hat was necessary. I was following the Harriers on Ginger when I rode her at a stone wall which did not seem very high. But the ground fell away on the far side. I remember seeing Ginger's ears coming at me as I sailed over them, then nothing.

Aeons later I was struggling awake with nausea and a blinding headache. An old countryman was leaning over me with a look of concern. 'Jayzez! Are ye kilt?'

Kilt and destroyed entirely I was, but speechless. An onlooker later reported that I had fallen with a foot caught in one stirrup, had been dragged a couple of paces and kicked on the head. Two sporting priests drove me home, where the cob had already arrived, causing alarm. Doctor Farrell came from Bagenalstown, diagnosed concussion and ordered bed rest for two weeks.

As it happened I never hunted again after the accident. With the normal folly of youth, I found other ways to test my nerve. I read in later life that head injuries could make you a sex-maniac or a serial killer. Nothing so interesting happened to me.

Father had taken up light Church work in his retirement, as Diocesan Secretary. In effect, he was running the bishop as he had run nawabs and rajahs in India. He did the work and urged the decisions. The bishop or nawab took the bows, signed his name and made the speeches. All this in the service of the Church of Ireland, which had become gradually marginalized since Disestablishment in 1870. It had gone into rapid decline with national independence.

The 1930s was spiritually oppressive for all Irish people. Ulster Unionists had voiced the slogan 'Home rule is Rome rule', and that was how it had turned out. The Roman Hierarchy had no real opposition in the Free State and its successor the Republic. Partition had removed the great counterweight of a large Protestant population in the north. This hurt Roman Catholics as much as it did Protestants. Divorce had been abolished, birth control prohibited, films and books were rigorously and stupidly censored and often banned. Education in the hands of the clergy was unabashedly sectarian.

A few spoke out, notably W.B. Yeats in the tiny Irish Senate. And in our County Kilkenny, the admirable Hubert Butler of Maidenhall, in a body of essays that are now part of European literature, was an advocate of liberty and local patriotism.

At Baymount I saw Senator Yeats from time to time when he attended school functions, a romantic figure with his shock of white hair, floppy bow tie and dark-rimmed glasses. We knew who he was and some of us could recite a version of his poem about Innisfree:

> I will arise and go now and get a Guinness free,
> And a small cabin build there of clay and bottles made.

His son Michael resembled him in appearance: a little ungainly, eyebrows perpetually raised as though in surprise. But in those days he did not wish to hear anything about poetry. He reported that his father could not spell – for 'gas' he wrote 'gass'. He hogged the family bathroom, chanting his poems in the tub. Passing Michael on the stairs, he did not notice him. My own admiration for his father was unbounded. The poet never appeared at St Columba's, though, because he disliked the Warden.

Throughout childhood and youth I was befriended by our neighbours Reggie and Linda Segrave-Daly. They lived about five

miles away at Orchards near Gowran where Reggie was busy growing apples. Reggie had tried to be a monk at Downside Abbey in
England, where he had been at school. But his fondness for pranks
– such as forcibly giving the novice-master a shower because he
stank – convinced his superiors that he was unsuitable. He was still
a strong Catholic though, becoming increasingly eccentric as he
joined Opus Dei, a right-wing activist society. Linda, very feminine
and sophisticated, was a Loftus of Mount Loftus. Before independence Major Loftus had been high sheriff of County Kilkenny; an
ancestor had been a founder of Trinity College. Now the family was
Roman Catholic.

In my teens, Reggie and Linda taught me to drink in a civilized
way. I remember gin and passionfruit juice in their lively company.
Witty and urbane, they seemed like a couple in the *Thin Man* or
Fred Astaire musicals.

Also during those years of adolescence, Hubert Butler was very
much a presence in my life. He was away during my early years – in
Egypt, Latvia, Leningrad and Zagreb. In 1933/34 he translated and
adapted Chekhov's *The Cherry Orchard* for the Old Vic in London,
directed by his brother-in-law, Tyrone Guthrie. In 1938/39 he was
in Vienna working with Quakers to arrange exit visas for Jews. In
youth he had worked with Sir Horace Plunkett, setting up county
libraries. He was kin to the Butlers, who had dominated Ireland for
many centuries from their stronghold in Kilkenny Castle.

As a local patriot, Hubert published his first book from his
family home, Maidenhall, near Bennettsbridge. After World War
II Lord Ormonde gave Kilkenny Castle to the nation. Hubert and
his cousin Lord Dunboyne founded the Butler Society, now flour-
ishing in several countries. Hubert's essays are now internationally
known, though he did not come to notice outside Ireland until he
was in his eighties. By then he had acquired a professional publisher. An Oxonian classicist, he applied his Latin to Irish hagiog-
raphy. Almost every townland of Ireland has its saint, each with
local cult and holy day or 'pattern' (corruption of patron). In a volume of curious learning, *Ten Thousand Saints*, Butler proposed that

the numerous Irish saints 'were the fabulous pre-Christian ancestors of pre-Celtic and proto-Celtic tribes and amalgamations of tribes, and that in their pilgrimages and pedigrees and in the multiplicity of their names, nicknames, cult-centres, we can read the true story of the wanderings of tribes'. Just as the Jews traced their origins to an ancestor called Israel as that was the name of their nation, and the Greeks accounted for the existence of Medes and Persians by inventing ancestors called Medea and Perseus, so Celtic and other tribes who came to Ireland claimed eponymous forebears. But the legends of Irish saints raised new questions.

'I'm so glad you like *Ten Thousand Saints*,' he wrote in 1977. 'No one understood it in Ireland, though I had good as well as damning reviews, but not long ago an English sociologist, quite unknown to me, wrote a twelve-page article about it. I suppose it would be much worse if I had any faint misgiving about possibly being not right in general, but I've never had a twinge of doubt and know I have just got to wait, if the Fates will.'

Hubert was an intellectual whose plain speaking infuriated many of his countrymen. Latin was not his only field of expertise. He was also well versed in Slavonic languages and the political history of Yugoslavia. He had taught at Leningrad and Belgrade. After World War II, Tito's government was holding Cardinal Stepinac under house arrest. At a public meeting in Dublin, Butler made known the facts that in Croatia during the war the Roman Church under this cardinal had been implicated in the massacre – or rather the genocide – of hundreds of thousands of Orthodox Serbs. The cardinal, it's true, had saved some lives by offering forced conversions instead of murders. In the Vatican, only the French Cardinal Tisserant had protested.

Butler was supported by Owen Sheehy Skeffington, whose father had been shot by the British. County councils passed angry resolutions condemning both men for insulting the Papal Nuncio, who had been present during Hubert's remarks. Butler had to resign as honorary secretary of the Kilkenny Archaeological Society, which he himself had revived. But he did have his few paternal acres to sustain him, psychologically if not materially.

I enjoyed visiting Maidenhall, with its rather austere culture. Hubert always seemed to be looking beyond the person he was talking to. He had a gentlemanly disdain for trade, and thought, for example, that the *New Yorker* magazine and many of its writers were vulgarians. It does seem like a trade paper for copywriters, its fiction displaying a formidable command of brand names. When I visited him from Canada after I had left Ireland he gave me, in his gentle way, a hard time. He thought I should have stayed home and argued for the liberties I believed in. I sensed that he thought I was in pursuit of the dollar when all I was seeking was a livelihood. I could see no future for myself in Ireland, since I had neither land, profession nor prospects. Butler's attachment to local and rural matters was attractive, but I thought he sometimes took a more rosy view of his fellow gentry than they deserved. Most were more interested in horses and pigs than in the arts and learning. True, their ancestors had created the national museums and learned societies, especially the Royal Dublin Society, dedicated to the improvement of Irish culture, agriculture and industry. But since independence, suffering the slanders of history (as Joyce Cary put it), most of the gentry had withdrawn from public concerns.

Hubert and Peggy Butler were always hospitable. I remember visiting them while I was on leave from the navy. Hubert led me downhill through the front lawn and across the road to the river Nore, where Peggy was watching two little naked children splashing in the shallows. Both were future writers, Julia O'Faolain and Joseph Hone. The Butlers were taking care of them for their absent parents.

While I was still quite small something happened that darkened my view of Ireland. Father had bought fifteen acres of the original Viewmount land from its owner, a Dublin tea merchant, who kept the remaining forty-five acres in the care of a steward called O'Mara. As children we sometimes visited Mrs O'Mara and her baby, and watched while she baked soda bread at the open fire in a Dutch oven.

When the tea merchant died, Father bought the remaining

acres. On a Sunday not long afterwards, the governess bicycled home from church while the rest of us walked. She found, tacked to the front door, a notice depicting a coffin with Father's name on it, and inscribed, 'Undo the Conquest or I will riddle your Orange Carcass!' Miss Caldwell, a good citizen, immediately bicycled to the gardaí barracks in Paulstown, our village, and showed them the notice. It then appeared that a gatepost had been sawn down and our cattle driven onto the road.

Father deplored the fuss, though he was greatly insulted at being called an Orangeman. Soon detectives were questioning everyone in range, collecting sawdust and examining saws at neighbouring farms. Police were posted at the gates to protect us, including a hardbitten detective who was said to be a marksman. He showed me his revolver; his partner alleged he could hit a flying pigeon with one shot. A barrel of Guinness was placed in the downstairs bathroom, from which Bernard and I fetched jugs of porter for the detectives. Every morning and evening we carried out jug and glasses to refresh our sentries. This was fun, but I was dismayed that we needed protection from our own people, not for our faults, but because of who we were.

Meanwhile Father was interviewed by the local garda commissioner, an old IRA man who advised him to give up the land. This enraged Father. 'By gad!' he said, 'I'll take that fellow down a peg!'

The culprit was soon unmasked. Steward O'Mara had believed he could get land, advised by someone influential, perhaps the commissioner himself. Father refused to prosecute. He was already respected and country people felt friendly about someone who never lost interest in their rheumatism. O'Mara was not a local man, and neighbours turned their backs on him. He left the county, and the disputed land reverted to Viewmount.

I thought about the episode when the excitement had died down. I felt that there was no place for me at home. The world outside beckoned. I dreamed of places over the horizon, and even wrote a poem about the South Seas 'and the long, roaring surf'. I had heard visitors talk of adventures in far places, captured by bandits in

Argentina, or treed by a rhinoceros in Africa. That was for me. Seigne and I vowed we would never settle for life in offices, but would go where we could work in the open air, with like-minded people. After the war, in which he flew Seafire fighter aircraft, Seigne emigrated to spend his life in the Australian outback as a prospector, a buckaroo cowboy and a longshoreman.

Four

By mid-1942 I was at sea in HMS *Caldwell*, as she yawed and rolled like a drunken pilot-whale. She was one of fifty old destroyers the US dumped on Britain in September 1940 in exchange for bases around the world. The Royal Navy had lost many up-to-date destroyers at Dunkirk and in other actions, and these American ships met a pressing need for escort vessels. During their British service, ten of them were lost – by bombs, by a mine, by torpedoes. Six others took part in sinking ten U-boats.

I had joined her in Boston, where she was refitting. My initial training had been in HMS *Raleigh*, a shore-base across the Tamar estuary from Devonport. I had missed some of the course, because of hepatitis after my typhoid and tetanus shots – doubtless a dirty needle. Though I had been classed as a CW candidate (recommended for a commission or warrant) I knew I had everything to learn, especially in the social sphere. I had made one good friend, a seaman of my own age who had joined as a boy and already seen action. I was lucky to know Soames, the kind of man you want beside you when there's trouble.

My mess was on the port side forward. The leading seaman, known as the killick, because of the gold anchor on his sleeve, took a strong dislike to me. A skinny, mean-looking bully, intent on the class struggle, he made my life unpleasant, giving me the nastiest jobs and calling me a 'fuckin' cap*it*alist boor-joys'. I decided to fight back. I told my messmates that I'd put a curse on him – an Irish one, which was the worst kind. Coming off the morning watch a few days later, I noticed, as I slurped my strong tea, my messmates giving me strange looks. No sign of the leading seaman. 'Where's the killick?' I asked.

There was moment of silence. Then someone said, 'In the fuckin' sickbay, is where 'e is. Fell and broke 'is fuckin' arm.'

'Broken arm?' I said. 'It's not enough.'

On his next run ashore the killick got stinking drunk. Coming off, he fell from the gangway into filthy water. The quartermaster jumped down on the garboard strake and hauled him inboard, where he found himself face-to-face with the officer of the watch. Charged as drunk and with conduct contrary to good order and naval discipline, he was busted down to able seaman.

After that, my mates treated me with respect. Even I treated me with respect. From now on, I would have to be careful with my curses. Sailors are superstitious.

Our lives were controlled by forces beyond us, by the elements and by instructions known only to the captain and officers. The most trivial decisions were made for us, what to wear, eat and do. We knew little about the war – civilians at home knew more. Being in it, we knew only that we had to win. We lived in a world of rumour. Our task was to escort and protect convoys of merchant ships and tankers from North America to mid-Atlantic, where escort groups from Western Approaches would take over. Often we escorted another convoy of ships steaming the other way – back to Canadian and American ports. Normally we would be zigzagging on the flank of the long lines of labouring ships, sonar pinging away in the search for U-boats, lookouts and watchkeepers scanning the ocean through binoculars for a periscope or even a U-boat recharging batteries on the surface. I learned the secret of night vision: to look away from what you thought you glimpsed, in order to see it better.

There were usually a few old destroyers, frigates and corvettes fussing around the convoy in an attempt at a screen. That was the theory. In fact we seldom made contact with the enemy before something nasty happened to the ships we were supposed to guard.

It was the merchantmen the wolf-packs wanted to sink, trying to cut the supply line to Britain. I don't think they were bothered much by the escorts. The commodore's ship was a favourite target, easily identified by the amount of signalling it generated. Some of the freighters had ordnance manned by naval gunners. The worst thing to see was a torpedoed tanker, the sea around it in flames as the oil burned off. Such engagements were rare. The constant menace to convoys and escorts was the violence of the ocean itself with its steep seas and heavy swells.

About my third convoy, we were keeping station on the starboard flank of a slow convoy about twenty-four hours from Boston. There was heavy fog, visibility one cable-length. My watch station was in the wheelhouse at the engine-room telegraph, my friend Soames, the quartermaster, steering. Every couple of minutes I had to sound the foghorn. The open bridge was overhead. The officer of the watch talked to us by voice pipe. We could also hear the reports from the radar and sonar operators.

Radar reported an unexpected blip on the port quarter. Soames muttered, 'Must be off station.'

Seconds later the port lookout just abaft the wheelhouse roared out urgently, 'Ship bearing red four five! Red four five, a ship!'

Over my shoulder I saw it bearing down on us at high speed from our port quarter, a huge liner with four funnels towering like a cliff. It looked like a twin of the *Titanic*. Absurdly I remembered the sailor who had told an Admiralty court what he felt at such a moment. 'Christ, you could have buggered me in me oilskins!' and the counsel's explanation, 'He means, m'lord, that he was taken aback.' The great liner was about to hit just where I was standing! Without thinking, I recoiled a couple of paces.

In the same instant I heard Mr Elliott, officer of the watch. 'Hard a-starboard! Stop both engines. Full astern together!' Soames repeated the orders as he put the wheel hard over, then jumped to the telegraphs to stop the engines. Then I was back at my station, furious with myself, just in time to put the levers to 'full astern together'. Only Soames knew that I had goofed.

The next orders were for me. 'Call the captain. Sound action stations! Sound off "D" on the siren – that's one long and two short!'

It seemed an age before our ship began to turn away and slow down. Towering over our heads, the liner struck us a heavy glancing blow on the port side just abaft the capstan. The whole bow crumpled like a concertina.

'Close watertight doors.'

The command for action stations was to clear lower deck and stress urgency. 'D' on the siren meant 'not under command'. Soames and I thought Mr Elliott had done well.

The cox'n arrived in the wheelhouse. 'Jesus – we've been tin-fished, right?' He thought we'd been torpedoed. The liner, which Mr Elliott now identified as the 42,000-ton Cunarder *Aquitania*, had disappeared into the fog. Then it was the captain's voice, telling us that we weren't going to sink, but would steam slow ahead for repairs in Boston naval yard.

In the fug below I said to Soames, 'You were stuck with my job. I stepped away!'

'Nah!' he said, shrugging. 'You were there, I only moved the fuckin' levers once!'

Soames was my age, an admirable sailor who had been trained at HMS *Conway* as a boy, then went with Lord Keyes to mine the Rhine in the retreat to Dunkirk. He had grown up in Dorset and liked to reminisce about poaching. Completely competent and fearless, he was exemplary. I studied him.

'Look wot that pig Elliott done to us,' a messmate sneered.

'You know fuck-all about it,' Soames said. 'He did his job perfect.'

New York was our favourite port, a wonder of the world with its bright lights and nightlife, its riches and towers, the lofty Chrysler, the still higher Empire State building. There and in Boston we found ourselves in Norman Rockwell's America. The war was new, the latest, hottest thing. We were feted like the stars of a new musical hit.

On my very first liberty I attended a colossal ball in the Statler Hotel thrown by Police Commissioner Tinahilty. This was my first glimpse of the Cult of the Bigshot, compensating for the boring religion of 'we the people'. Another glimpse came when I swam in the governor's pool in Brookline, introduced by Jinks Reggio, a girl I had met in the USO on Boston Common. The names of the bigshots told me that the Irish were running politics there.

I was even more impressed when I met the men and women who called themselves working stiffs. With F.D.R. in the White House, they were coming into their own.

Chipping paint aboard one day, I made friends with a riveter. The navy-yard maties (as we called them) were working three shifts, something unheard of in British dockyards, where working at all was almost unknown. My new friend Bruno invited me home to eat with his family. He drove me there in his car. 'What a great car!' I said, admiring the bulging vehicle with its shiny paint and chromium.

'Dis? Oh dis is jus a poor man's car!'

A poor man's car! It was a new idea to me, a wonderful idea. As an ordinary seaman I was earning about $7 a week, all found. Bruno was making $3000 plus a year and proud of it. His wife had put out a spectacular spread of all sorts of fresh produce, pasta and roast chicken, salads and plenty of chianti in straw-wrapped flasks, followed by ice cream. My heart was warmed. I saw that this was what was going to win the war – the commonwealth of men who worked three shifts for a decent wage, owned cars and ate like bishops.

The great republic had been at war only a few months, forced into it by the treacherous Japanese assault on Pearl Harbor, which had destroyed the capital ships of its Pacific fleet. Before that the US had been supplying the beleaguered British at great profit, spending money rather than precious American lives. But now the mighty engine of US industry was geared for total war. Henry Kaiser was launching a Liberty ship every day. Huge aircraft-carriers were on the stocks to replace the obsolete battleships destroyed at Pearl Harbor. Troops were training in hundreds of thousands. Thousands were learning to fly. Civilians, fired by propaganda from Hollywood and New York, were raising money, singing patriotic songs and wearing buttons with General MacArthur's head on them. The slogan was 'Remember Pearl Harbor'. The MacArthur cult was disquieting, but this kind of Caesarism had always been lurking in American democracy. Meanwhile most Americans wanted to do something nice for the boys, including us.

In New York the hospitality was lavish and exhausting. Adrian, Godfrey and I were adopted as a special project by Miss Gretchen Green, who worked from The Whole World & Company Inc., her shop off Park Avenue. There was no one in sight when we arrived. We were wondering what to do when the door of the grandfather clock sprang open. A tall lady with a shock of white hair sailed into the room, spread her arms and cried, 'Well, boys, this is bully!'

She had steeply sloping shoulders, a long neck, and a spare, straight figure. Perhaps in her sixties, her radiant charm and benevolence shone on everyone around her. *Of course* she could get us tickets for the show we wanted to see.

Gretchen Green, daughter of a Dixieland bishop, seemed to know or have known everyone influential in the world, from Lord Wavell to Wendell Wilkie, from George Santayana to the dowager Empress of China. For Wavell she had run a soldiers' canteen in a houseboat on the Nile; she had campaigned for Wilkie in his failed attempt to unseat Roosevelt; Santayana had advised her aboard ship in an Atlantic crossing, 'Morality, my dear young lady, is the art of spreading pleasure thin'; the Empress had given her a gold ring. She had leased her Venetian palace to Ezra Pound, whom she disliked. She used her contacts to provide comforts and respite for British servicemen, not forgetting the Beefeaters of the Tower of London. When she learned about the Warders' exiguous meat ration, she exclaimed, 'Beefeaters without beef!' and persuaded Macy's in New York to supply a whole sirloin every week, then got RAF transport command to deliver them. The Warders responded by presenting her with one of the Tudor ruffs they wore. She flaunted it everywhere. Since no New World laundry could clean and press it, the RAF flew it home to the Tower to be laundered there, then returned it to New York. After the war, Gretchen was decorated with the MBE. That too she wore constantly.

She took us over, calling us her Three Musketeers. We called her GiGi. To me she was a fairy godmother. She gave me a guitar, a wind-up gramophone, books (all of which I passed in due course to my messmates) and other things to send home: for example, instant cake-mix, a novelty at that time. Believing I had talent, she introduced me to literary people and the lovely daughters of the rich.

In the apartment of Miss Caroline Newton I saw a self-portait of Alexander Pope, a Reynolds portrait of Dr Johnson, Blake watercolours, and a manuscript of W.H. Auden's work. 'You *must* meet Wystan,' Miss Newton said. Similarly with Geraldine Fitzgerald (sister of my brother-in-law David), whose beautiful face that summer was on the cover of *Life* magazine. She told me about her friend Orson Welles, 'You *must* meet Orson,' she said. They had worked together at the Gate Theatre in Dublin, before both of them came to Hollywood. She said we'd understand each other. But he was out of town and I was off to sea.

I was happy enough to be friends with Geraldine and her first husband, Eddie Lindsay-Hogg (later Sir Eddie). Eddie told me where to buy a good ten-cent cigar. Orson he taught how to dress like a gentleman.

Thanks to GiGi, the three Musketeers lunched with Ruth Draper in her apartment. In 1942 she was big-time, famous for her solo performances in witty and satirical routines. Henry James had written a sketch for her that she never performed. The dining/living room was decorated with a big map of the world, on which every city where our hostess had performed was marked with an electric light. They twinkled like a galaxy. I made friends with a girl who urged me to join her at the piano in a duet of 'Chopsticks'. To our humiliation, we were asked to make way for the virtuosa Madame De la Rocha, who played a Chopin nocturne. She told us we played nicely for people who did not play piano.

We heard Hazel Scott playing 'boogie-woogie' in Café Society Uptown and the composer of 'The Birth of the Blues', a skinny old black man, blowing it out his trumpet in Billie Rose's Diamond Horseshoe. We lived it up in the Stork Club and Jack and Charlie's Twentyone, where Robert Benchley paused at our table to tell a joke. With Geraldine, one was always welcome.

One day Geraldine asked what I had been writing and I said, 'Nothing. I may have lost it. Hamlet calls it bestial oblivion.'

'You sound like Orson,' she said. 'I'm going to remind him of that phrase *bestial oblivion*. He's forever saying he can't work. But he *is* threatening to play *Hamlet*, saying he too is fat and short of breath. It could be a disaster – everyone's out to stop him.'

Geraldine sent a cable to my ship after reading some of my poems, declaring that I was very talented. Later she sent a photograph of us sitting together in the Stork Club. Eddie had removed all signs of alcoholic drinks. Hollywood kept close watch on the image of every star.

On one of our New York liberties GiGi noticed that Adrian had a hole in the seat of his bellbottoms. He scowled when she pointed it out. To his embarrassment, she telephoned the British naval liaison officer to find a new pair. Impossible, she was told. Adrian offered to colour his exposed skin with blue ink. This was ignored.

'We'll just have to patch them,' GiGi said. 'Who owns navy blue? I know! Kitty Lehmann was at a British girls' school where she wore a blue blazer. Bet she still has it.' And almost at once we were all three with GiGi in Senator Lehmann's two-storey apartment on Park Avenue. Adrian, still scowling, huddled on a sofa debagged and kilted with a bath towel. Kitty Lehmann, a modishly slim blonde, sat cross-legged on the floor cutting a patch from her Roedean cashmere blazer to sew onto Adrian's serge trousers. Godfrey and I were encouraged to inspect the priceless collection of art treasures. One room was lined with cabinets displaying Medici jewels against black velvet. Others glowed with French impressionist paintings. They may be seen today in the Lehmann wing of the Metropolitan Museum.

During that same visit our ship underwent repairs in Brooklyn naval yard. Max, a welder, gave me a dollar and said, 'Hey, sailor.

Why'n't you go over to the canteen and get me cigarettes – whatever they got. An keep d'change.' I obliged, making about half a dollar on the deal.

I said, 'You're Jewish, aren't you?'

He admitted it. 'We got all sorts. See dat guy over dere?' I looked. There was a short man welding the deck. 'Dat guy's a Guinea.'

'A what?'

'A Guinea, a *Wop.*'

The short man stood and pushed up his mask. He looked at me. 'Ever hear tell of Garibaldi?' Of course I had. 'No relation of mine,' the short man said, bending to his work.

At this moment one of my Welsh messmates hove into view. 'See him?' Max said. 'Fuckin' Taffy! – Limeys say Taffy was a thief!'

The Welshman scowled. 'Wot are you then? Fuckin' *Jew.*'

Chuckling, Max offered him a cigarette.

With winter, gales and storms became more frequent and violent. By now I could take care of myself, one hand for Jack, one for the Andrew – as we called the navy. When the sea was merely boisterous, we enjoyed it. If we crashed into a big sea the watch below would sing out, 'Who's on the fuckin' wheel then?' Sometimes in the middle or morning watches I would be spellbound by the dark seas and phosphorescent foam. A school of dolphins surfing the bow-wave would make everyone happy.

From Soames I learned to steer, altering course with precision. The ship did not answer at once to the wheel, hanging between waves, then would suddenly swing to port or starboard until opposite wheel was applied; and keep swinging until the rudder bit. After a while you could feel the inertia in your feet and lean into it.

We slept about four hours most nights, waking to the pipe, 'All the Blue watch, Blue watch to muster!' Some mornings it would be the Buffer himself, moving through the messdeck. 'Come along then, let's be 'avin' yer! Chop chop! Else I'll be in alongside!'

'O Chiefie!' a sailor would squeak, 'That's a promise?'

'*And* I'll bring yer a cup of char! Rise and shine!'

By then we'd be scrambling to our stations.

In December 1942 we were with a slow convoy in half a gale toward mid-Atlantic. A few days out we had to send our surgeon aboard a merchant packet for an emergency. We lowered the whaler with the sawbones and his bag and our five Newfoundlanders to row him. There were cheers as they moved through the huge swell with steady strokes. This was seamanship of the first order. Newfoundlanders were bred to the sea, acquiring their skill along with a strong sense of duty. When they returned, operation completed successfully, the captain piped, 'Clear lower deck!' Everyone except those at special sea duty turned to, to haul in the whaler by hand. The orders came, 'Man the falls! Walk back handsomely! Marry to the mark!' And then 'Light to!' The words had not changed since Nelson's time. We just hoped the sawbones had been more up to date.

Still later, we took up station to refuel at sea, leaving the convoy to the flotilla from Western Approaches. For the first time I would have to spend days looking death in the face.

Already the seas were high, the wind blowing like a bastard. Long streaks of foam striped the ocean. We did our damnedest to grapple the floating hose. The tanker tried over and over to float the line in our direction, but it always drifted away in the gusts of what was now a full gale. After some hours, both captains agreed that it would be dangerous to stay bucketing around here any longer. U-boats were lurking. Turning west, we stood for home.

And ran smack into the most violent hurricane anyone aboard had ever seen. At first we laughed when a big shock sent our dinner of pork chops flying in a shower of knives and forks. Our spirits were high. After some hours of violent motion, though, we began to tire of it. Although we were now at half-speed, the bows were crashing into waves in a way that made us uneasy. We still had no idea that we were heading into worse weather. The destroyer was shipping them green as she ploughed ahead, then shrugging the waves off like a dog as she rose shuddering. The buzz was that we were steering for a Canadian port. But with seas now breaking over the ship's narrow waist as well as the bows, those of us not on watch were told to stay below.

Some of us were seated at the mess table, holding on with both fists, when there was a tremendous crash and tearing sound. The ship was slowly rolling over to port until she was almost on her beam ends. Water was pouring down the companionway. The alarm of the master-gyro began to shrill as it went off the board. She hung there while we held on, leaning against the tilt, for agonizing minutes. We were sure the ship was going to capsize until, ever so slowly, gyro still screaming, she began to roll back.

Our first thought was tin-fish! Always our secret fear. In fact we were now in the grip of the full hurricane, the air dark with flying spray and rain, mountainous seas rising before us or throwing us to the tops of range after range of vast, confused waves. Lightning played about the mast, the wind loud with thunder and crashing water. Special sea dutymen were at stations, the captain on what was left of the bridge, all fighting to keep steerageway on the ship, her head to the weather. If she broached to, turned beam-on to a breaking sea, she could be engulfed and founder. All this came home to us – no rumour, but stark reality.

Half the bridge had been torn off the starboard side, one of the four funnels was ripped away with most of the Carley floats, and all that was left of the boats were a few splintered timbers swinging from the twisted metal of davits. On his way to take the wheel, the cox'n muttered, 'Forty years at sea and I never seed it like this. We come through this lot, you'll have summat to tell!' He was pale with fright.

The storm raged with growing fury and violence. In the uproar of the elements you could imagine the yelling of malignant spirits, the deep bourdon of evil. I did not want to die just yet, with all my shipmates and no one to know. We had not even met the enemy. Terror had a strange effect on me. I became icy calm, stolid and withdrawn. All sorts of heavy stuff was rolling around on the deck, oil-drums, rolls of wire, loose floats. The Buffer called for volunteers to secure the loose gear. No one came forward. I tried to make myself volunteer. But in my coldly rational state, I knew I did not yet have the skill to be useful in this way. The Buffer picked half-a-dozen men who did have it – stalwarts from the rigging party. They did the dangerous job quickly and efficiently. None of them was hurt.

I think the worst of it lasted two or three days, but after five days the seas were still high and breaking and we were afraid and sleepless most of the time. The ship could not take much more. The galley had been wrecked and we were issued with hard tack, the first time I'd ever seen the big, iron-hard biscuits. One could only nibble at corners. An extra rum ration helped keep out the cold. There was cold bully beef from cans.

After three sleepless days I was hallucinating. In the face of the black ocean, monstrously swollen and bursting over us with millions of tons of salt water, I felt something break in me, some part of myself tear away.

Someone said, 'Shit, it could be worse.' And at once it did become worse. Word came from the bridge that we were to turn to and break up everything made of wood in the messdecks and flats. We were running out of fuel. Unless the engines could be kept going we would be at the mercy of breaking seas. The chief engineer and chief engine-room artificer were adapting the boiler-room furnaces for firewood. As a backup, the captain had a plan to sew together our hammocks and rig a jury sail. No doubt he was also thinking of streaming a sea anchor to keep us hove to.

We set to work wrecking our living space. There was no talk, by the way, of breaking up the wardroom panelling. Our firewood kept the engines going for a few hours.

Meanwhile the sky had cleared and the wind let up, though the sea was still running very high. Sparks, the radio operator, gave chilling news that around us several ships had foundered. We were afraid the *Caldwell* would break her back. It was strangely quiet below decks, just the thud of the propellor-shafts and the rush of water along the side. None of us said much. We looked at each other with doubt in our eyes.

A lookout announced that an aircraft was in sight. It was a

Catalina, a coastal command flying-boat that made eleven-hour reconnaissance patrols. We sent up flares as distress signals. Later we heard that the pilot reported us 'under command' and in good shape. He also gave our bearings incorrectly. Or that was the buzz. Sailors were always ready to think ill of the RAF. None of us knew how frightful their casualties were or how thinly they were stretched.

The temperature had fallen and, without heat in the derelict mess, our spirits sank. We kept on our duffel coats and all the sweaters we could find. Still we were cold and wet. I had a wind-up gramophone and a few Christmas records – alien, sugary carols – and Ginge, my red-headed messmate, kept putting on Bing Crosby groaning 'I'm dreaming of a white Christmas'. I hated the record then – the song and the voice – and still detest it. It was played over and over.

There was thick ice on the fo'c's'le and rigging when we sighted an ocean-going tug, come from St John's to take us in tow. We were too tired to cheer. This time I did volunteer for the party on the fo'c's'le. There were five of us including Soames. First we rigged lifelines – the taffrails had been torn away. Then as the *Frisky* came near, we stood by to catch the line shot from a Costen gun.

Seas were still steep and the wind gusting. It took five hours to secure and bend the line to our heavy hawser. Lines were stiff with ice, cutting our hands, but at last we had the tow secure. The *Frisky* took the strain. We were on our course to safety, provided the cable held. Newfoundland was about 300 miles away. A lookout was posted to watch the tow.

Some men were cut and bruised from being thrown about. An officer had broken his back and had to be strapped into a special cradle. One of the chief stokers had disappeared. No one had seen him go. He'd been unpopular; we thought he might have been pushed. This was not said out loud. A few men were now in an ugly mood; fatigue and fear making them fretful. They felt like bashing someone. The sea had gone down enough for us to go on deck to breathe – it was no colder there than below. A quarrel broke out between an able seaman and a fat stoker petty officer. When they swung at each other, Soames and I, with some others, grabbed and held them till they had calmed down.

Soames said, grinning, 'Maybe I see why they give some fellows commissions.'

What he had observed was fear.

It was 0200, Christmas morning 1942, when we came alongside in St Johns, heaving out lines to secure our breast-ropes and springs.

In the snowbound town, which enfolded us like the tiers of a theatre, lights showed here and there. Silent night! Soon the children would wake up to look in their stockings. From 0800 aboard our shattered ship, there would be leave for both watches.

When I think about that time, though, I do not dwell so much on storms and air-raids as on insomniac visions of dimly lit English railway stations. Couples saying goodbye in the blue lamplight, faces ghastly with fatigue, drafts of servicemen and women lugging kitbags as they stumble in search of their trains. Daylight comes in through broken glass, steam hisses with smells of hot oil and sulphur, the big, black steam-engines pulsing, with now and then a little shriek of whistles as a train pulls out. Nagging posters say, 'Is your journey really necessary?' and 'Careless talk costs lives.' Those lovers with their arms around each other, those young men who will not be coming home, the grief of everlasting farewells – none of this could ever be redeemed by any victory, however glorious. Every life, every death would add its increment to the sum of irremediable human sorrow.

Five

In spring 1943 I was in England learning to impersonate an officer. Facing a board of three admirals and a schoolmaster captain, I'd answered their questions while looking them each in the eye. I had been told they liked that. They sent me to train at HMS *King Alfred* in Brighton/Hove and at Lancing College, a neo-Gothic public school nearby.

As cadet-ratings we wore square rig, with a white ribbon round the cap. As officers we dressed as gentlemen in navy blue reefer jackets with gilt buttons, white shirts with hard collars and black tie. The difference made all the difference, but really all I had was the uniform. The course was so fast and tried to cram in so much knowledge that I couldn't retain it after the final exam. I was capable only of looking keen and alert and giving orders. My rank on passing out was Midshipman RNVR, and not long afterwards I became Probationary Temporary Acting Sub-Lieutenant RNVR with one wavy gold stripe on my sleeves. Every few months I shed an adjective: first I lost Probationary, then Acting, though the war did not last long enough for me to lose Temporary. I believe this was to reassure regular officers with straight gold stripes that they would not be stuck with us jokers for long. We were good enough for coarse work like wars, entitled to die in action, but not for the real naval business of kissing gilded arse.

The commission came just in time. Another few months and

I'd probably have told them to stuff it. Living at close quarters with men and sharing their dangers, one develops loyalties.

I did enjoy being an officer, though – anyone would. Life on the lower deck at sea had been hard. Officers lived as comfortably as anyone in embattled Britain, waited on by stewards. Our travel-warrants were always first class. And in the officers' mess we used first names, did not grovel to seniors and drank duty-free gin for tuppence a glass. On the other hand we had to pay for food and uniforms, and once again I was more or less permanently indigent. And at the bottom of the scraped barrel, one had to take all the nagging.

Liberty in London would have been more fun with money. Well-paid Americans had taken over. They monopolized the taxis. GIs lounged at street corners or squatted on pavements shooting craps. Loose-limbed, they threw balls at each other in the parks, catching them in big leather gloves. Officers in olive-drab tunics and pink trousers wined and dined young Englishwomen in restaurants and nightclubs. Some of the women had husbands fighting overseas. There were many divorces.

I was lucky enough to meet my sister Lucinda on leave. She was now a lieutenant in the ATS, attached to the Royal Artillery. Her anti-aircraft battery near Portsmouth was often in action. One morning after a hard night's drinking with the boys, she came to breakfast with a terrible hangover and a story of having dreamt that she'd shot down a Luftwaffe bomber. She was shocked to learn that the dream was true, that at the plotting table she had called the successful shot. She told me this story at dinner somewhere near Piccadilly. I was walking her to the tube station at the Circus when air-raid sirens began to wail. Before long Pall Mall was in flames. We offered our services to an air-raid warden. Could we help? 'Yes,' he said, 'just fuck off!' We saw how fearlessly London firemen worked while buildings collapsed around them. The noise was shocking, mostly from ack-ack batteries in the parks.

Londoners were at their best under attack, cheerful, friendly and unselfish. After a bad night they'd give thumbs up. True, there were also the power-crazed butchers and grocers who snarled, 'There's a war on – d'you mind?'

During a brief stint at Westward Ho! Devon, the secret experimental research station, I was able to spend some evenings with my sister Kitty, who was now a WAAF driver on an RAF bomber base nearby. She had served first in the FANWY or 'fannies', driving stretcher-parties in the Blitz, and then Air Chief Marshall Sir Cyril Newall, head of the RAF. We drank with aircrew, a fresh lot each week, since the ones we had been with the week before were already missing. I noticed how intense were the loves of airmen and WAAF in the face of death. Joan was back at Viewmount with her baby boy; her husband, Gibbon FitzGibbon, a born warrior, was away with the 1st Army in North Africa. I saw her there when I came home on leave.

Leave in neutral Ireland was a strange experience. The mailboat from Holyhead to Dun Laoghaire was always crowded with servicemen and women unaccustomed to being in plain clothes, Ireland being studiously neutral. Immigration formalities were tedious. There was a long queue to show papers. On one arrival I was at the back of the line when my name was called, telling me to report to the purser's office. Passing admirals and generals in civvies, I came to the desk, only to be arrested by two sailors of the Irish Marine Service. One of the sailors carried my bag. In the customs shed I was greeted by a chuckling lieutenant – my friend Buddy Thompson. He had used this ruse to save me from standing in line. He took me into an office to join the superintendent of the gardaí in a dozen Guinness. Buddy (Basil), a respected solicitor, was deeply eccentric and very funny. He looked like an Arab. A major passion was his yacht *Rosemary*, which he kept at the moorings of the Royal Irish Yacht Club at Dun Laoghaire. Once he took a lobster from a pot in Dublin Bay, carried it home and boiled it. Then, chuckling, sailed back and returned it to the pot. Something for the fisherman to think about, he said. I stayed with Buddy and his pretty wife Peggy before going on to Viewmount.

My father took me into his study, where he grilled me about

the war. He soon became bored. The trouble was that I knew less about the war than he did. Deeply pessimistic, he expected the Germans any day. He corresponded regularly with old friend R.C.A.S. Hobart, brother of Sir Percy Hobart, the general who trained the Desert Rats of the Eighth Army. My father's friend had been in the ICS with him and was known as 'civil' Hobart, while the general was notorious as 'uncivil'. Another correspondent was a retired civil servant who had been personal private secretary to Lloyd George in the Great War. The former PPS told a story about a recent dinner with Churchill at 10 Downing Street. One of the guests was Stanley Baldwin, former Tory prime minister. Churchill called for his cognac and lit up a big cigar, preparing to relax and enjoy himself. Baldwin rose and took his leave – 'I must be off,' he said. 'I'm a busy man.'

Father told me to help myself to beer. The house was freezing; we dined in overcoats. There were only two servants now. The tennis court had been ploughed to grow wheat. Gandhi, the big hunter I'd ridden, had learned to pull the plough.

Since I found myself appointed to Combined Operations, I volunteered for Naval Commandos. It was my own choice and, I thought, a chance at adventure. Accepted, I was posted to RN Commando 'U', to train in Scotland at Ardentinny on Holy Loch, quartered in a baronial mansion commissioned as HMS *Armadillo*. The course was gruelling but fun. We ran up and down mountains and jumped into the loch in full gear. This butch stuff was to inure us to cold and wet. By day we wore khaki battledress with Commando flashes and navy epaulettes, changing into gentlemanly blues in the evening for nights of happy carousing. It was up with the larks and to bed with the Wrens – the latter only for young officers who could afford sexy weekends in Glasgow. Not for a commissioned pauper like me.

Bored with seeing the same crackers served up every day with dinner, I wrote the date on one of them. A couple of days later the Wren chief steward, a lovely blonde, berated me for this.

'Why give me a hard time? It's just a joke,' I groaned.

Her smile was dazzling. 'Hoping to get your attention!' she said. I'd have loved to respond. But without money for the Glasgow excursion, it was no go.

There was a Canadian unit and at least one American officer. Lieutenant Kittrick had been decorated for gallantry in the Sicilian landings. I asked him why he hadn't joined the US Navy. 'Well,' he drawled, 'reckoned our ships were kinda *dry* ...' No rum or gin in the USN.

We learned how to kill with our bare hands, with piano wire, with a matchbox. The instructor was a pock-marked leading seaman, perhaps a psychopath. We exercised with stabbing knives and coshes. With relish the killick showed us how to grab an attacker's testicles and disable him. I knew in my heart that I could never win at unarmed combat. My formula had to be, 'Carry on, petty officer!' In reality our job was to land with assault troops, take charge of the turnaround of landing craft and clear the beach of obstacles. Which did not stop us from indulging fantasies of charging an enemy pillbox and dropping grenades through the loopholes.

Meanwhile we had to train our men – petty officers and lively young toughs. Our unit was commanded by a short-arsed two-and-a-half striper we called Twinkletoes.

Commanding the training establishment was an elderly RN commander known as Benghazi Bill. He shared one characteristic with Patrick O'Brian's fictional hero Captain Aubrey – he kept getting his proverbs and clichés wrong. 'You can't pull the wool over my ears!' he'd say. 'It's all water over the bridge,' and 'A rolling stone gathers no moths.' Once, mysteriously, he told an officer, 'You're spreading your eggs too thin.'

We spent our whole time exercising for assault landing. From romantic Inverary we practised beach landings with successive army units, including a battalion of Norwegian mountain troops. The blond beasts were strangely indifferent to the things that interested us – girls and drink. We felt like sissies.

Supervising the war games, with live ammunition, were gallant instructors. Major the Baron de Styger, known as Tiger, was the most glamorous. I heard his exchange with an infantry officer: 'I hear you're married, Tiger! Good show – no more orgies, what?'

'Well, thanks old boy, but you've got it wrong. I *met* my wife at an orgy.'

Another instructor was Captain Sholto Douglas, always chivvying troops on the beach, a neat figure in Balmoral bonnet, sea boots and duffel coat over plaid trews. He was armed only with a swagger-cane, tapping his boot impatiently. 'Come along chaps, chop-chop!' On D-Day, similarly accoutred and unarmed, he was seen under fire on Sword beach, encouraging the attackers.

I was on a road somewhere in the north of England, speed-marching with my sub-unit, on 6 June 1944 when news reached us of the landings in Normandy. We were trained to the top of our form, absolutely fit and ready for this action we'd been working towards for almost a year. And here we'd been left behind. The excuse was that heavy casualties had been expected but had not materialized (something we could not regret). I felt the futility keenly. I looked at my lean and active sailors and petty officers and saw their disappointment – *ah, fuck*. True, there might be another big combined operation in South-East Asia – and in fact we were soon sent to India for it. But there was no way we could ever again come up to the pitch we were at now. And for myself, this was what had become of my attempt to control my life by volunteering. In the Atlantic war there had at least been depth-charge attacks on the hidden enemy, the adrenalin rush of action and, in the seas around Britain, Junkers 88s to shoot at. After all the strenuous exercise, after giving up duty-free drink and tobacco for a year, after preparing for desperate fighting, after training the assault troops, this anticlimax, bathos, futility! We were reduced to listening to BBC broadcasts, the cricket commentator drawling on about the style of the assault troops. It would be a fine frosty Friday before common sense kicked in to remind us that we had been spared the dirty work for a while.

We were plunged into boredom. Discipline suffered. Posted to Lowestoft on the coast of East Anglia, we watched the buzz-bombs fly over to London. We watched the morning sky full of US bombers in tight formation as they headed for Germany. We saw the afternoon of their returning remnant, more gaps than aircraft in the formations. Spectators at the horror show, we were out of it, except, of course, when we were on leave in London.

My friend Harry Lomax and I were staying in an officers' club on Piccadilly, listening to buzz-bombs. We were in bed when one of them stopped right overhead. When the racket stopped, they started to come down. With pillows over our heads, we waited for the bang. Luckily the bomb fell some streets away. It was different with the V2 rockets. First, there would be a terrific explosion as they hit not far off, and then we'd hear them coming as the sound caught up.

Walking about in the ruins, where some bomb sites were already blossoming with wildflowers, I thought my life had shrivelled to banalities. My depression was increased by poverty, though I did have food and shelter. But the freedom money brings was missing. True I had my books with me, *Ulysses* and Flann O'Brien's *At Swim-Two-Birds*, which opened another world, lost Ireland.

In 1944 we were sent on courses to keep us out of mischief. I was doing summer busywork in Dartmouth, enjoying the fine, classical buildings where, in peacetime, cadets learned the elements of our profession.

A long, high corridor ran from the palatial wardroom to a distant wing. The commander set up races in early evening for junior officers. A Wren took off her shoes and sprinted down the corridor, fleet as Atlanta. She was the hare. Junior officers started in pursuit. No one ever caught the Wren, but the first to reach the far end drank free all evening.

In the Dart estuary one afternoon, I swam out to a rock where two pretty women were basking in their swimsuits. We began chatting and I found myself strongly attracted to the slim girl with auburn hair who said she was a VAD nurse. This was Patricia Parsons, who became my first wife. In a desperate commitment to life, we were married in London later that year, though we both knew it was a mistake and everyone advised against it. Pat's father had left her mother to bring her up on her own. She had been deprived of love, her mother being away at work throughout her childhood. The little girl had only a sketchy idea of how to give love, and growing up in this way became distrustful of receiving it. Still, we were to tough it out for ten years, in which time our two sons were born. But we were too different in temperament to make a go of it.

What Pat really loved was nursing and the structured, busy life of hospitals. Her maternal grandmother, whom she adored, had been a hospital matron. We had a lot of fun in those early days, drinking rough cider in rural pubs and staggering back to our lodgings, legs partly disabled by the deceptively strong drink. We were married in Holy Trinity Church, eclipsed by the Brompton Oratory next door, that most opulent of Roman Catholic fanes. My best man was a brother officer and we carried swords, mine on loan from Austin Reed, the Regent Street haberdasher.

The honeymoon was not a success. Pat insisted that we spend it with her great-uncle in his manor house in Devon. The rich old fellow, his hands clenched in carpal tunnel syndrome, showed me the treasures in his strongroom. He collected Plymouth China and gorgeously illuminated medieval books of the hours. He did not think much of me. Nor, I feared, did the bride. I came down with nervous colitis. I had to notify the hard-nosed commander of my naval base at Tamerton Folliot that a civilian doctor had declared me too sick to return to duty. He sent a naval doctor to check on me. This was the commander who had the bugle-boy caned for playing a wrong note.

Pat was posted as assistant to a naval dentist in Lowestoft. She enjoyed the work, I think, making many jokes about it, though after a while it became stressful. My letters from overseas were full of complaints about inaction so she took a short leave to contact personnel officers in the Admiralty. She charmed them. Thanks to her energetic efforts, I was transferred to seagoing duty. But that was to happen many months in the future.

I was in London on 8 May 1945, the historic 'VE Day' celebrating victory in Europe. 'My dear friends,' Churchill broadcast, 'this is your day ...' It was a happy day, no more war and bloodshed at home, and the odd thing is that I can hardly recall any of it. I do remember crowds after dark along the Embankment (I hate crowds), huge peonies and carnations of fire opening in the sky with loud explosions, while from speakers on lamp posts came Handel's 'Water Music' and 'Firework Music'. Bells had been ringing changes all afternoon, a wonderful sound. I was just tired and disillusioned, and now that I look back, I am sure all Britain was weary beyond measure. All of us had lost friends and relatives. I grieved most for Peter Morrice, the poet, shot down in flames over Milan.

Strangers kissed, there was dancing in the streets, yet we knew the misery wasn't over. Japan still resisted fiercely, and there was a weary way to go in rebuilding shattered cities. We knew from magazine pictures that Berlin was in ruins, hardly a building unscathed, and the beautiful city of Dresden destroyed by a single firestorm. There was a suspicion that our Russian allies had borne the brunt of the war. But in Britain too everything was run down, broken or wrecked.

Someone had said this was the century of the common man – and even the common man was depressed by the thought.

Six

I arrived a term late for my first year at Cambridge. Jesus College had obtained my release from the service and I'd been demobilized and paid off in Belfast, where I'd joined. I was now a civilian, in possession of such unfamiliar objects as a ration book. Presently I received a letter from the Secretary of the Admiralty, conveying the thanks of the Lords Commissioners for my service. The good wishes of their lordships, he wrote, go with you on your return to civilian life.

Patricia had been invalided out of the nursing service on psychiatric grounds after a nervous breakdown. I never did learn the details. She told me the doctor had said, 'I hope your husband has broad shoulders.' We both did our best, though in the end it wasn't enough.

In addition to my gratuity from the navy and my share of prize money, I had a state grant for my time at the university. Wearing my itchy demob suit and ersatz leather shoes, I called on the Master of Jesus College in his lodge to introduce myself. Dr E.M.W. Tillyard was a gentle, cricket-watching scholar who looked like a beardless Santa Claus. A former archaeologist and now a Milton man with a strong interest in Yeats, he spoke kindly about my exhibition, and my promise as a student. I told him I wanted to read philosophy.

'No, no, no, you don't!' he said, appalled. 'You'd hate the way they teach it here – Logical Positivism and the impossibility of saying anything that means anything. Oh, I think I know what you want – to understand the things you've been living through. Moral Science as taught here wouldn't help you with that at all. Much better to read the English Tripos. You can learn about life in poetry and fiction; that's what it's for. And if you want formal philosophy, you can always opt for a paper on the English Moralists in part two of the Tripos.'

I gave in. The Master knew what he was talking about. I was having trouble being a returned husband and a civilian, and I saw the university as my lifeline. The war had left the place shabby, in need of paint and cleaning, crowded with leftover Polish and American airmen, yet still a beautiful refuge of learning and understanding. Here among medieval and renaissance surroundings I might find my way.

In the gatehouse under the tower a porter in a dark suit and bowler hat stepped out to meet me. He tipped the hat, 'Morning, sir! May I know your name, sir?' I told him my name. That was the last time I had to give it. Henceforth all the porters knew me.

I passed into the front court, dark red-brick Tudor ranges of rooms on three sides, the fourth enclosed by a wall topped with revolving spikes. Doorways led to staircases, off which suites of rooms opened. Beside the entrances occupants' names were painted white on black. On the staircase facing the gatehouse Samuel Taylor Coleridge had lodged. Another stair led to the former rooms of Laurence Sterne, author of *Tristram Shandy*. Jesus was also the alma mater of Thomas Malthus, a Fellow and author of the influential *Essay on Population* (1798).

After the first two terms, when Pat and I rented a flat near Fenners cricket ground, I moved into college. Pat and baby John spent that year in Dun Laoghaire, in the former German minister's residence. I was able to study now without domestic distraction, although – perhaps perversely – I missed it. This, despite the fact that Pat and I did not get along together too well.

My rooms were in a Victorian range. There were two doors, a light inner one, to keep out draughts, and a heavy outer one, known as 'the oak'. Closing the outer door was called 'sporting your oak', a signal that you must not be disturbed. There was a lavatory on the landing. To reach the baths, you had to cross two courts in the open, a daunting ordeal in winter. In this academic squalor I hoped to receive an education. What I did receive was a degree. But perhaps the spirit of the place infused me too because of 'incubation', the simple fact of sleeping there.

My supervisor, for whom I had to write an essay every week, was A.P. Rossiter, a sardonic don whose specialty was the Elizabethan stage. In addition to his scholarly works, he had written a gritty novel, *Poor Scholars*. A Fellow of the college and a BA, he refused to proceed to an MA, which he insisted would do absolutely nothing for him. He had a degree in chemistry and was an enthusiastic mountain climber and motorcyclist. I greatly enjoyed our weekly sessions and, for all his ironic comments, I think he did too.

Though Rossiter thought me promising, I was still an awkward student. It could be said of me, as of Coleridge, 'He was very studious, but his reading was desultory and capricious.'

My tutor, the don who oversaw my studies and conduct, was a much decorated ex-bomber pilot and classicist called David Balme. At the end of my first year, personal difficulties impelled me to tell him that I would like to take psychology instead of continuing with English.

'You wouldn't like it at all!' Balme said. 'I imagine you want to learn more about yourself and, believe me, psychology wouldn't help in the least. You'd hate it, the way they teach it here. Nothing but rats in mazes. Listen, I was interviewed by a psychologist in the RAF. She asked if I'd prefer to fly bombers or fighters. I said bombers, and I saw her write down, "Says bombers, but would really prefer fighters."'

'You were reading upside down!' I said, lost in admiration.

With the postwar surge in enrollment, as we warriors came squawking home to roost, students had to share rooms. My roommate was Willie Watson, a decorated RAF veteran of Mosquito bombers, a Lowland Scot whose vivid personality more than compensated for his lack of inches. What's more he quickly earned his

Blue for boxing, becoming inter-university bantamweight champion. A beautiful boxer who always fought close to his opponent, he was also a formidable golfer, and older: 'Kildare,' he'd cry, 'you're just a *boy*! Me, I'm *thairty*! *Thairty*! Jesus, I'm an old man!'

I learned a lot from Watson. In his teens he'd been a street orator for the Communists in Glasgow. He'd quit the Party in disgust when Stalin signed a non-aggression pact with Hitler, but he could still make a powerful speech for the workers. In the RAF he'd survived four tours of operations flying with a Canadian pilot called Bob in a Mosquito, that wonderful plywood twin-engined aeroplane. A group photo of his original squadron showed a great crowd of faces. Only three or four were still alive. Willie described the fatigue of later operations, the kite flying on automatic while the airmen nodded off over Germany until, awoken by flak bursting around them, they'd gasp in terror, 'God! What was that, what was that?'

Watson had flown many sorties harrying retreating Germans in northern Sicily. He was convinced that aircraft were grounded to let the enemy escape to Italy, to keep them strong enough to fight the Russians. This bee in his bonnet got him discharged on psychiatric grounds, his Distinguished Flying Cross making it impolitic to discipline him. He was sent to a rural hospital in England, where he said he played golf and fucked the WAAFs and nurses until his release. He was anxiously protected by ex-comrades – William Howell, for one, of Gonville and Caius College. Howell was an artist reading architecture and a kind of mother-hen to his friends.

Howell was a prime mover behind the new Cambridge Arts Society, which put on public lectures. There I heard Barnett Freedman and Osbert Lancaster deliver sarcastic talks. Freedman said that art curators stood in the same relation to art as bishops did to Jesus Christ. Lancaster, trashing Herbert Read, said of children's art, 'By all means let the little beasts express themselves but for Christ's sake don't call it art!' I remember best James Laver, keeper of prints at the Victoria and Albert Museum, expounding the history and meaning of costume.

My roomie was busy writing a novel about professional boxing, yet he also found time to promote not only Marx and Engels, but Carl Jung and a social historian called Lewis Mumford, an American sage then popular with younger intellectuals. I diligently read Jung's *The Psychology of the Unconscious*, and then Mumford's books, *The Culture of Cities*, *The Condition of Man* and other ambitious studies. Another of Watson's enthusiasms rubbed off on me – Wilhelm Reich, a Freudian apostate who combined psychoanalysis with Marxist politics. I admired *The Mass Psychology of Fascism* and *The Function of the Orgasm*, works thought unsuitable for students, so I had to buy them from the Freedom Press in London. The orgasm study showed a photograph of a female anus in a state of sexual arousal, and compared it with the electric potential of a damp towel. The oddest thing about Reich was that he came to believe one could collect psychic energy by using a simple funnel and directing it at one's body. He also designed an empty box which he insisted preserved the 'orgones' or energy usually discharged in orgasms. He was sent to jail for selling these empty boxes with the promise that they could cure cancer. This was exciting stuff for an ex-sailor trying to find meaning in his life.

From hints in Jung, I became interested in alchemy and Gnostic Mysticism. These studies, which had little to do with anything in the Tripos, happened to coincide with the coldest winter anyone could remember (1947) and a severe fuel crisis in England. Cambridge is in any case the chilliest place in England and without heating it was unbearable. The only place of comfort I could find was a corner of the stacks in the university library. Books, after all, had to be kept warm even if persons *in statu pupillari* froze. My corner happened to contain a great many volumes on early Christianity and Gnosticism. I read Mossheim's *Commentaries* with close attention, though from time to time the cosiness of my nook induced naps and dreaming. I'm afraid these lucubrations rather got in the way of close reading of the books set for examination. Lectures, I should explain, were voluntary, so that we were ruthless in skipping boring ones. I favoured Mr Potts on Aristotle's *Poetics*,

George (Dedie) Rylands on Shakespeare and Matt Hodgart on the *Lyrical Ballads*. Potts, with his hesitant precision, helped me to understand Platonic Ideas. I can recall the moment I fully saw them, under a lamp post in Petty Cury Street.

Rylands was a Fellow of King's, an old Etonian and evidently an old queen too. The story went that he had watched a wedding celebrated in King's College chapel. 'Oh dear, oh dear,' he said. 'It will never work.' And when he was asked how he knew that, he said, 'I ought to know! I've slept with both of them!'

My straying from the curriculum helped me in intimate ways, even though I now recall very little of what I learned – though surely not less than I remember from the curriculum itself. It helped by showing me experiences similar to my own.

I wrote some poems, but when I showed them, they were scornfully dismissed. The influence of F.R. Leavis was strong at this time. Young sophisticates believed that nothing written by anyone they knew could conceivably be any good. True, it was entirely possible that nothing I had written was any good. Leavis offered a brilliant technique of analysis, but apparently it did not permit him to enjoy contemporary literature, except D.H. Lawrence and T.S. Eliot. He also believed that other scholars were out to get him, a paranoia complicated by the fact that other scholars were out to get him.

Rossiter was disappointed by my results in the Tripos. I had come somewhere near the top of the second class. He glowered over the half-moons which had slid to the end of his big, north-country nose.

'A good second – it's not what I'd hoped,' he said. 'If you'd done the reading, you should have taken a first or else failed! There's no distinction in a good second.'

He was right, but what was the point of a first? People who took firsts never left school; they were institutionalized for life. Sour grapes, to be sure.

The trouble was that a good second – *aurea mediocritas!* – would be just right for a government or corporate bureaucracy. Bureaucracies don't want brilliant men, they want safe men. I put off that thought as long as I could. I had a family to support and the jobs I applied for in, for example, publishing, offered very little.

After demobilization, I had the idea that I might try for the Irish diplomatic service. My sister Nancy FitzGerald, now a Roman Catholic and acquainted with the new Irish elite, introduced me to Freddy Boland, at the time Minister for External Affairs. He interviewed me in the splendour of Iveagh House, formerly the residence of Lord Iveagh, the Guinness plutocrat, where Mother had danced at many a grand ball. Boland was an affable, cultivated man who advised me to learn Irish and, if I were to study philosophy, to avoid Hegel. It was kind of him to see me and I thanked him. My failure to find instruction in Irish at Cambridge killed further ambition for the Irish diplomatic service.

I wanted work that would take me out of the British Isles. Everything there seemed worn out, the cities gap-toothed with bomb sites, the people run down and bloody-minded. The only promising thing I could see resulted from the Welfare State, a generation raised on free milk, cod liver oil and subsidized dinners noticeably sturdier and healthier than earlier generations. Then I had a break. A friend of Mother's, a monocled executive in Anglo-Iranian Oil, said he could give me a job teaching English to Iranians in the Persian Gulf. Pay and benefits were excellent. All I had to do was pass a medical exam.

The company doctor was surly. He rejected me on the grounds that my blood pressure was too high. It was high when *he* tested me, at any rate. The hotshot asked him to try again, and this time he was so nasty I tested even higher. Result, no job with the oily boys. 'You'd die in that heat,' the doctor said. I was supposed to be grateful.

The fact I was looking at opportunities of that kind should show how lost I was. Back when I was a volunteer fighting mad dictators I had thought my life useful. Now I was just looking for a livelihood. I sank even further when I agreed to be interviewed for a post with the Colonial Education Service. I ought to have noticed that the empire was finished. Churchill was to say he would never preside over the dismantling of the British empire, but that is exactly what he had done.

I had my interview and while I was awaiting an answer took a temporary job as a supply teacher in the boroughs of central London in 1947. Supply teachers were temporary replacements for staff who were sick or absent for some reason. I was sent to fill in at modern secondary schools, sort of dead ends in education for students who had not qualified for elite grammar schools. The principal of one such school came into my classroom while a boy was on his feet telling a story. The principal glanced at him and said, more or less to his face, 'That boy, Mr ah, Mr ah – that boy ought to be *emasculated* – ' smiling at the lad, who smiled back, 'to prevent him propagating his species.'

In another school, the children in my room were always noisy and unruly, hurling spitballs and paper darts, while across the corridor in another room, children were bent over their work in silence, diligently writing. I asked their teacher, a saturnine man with magenta bags under his eyes, how he achieved this amazing discipline. 'It's simple,' he said in tones of deep gloom. 'I *hate* the little bastards … and they know it.'

But there was one young teacher I could not forget, who knew every child in his class and treated each one of them with respect.

Meanwhile I received a letter appointing me to the education service of Tanganyika in East Africa. 'Sir, I am directed by Mr Secretary Creech Jones to refer to your application …' Creech Jones was the colonial secretary in the Labour government. I was to go on half-pay in January 1948 (half of £550 a year!) and start courses at London University. I was to take a Teacher's Diploma at the Institute of Education, to start learning Swahili at the School of Oriental and African Studies, and be instructed in tropical hygiene by the senior medical adviser to the Colonial Office. Again, there would be a medical examination. This time I had no trouble. A Dublin physician found me in excellent shape.

After a term as supply teacher I worked as a film extra. I had to join a union called the Film Artistes' Association and check with an agent, a hardbitten blonde named Streaky Bacon. She told us where to report for work, or rather, for auditions with casting directors. I earned about three guineas a day. A guinea was a kind of snob currency, worth a pound plus one shilling. I soon found that I could earn an extra five shillings a day if I could sport a beard. I reported for a beard whenever I could get away with it. Make-up artists would spend up to half an hour gumming hair to your face.

I was a bearded soldier in Fortinbras' army in Laurence Olivier's *Hamlet*, marching for a whole week around an artificial hill on the lot of Denham studios. I sweated in a helmet and a heavy suit of knitted wool, sprayed with aluminium paint to look like chain mail. The whole sequence was left on the cutting-room floor. On my way to the dressing rooms I would pass the tiny figure of Jean Simmons in a blonde wig as Ophelia. Sir Laurence had his own caravan.

I had resumed my street clothes one day when a man who had been staring at me on the set approached and said, 'Are you by any chance an actor?' I wrung his hand, choking back a sob of gratitude. He told me he was scouting for a producer who sought a fair-haired man for an important part. Given the name of Brian Desmond-Hurst and an address in Chelsea, I was to report there after work the next day.

The door was opened by a muscular type in a T-shirt. The man who strikes the gong in the Rank Pictures logo! He said, 'Brian'th at the Dorchester. He'll be home thoon. Come in and thit down.'

I followed him upstairs to a big room open to the rafters. There was a grand piano, an alcove with a coffee table and an armchair. Butch pointed to the chair. I sat. On the black table there was a script, 'Lawrence of Arabia, by Robin Maugham'. Well, well. The writer was Somerset Maugham's nephew. Butch was speaking.

'Robin has this fantastic relationship with Arabs, you know, like Lawrence.' I tuned out. I was remembering that Desmond-Hurst had directed *A Christmas Carol* with Alistair Sim, a cinema classic, and that he was Irish. Surely he was a serious director. Maybe I was about to be discovered. I could learn to ride a camel.

The great man arrived, out of puff from climbing the stairs, an obese figure with a sharp, cruising eye. He questioned me about my film work and other experience. I said it was getting late and my wife was expecting me.

'You're married?'

Yes I was, and with a little boy. The director looked bored. I had wasted his time. 'We have your number? We'll call you.'

A couple of years later I met Robin Maugham in East Africa, where he lived near Iringa in the Southern Highlands of Tanganyika, a small, tough man with a big Swedish boyfriend. He was a successful author of sensational books. His script of Lawrence was never performed, like most filmscripts.

And of course I never heard from Desmond-Hurst. Geraldine Fitzgerald was in London, making a movie called *So Evil My Love* with Ray Milland. She laughed. 'So it was the casting couch for you – and you didn't come across!' Later I heard from a real actor that this director always expected to score a few boys wherever he went.

My great moment came in Shepperton Studios, when I played a bearded Ernest Shackleton in his Antarctic tent, listening to a recorded hymn on a wind-up gramophone. The hymn was 'Abide With Me', which was also the title of the film, a short feature made by Religious Pictures Inc., a subsidiary of J. Arthur Rank. The Shackleton bit was shot in the morning. In the afternoon, when the extra who was to play a German officer failed to turn up, I became the officer who marched the heroic nurse Edith Cavell to her death by firing squad.

One evening, just for laughs, I decided to appear at our Holland Park flat with a beard. But as I arrived, Pat ran out of the house calling me to come in and look at the living room. Distracted, she did not notice the beard, and when I went through the house I saw why. The whole back of the building had fallen into the garden at the rear, covering grass and flowerbeds with piles of rubble. A canvas tarpaulin hung as a temporary shelter. Little Johnny in his playpen had been narrowly missed by falling bricks. The structure, weakened by bomb blasts in the Blitz, had finally collapsed.

While I was at London University, Pat stayed on in the Dun Laoghaire flat and looked after Johnny. The house was called Gortleitragh. Our second son, Christian, was born there in January 1949 in the room from which a Nazi spy-master had radioed intelligence to Berlin. Dr Eduard Hempel, former German minister, was still the landlord, afraid to go home. His part of the house was richly furnished with Oriental treasures. In the basement Frau Hempel ran a bakery, selling fine pastries. I can still hear Dr Hempel shouting 'Eva! Eva! *Komm hier!*' She always came. To us his manner was stiffly polite. Mother came to visit one day. Dr Hempel was introduced and I could see he was charmed. We were then treated with greater respect. As Ireland prospered after joining the European Economic Community, the building was bulldozed away to make room for a shopping centre.

During Christian's birth, the midwife – who had been trained at the expense of W.B. Yeats as a reward for having looked after his chidren – suggested that I go to my sister Joan in Dublin and wait for a call. I bicycled off to lunch with her. The phone rang early afternoon: 'You can come now,' the midwife said, 'Dr Davidson is after leaving. You have another fine boy.'

And away I rode on my bike. A thin rain was now falling and the streets were slippery. I rode carefully. But when I was nearing home, I think in Monkstown, my front wheel slipped into a tramline and I took a horrible fall. I'd thrust out my hands to break the impact; they were skinned to the wrist. Luckily there was a small hospital nearby. In shock, I felt little pain when the wounds were cleaned and dressed. I was given an anti-tetanus shot. A doctor going off duty kindly drove me home.

I went in to see Pat and the beautiful baby, my heavily bandaged arms hidden behind my back. She caught sight of them, at once accusing me of trying to upstage her in her moment of triumph. I thought she was joking. But when my eyes began to close and my whole body came out in thick hives, while I could hardly breathe, she was clearly in earnest when she charged me with a psychosomatic demonstration, intended to belittle her own suffering.

It was pointless to protest that I was suffering an allergic reaction to my anti-tetanus shot.

I told myself that Pat was reacting to her painkillers.

We had spent Christmas 1947 in the London flat along with our guests, an American graduate student called Harry, and two German prisoners-of-war on parole who had been cleared of Nazi affiliations. The Nuremberg Trials had taken place, with their dreadful revelations. The systematic murder of millions of Jews, Gypsies, homosexuals and others was the worst thing that happened in my lifetime.

Once more I was a poor student. The best part of my teachers' course was a seminar in anthropology. More useful was teaching under supervision to a class of wonderful children of seven or eight years of age. At The School of Oriental and African Studies, Mrs Ashley, author of the best grammar of the language, taught me enough Swahili to get me started in Africa. I carried her grammar book with me and studied it whenever I could. I was ready for the new adventure.

Seven

I sat on the veranda of our house on Kilimanjaro, Tanganyika, in 1948. Onesmo brought tea. He was a sturdy young Chagga, elegant in his white *kanzu*, the long shirt worn with a white embroidered cap. In the first light of day his honest face shone. He looked off to my right. I turned my head to see, above the hibiscus and frangipani, and far above the forest canopy towering over them, the shining snows of Kibo, at nearly 20,000 feet the highest point in Africa. The glacier was touched with rosy tints of daybreak, the light changing every moment. Kilimanjaro lay like a vast Brahminy bull on the plain 3000 feet below us. Onesmo loved the mountain, home of his tribe and ancestors. It was something we shared.

In the house Ndeo, the other houseman, was already at work cleaning, under Pat's direction. Any minute now Paolo, the dignified cook, a prominent Lutheran and a man of substance, would arrive to inspect me. 'A young officer like you – you will not have much money,' he had told me when he first arrived, natty in blazer and fez. 'I'm not interested in money – I have plenty from my coffee and other crops – but I'm a good cook and want to keep my hand in. Pay whatever you can.' He was a legendary cook, trained by a Goanese chef. Wives of visiting dignitaries kept trying to lure him away from us without success. Paolo would tell me about it afterwards.

There was no electricity up there, so the house was lit by paraffin lamps. Paraffin also supplied energy for the fridge. Water for bathing and washing came from a big oil-drum heated by a wood fire.

Veils of cloud were straying over Kibo. The peak would be hidden throughout the day. Below the glaciers there was scree, below that heather and giant groundsel, then rain forest. I looked out over the plain. Hidden at the foot of the mountain was the town of Moshi, district headquarters, garrisoned by a battalion of the King's African Rifles. From there the district commissioner and his two district officers, with police and other specialists, administered the Chagga country. There were a few European and Asian planters on short-term leases. Beyond Moshi was the plateau of Tanganyika's Northern Province, the Maasai steppe, savannas stretching away to the blue foothills of Mount Meru. At night the plain was a galaxy of twinkling fires marking the hearths of nomads, Maasai and Warusha, with their donkeys and cattle, and Wanderobo hunters and foragers. Grasslands and bush teemed with wild animals.

After ruined England, after the three-week voyage in the MV *Dunnottar Castle* and the hot, dusty train journey through dry thorn bush from Mombasa, the place seemed like paradise. Roses, canna lilies and daffodils bloomed together.

Tanganyika was a trust territory of the United Nations, under British administration. I had been posted as teacher and education officer to the Government Secondary School at Old Moshi, a self-contained community at 7000 feet above sea-level. The headmaster was Ralph Elwell-Sutton, emaciated from fever, a kindly man of acute intelligence. An Oxford graduate, he had soldiered in the war and made a start as a writer, published in *Penguin New Writing*. Now all his energies went to his work at the school, preparing a generation for self-government. A third European was the industrial instructor, Cecil Rice, a former missionary and also a brilliant organizer of events like school sports. The 250 boys, nearly all Chagga, would have been remarkable anywhere. Teachers from various African tribes were well educated, trained and committed.

After breakfast I walked down to the field where the school assembled each morning with the band of drums, fifes and bugles. Banging the big drum in 'Marching through Georgia' was Gabriel, a tall, coffee-coloured boy who was the son of Old Moshi's *Mangi* or chief, deferred to by his schoolmates. The boys loved the band and sang Lutheran chorales and spirituals learned from missionaries.

The Chagga, numbering about 250,000, were strongly in favour of education and development. Their clans, each with its own *Mangi*, were separated by deep ravines. They had learned co-operation from experience in irrigation. Along the sides of valleys, *200-300* feet above torrents at the bottom, ran the furrows that carried water to banana groves and shambas. They followed the contours so accurately, the line chosen by eye, that they seemed to be flowing uphill. Directing this enterprise was the coffee co-operative that had made them rich, the Kilimanjaro Native Cooperative Union (KNCU).

The country had been a German colony from 1886 to 1918. The notorious Dr Karl Peters had ruled the area from Old Moshi at around the turn of the century, hanging several chiefs nearby without trial in 1900. Dismissed in 1906, in a later age he became a hero to the Nazis. The British captured Old Moshi in 1916, but did not begin administration there until 1920. It was here that General Jan Smuts had had his headquarters in the long campaign against Germans and their askaris under General von Lettow Vorbeck, whose scorched-earth retreats laid waste to the country. Fevers and forced labour had ravaged the tribes. Smuts could never bring Vorbeck to a pitched battle. Even after the Second World War Tanganyika had barely recovered from the first. The campaign was vividly described by Francis Brett Young in his unjustly forgotten book, *Marching on Tanga*. After describing the wild, beautiful country, Young wrote, 'But no man, in after years, will visit the battlefields of Pangani. No man, unless he wander there in search of game, will seek to look upon her sinister smile in the lovely winter weather of that deadly land.' Such a man, in my innocence, was I.

The first British district commissioner of the Chagga was the Hon. Charles Dundas, who helped the tribe to organize coffee cultivation and marketing. Dundasi, as they remembered him, was revered and given the honorific title of Elder of the Chagga People. His part in Chagga development is not mentioned in recent histories. It does not fit with Nyerere's 'self-help' socialism.

In his admirable book, *Kilimanjaro and Its Peoples,* Dundas acknowledged two informants, Nathanael Mtui and Joseph Merinyo. Merinyo, a wiry figure in his seventies with a goatee beard when I met him, wearing a topi, breeches and leggings, told how he had been schooled and made much of by the *Wadachi* – the Germans – who had taken him to Berlin to show him civilization. He spoke German as well as English, Swahili and kiChagga. Deeply versed in the history and lore of the tribe, he loved his country.

At a race meeting, he was presented to the Kaiser, who gave him a gold coin. Merinyo said the Germans, on the whole, had ruled with wisdom. They had introduced cash, Christianity and a railway. He did not mention the massacres following the Maji-maji Rebellion in 1905-07, in which as many as 40,000 Africans perished.

Some weeks after our first meeting, Merinyo invited me to a large meeting. This *baraza*, as it was called in Swahili, was to consider ways to make local government more democratic through a body called the Kilimanjaro Citizens' Union. They were proposing to elect a single paramount chief for the whole mountain, abolishing the local *Mangis.* This was not an initiative of the district commissioner, who thought it retrogressive. It was a grassroots project. I saw no chiefs there. My presence was to show that the tribe was not hostile to *Wazungu* (Europeans), although one aim was to resist further encroachment on Chagga lands by white settlers. I hardly understood the proceedings – conducted throughout in kiChagga, not Swahili. Merinyo introduced me to the tribesmen as a new *mwalimu* (teacher) friendly to the Chagga and willing to help them. There was unanimous support for education and enthusiastic pursuit of *maendeleo* (progress).

The DC, Martin Lewis, was a sandy-haired South African, whose intelligence was matched by experience. Over sundowners in his house he told me that police spies sent to the *baraza* had been ejected, but he understood I had been present. That was fine with him, he assured me – indeed it was creditable – but could I let him know what it was all about? I said I had not followed the discussion closely, since it was all in kiChagga, but that everything had been orderly. Thinking that if the Chagga had barred the police spies they would not want me to take their place, I added that Joseph Merinyo could probably tell him more. Elliot smiled and said, 'Yes, of course. Point taken. You don't want to lose their trust.'

One day he asked whether I had considered asking for a transfer from education to administration. He suggested that as a district officer I'd have more scope for work with Africans. By this time I also knew Tim Revington, the provincial commissioner, who was deeply committed to early independence. He said that if I wanted a transfer he would support my request.

I began to face up to my discontent with teaching. After a little over a year when Elwell-Sutton went on leave, I was headmaster. The school more or less ran itself, though I had to draw up the budget and defend it to auditors; and to teach subjects like mathematics, which I needed to bone up on before each class. Luckily some of the boys had more insight than me, including more than one of genius intelligence. Conditions for teaching were ideal: everyone wanted to learn. They had never been taught anything but tribal lore in their own language – schooling was always in English or Swahili. Learning foreign languages slowed progress. Some of the students were fully adult, and even married, which distressed Mr Rice, a crusty bachelor.

Education was clearly the key to development and better lives. I admired what Elwell-Sutton was doing, and Nancy King no less at her girls' school on another part of the mountain. By educating women, Nancy hoped to set off a kind of chain reaction as educated mothers sought schooling for their children. Tribal authorities trusted and respected her.

But I couldn't help feeling useless, as I confessed in a letter to my father that year. Socially we were somewhat isolated, without transport, though the school lorry did make regular trips into Moshi town. We made friends with some of the soldiers and their families, and with other government people, district officers, doctors, agricultural and other specialists. We played tennis at the club and attended dances, and we dined or drank at the Pink Elephant Bar, meeting settlers in both places. We got to know some of the Poles from the refugee camp just out of town. It was British suburban life, busy and vapid, although I enjoyed the wild sundowners and flirtations.

Germans had angered the whole world with their violent insistence on racial superiority. The British didn't talk about it openly, but were perfectly sure that they stood head and shoulders above every other breed on earth. Their trouble was, they let it show.

Lewis and Revington were different from most colonial officials. Lewis's mother Ethelreda had discovered and edited the South African classic *Trader Horne*, about a Boer pioneer. Her son was a man of wide sympathies. He told me once that a mutual friend of ours, a garage mechanic called Penfield, was the subject of secret service reports as a Communist. 'But I happen to like him. Dine with him any day!'

Revington was a man of refined sensibility, committed to public service. His attractive wife was free of the suburban airs that sometimes afflicted memsahibs. She gave me a bluepoint Siamese kitten.

I played beer rugby with the Moshi team and enjoyed it. For Saturday games I stayed overnight in the town, usually with a big second-row-forward, an Afrikaner called Len Bekker. At breakfast he poured Worcester sauce and Tabasco into the yolks of his eggs. 'Good for the hangover, man!' he declared.

He sold me a second-hand Mannlicher-Schoenauer 9.5 mm rifle. From a Czech manager in Bata's shoe shop I bought a Brno .22. With these weapons I discovered the absorbing craft of game hunting and the life of the bush with the tribes of the savanna, Kamba, Wanderobo, madmen and outlaws. The hunter's view of wildlife differs from that of the spectator. Himself a predator, he's part of the scene.

The country was seizing my imagination and entering my dreams. Still, I could not help being aware that I was a transient, a creature of the Colonial Office.

After a few months I noticed that Patricia looked unwell. She did not have a fever, but she was pale and listless. And one evening, while Ndeo was serving dinner, there was a disquieting episode.

Patricia was sitting across from me under a painting by Thanos Papadopoulos, a local artist. It was a nude portrait of the African girl he lived with. He had lent us the picture and we'd hung it as a kind of statement to visitors.

Ndeo brought in plates of peanut soup from the kitchen outside. He wore his long white kanzu and white kofia skull cap. I was looking at the painting, which racist visitors found ugly. The lamplight softened its harsh colours. I was wool-gathering when Ndeo set down my soup before me. Then he went round the heavy *mvule* table and served Patricia.

She stood and screamed at me. 'He served you first! You *let* him do it. He's supposed to serve me first. ... You said nothing! You didn't even *notice!*'

She burst into tears and, sobbing, ran into the adjoining bedroom. That room opened into the nursery where our two little boys were asleep. I sat frozen in my seat, stunned by the usual northern male hatred of a 'scene'.

The next moment I heard a metallic rattling followed by a tremendous explosion. The sound was shocking. I remembered that I kept my rifle in the big armoire. The rattling must have been Patricia loading a round. What was she doing? I ran into the bedroom.

Ndeo ran the other way, out the back door.

I found Patricia weeping and fumbling with the rifle. I took it from her and removed the bolt. I set it down on the bed.

'For God's sake, calm down!' Easy to say, and now I was in a rage myself. 'Who were you going to shoot? Ndeo or me? Or yourself?'

She muttered something incoherent about going to the visitors' rondavel to tell the provincial director of education how she was being treated, or rather tell his wife. They were visiting, and must be wondering why they'd heard a rifle shot.

'Good idea!' I said. At that moment I felt no sympathy. I blamed myself for having the rifle in the house and decided to keep the bolt and ammunition separately in a drawer in my office.

Now I had to go and calm the servants.

Coming out the back door, I saw them standing by the kitchen shed, staring at the house: Paulo, Ndeo and Onesmo – the nursery boy, a teenager who took the children for walks, had gone home. When the Africans saw me, they turned, hitched up their kanzus and fled. When they reached the low, cactus hedge that marked the border of our canonment, they leaped it like thoroughbreds in a steeplechase.

Patricia had gone bawling away in the other direction. I watched until I saw her go into the rondavel and went into the house to simmer down. I looked for the bullet hole. It had hit a bedpost in the nursery and smashed into the distempered wall.

I sat in the living room, my hands shaking. Paulo came back, blazing with anger.

'You are a very bad man!' he said. 'Shooting the memsahib just because she used sharp words!'

Dear Paolo. 'Oh, Paolo, it didn't happen like that. The memsahib fired the shot. She lost her senses and fired the gun. She didn't know what she was doing.'

Paolo took this in. 'The poor lady. I should have known. She's a good spirit, but sometimes she can be childish. Myself I've told her so, when she shouts at Ndeo. Well I'm sorry, *bwana mkubwa*. Where *is* the memsahib?'

'She's with the director's wife.'

'You'd better eat your soup, bwana.'

'Hey, Paolo, you can run and jump like an impala! I had no idea.'

He went out laughing.

Later, the director's wife told me I should pay more attention to Patricia, bring her flowers now and then.

As a hunter, I learned from Solo Mganga, plumbing instructor at the school, and his friend Tiba, a retired game scout who had spent his life in the bush tracking and hunting rogue elephants, man-eating lions and hyenas. Attacked by an elephant, he had escaped with his life and a broken arm. Solo was a muHehe from the Southern Highlands, exiled from his homeland for murder many years previously. He was passionately fond of hunting and safaris in the bush. A British officer had given him a twelve-bore shotgun. Loaded with grape-shot, the weapon had slain many antelopes, big eland in open country above the rain forest, Grant's and Thompson's gazelles down in the savanna. But Solo longed to attack more dangerous game.

Tiba, a small, wiry sixty-year-old taught me tracking. Solo helped me recognize the many species of wildlife with which the country teemed. Using his forearm as a blackboard, he scratched pictures and words on his skin with a sharp stick. KIFARU for rhinoceros, SWALA for bushbuck and so on, white on black. Solo, his eyes widening with excitement, also told stories with dramatic sound effects, Swahili ideophones. 'Rhino is trotting through the thorns, trotting through the thorns – ka-ka-ka-ka-ka! Here is my gun, I take aim, I press trigger, shooty! paa! paa! He falls! He's dead – finishy, *amekufa*, pfui!'

Tiba, a quiet man, would watch his friend with a smile, enjoying the performance.

Whenever I could get away from work, we took to the bush on foot – Solo, Tiba and Onesmo, with a local guide and a porter to carry the water can. With my .22 I'd knock off a guineafowl or a dik-dik antelope no bigger than a terrier, and that with boiled rice would be our dinner and breakfast. We slept on the ground by a fire of dry wood and sticks. Onesmo carried brandy for a quick hit when we needed it.

Our excursions began in the Rau Forest, at the foot of the mountain, where I watched beautiful, pied colobus monkeys while they watched me, making curious drumming sounds in their throats. We made forays into the savanna toward the Pare Mountains and Lake Jipe, and sought in vain a legendary bull elephant known as Ngalantini, who sometimes came to drink the run-off of fermented sugar cane into the Pangani River, which ran deep between wooded banks, showing like a smudge of verdigris through sunburnt, tawny grasslands. We walked as far as the pure springs of Nyori-Nyori, where thousands of birds and animals came to drink the crystal-clear water.

We hunted through the country evoked so passionately by Francis Brett Young. The terrain along the Pangani River was through Pare country shunned by Maasai and Wanderobo, where humans could not live. Beautiful but deadly, the forests and parklands were infested with tsetse fly carrying the trypanosomes that caused sleeping sickness in humans and domestic animals; the waterholes seethed with bilharzia and mosquito larvae, causing malaria and other fatal infections. The teeming animals were immune. In open grassland scattered acacias gave narrow shade, with now and then a mighty baobab, a tree that resembles an anatomical diagram of major blood vessels – the thick trunk and branches that diminish to twigs like capillaries. Here and there were raffia palms and candelabra trees, and along the fast-flowing river, tall forest trees. But worst was the bush of dry thorn, its tangled thickets like grey embers incandescent in the midday heat. The spirit of those dry places, wrote Francis Brett Young, was the lesser hornbill, whose melancholy call seemed to intensify the desolation. And wherever we trekked, at first light and at the brief hour of dusk, the immense, unearthly bulk of Kilimanjaro loomed to the north like a shadow.

On dark nights, under a vast sky lit with stars, the remote and familiar constellations of Sirius, Orion and Aldebaran glowed in the Milky Way. Listening to Solo's tales and sound effects, we were in a cave of firelight. Outside was a dark wilderness in which we often heard, above the crackle of blazing thorns, the whoop and chuckle of hyenas, and not seldom the grunts of hunting lions.

There was an ethic in hunting. No killing except for the pot, for ivory or to save lives. Any wounded animal had to be followed and put out of its misery. Often we would attract a human following. As well as the guide we'd have a witch doctor in attendance, eager to collect fat and bones from any fierce animals we might kill. It was useless to say that we were not going to shoot predators, unless they were attacking humans or cattle. He could do brisk business with elephant fat.

I was living a triple life: sharing safaris in the bush with Africans, playing social games with white expatriates, doing my job as a minor official and teacher. I was making friends with the movers and shakers on the mountain – Mangi Petro Itosi at Marangu; his ebullient British-educated nephew Tom Marealle (the future elected Mangi Mwitori); clever old Joseph Merinyo.

In a Moshi theatre, Ralph Elwell-Sutton directed an amateur production of Wilde's *The Importance of Being Ernest*, casting me as Jack Worthing. Ralph was a director of great patience and persistence, hauling me out of the Pink Elephant Bar for rehearsals. The butler was played by a police superintendent. There were two well-attended performances. Some of our students in the audience were fascinated by the butler. 'So in England you have European orderlies!' Strange to see white men as servants.

At home we were struggling with debt. Neither Pat nor I were any good at managing money. My father helped out, with increasing frustration. His health was failing; he had moved to his Dublin house and put Viewmount up for sale. So far there were no takers. On my side, his help, accompanied by rebukes, kept me in a dependent state.

I escaped to safaris in the savanna. At dawn I could look up and see blue mountains far off on the horizon. With African friends I would walk all day and arrive there by nightfall. In my pocket I carried Dylan Thomas's *Deaths and Entrances*. The young hunter who walked in the bush was different from my later self, 'King of your blue eyes / In the blinding country of youth'. I was happy then, taking my part in nature.

Under Tiba's tuition I became a passable tracker. Tracking was an exercise in deductive logic. The natural increase of elephants in those days, when poachers were few, was about 3000 a year in the whole country. Unculled they would have multiplied to the point where there was no food for them, making deserts of their habitat. The game department culled most of the increase, the rest being shot on licence by sportsmen. On licence, I killed elephant, hip-popotamus and – unwillingly – rhinoceros, then very numerous.

Ivory brought a small profit, small because there was a limit for each licensed hunter of two tuskers a year. But the death of an elephant is a large, even a tragic, event, like the loss of a ship, followed by a bloody shambles as professional meat hunters butcher the carcass. Despite the thrill of the chase, I no longer care to remember it. It should be said, though, that even when 'sporting' hunting is stopped, elephants still have to be culled for conservation. Their only natural enemy is man, and without his predation, their increasing numbers destroy their own habitat.

For the greater part of our evolution our species were predators, and there is no virtue in feeling guilty about it. The instinct is still with us. There's nothing admirable about pretending that wildlife are like the soft toys of middle-class childhood, but the sentiment persists, for example, that big cats and wild dogs, unless crippled or sick, are too nice to eat people. The fact is that we are meat and if they are hungry they see us as food.

The hippo I shot in Lake Jipe fed villagers who had eaten hardly any meat for a year. The rhino, one of many I watched at close quarters, came at me in a blind charge. I had to bring him down. I told those stories in *Running to Paradise*, my first book.

After some months Pat left Old Moshi to work in a nursing home in Nairobi, capital of Kenya. She had always been fascinated by nursing, but this was also partly to increase our income. She never said much about it, but she came down with a mysterious illness. I did not hear about it until she arrived home in a debilitated state, having undergone major surgery.

Not long after that, my transfer to administration came through. Posted to Iringa in the Southern Highlands as a cadet district officer, I was to begin yet another career.

Eight

Thomas Monier Skinner was district commissioner of Iringa, an immense tract of mountains, forest and upland savannas south of the Great Ruaha River, sparsely inhabited by the warlike Hehe tribe. An Oxonian, he was a suave, ambitious officer from County Offaly with a glamorous family history. An ancestor had founded Skinner's Horse, a regiment of Bengal cavalry. The cavalryman had married an Indian princess, whose genes showed strongly in Tom Skinner's ivory complexion and eyes dark as bunker oil. The Hehe called him *Bwana Mwarabu*, Mr Arab. He had the indolent grace of a nawab. At thirty-eight, he was not the kind of officer who goes native, more at ease with the exiled socialites of his district. The English had a saying, 'Are they married, or do they live in Kenya?' The white highlands of Iringa and Mbeya were an annex of that Kenya.

Skinner drank scotch and smoked black cheroots made by missionary nuns. He played bridge at the club with Police Superintendent Mitchell and both their wives. Clean-jawed and moustached, Mitchell learned his part in a wartime officers' mess.

I relieved a breezy district officer called Green.

He told me to watch out for Skinner. I should have paid more attention to this. Thanks to my stupidity, Skinner would put an end to my career. He was supposed to be my mentor. For the present, I would have to concentrate on learning my job.

Green told me how to try petty cases. His advice made me think of A.P. Herbert's *Misleading Cases*: 'It is a rule of practice amounting to a rule of law that justice need not necessarily be done, but should manifestly seem to be done.' I was now a third-class magistrate, empowered to adjudicate petty disputes, and impose small fines and prison sentences of up to three months. Every case would be reviewed by the High Court. 'So keep good records,' Green said, 'and don't forget that as a magistrate you're independent. The DC can't interfere.' One of Skinner's virtues, though, was his willingness to delegate. There was so much work that micro-management was out of the question.

I was to take charge of the jail; oversee three sub-chiefdoms, checking the tribal court accounts; and be responsible for mining licences, education, the game department and a number of other matters. The provincial commissioner had ordered that ten days of every month must be spent on safari, listening to the people and looking into complaints. All safaris by junior officers were to be by the Treasury lorry or on foot. 'I love safari,' Green said, 'but it's a royal pain to come back to the files. They pile up.'

If you listened carefully, you might have heard in the *boma* – the district office, an old German fort – a tiny, rustling crepitus. That was the sound of millions of termites nibbling away at the files and other records. Only the *District Book*, kept in a termite-proof safe in my office, was immune. The *Book*, which was confidential, recorded everything known about the district before the Germans came, during their reign and finally during the British regime. I had the key.

Pat was recovering from her illness and found a job selling clothes in a shop run by Joyce McQueen. Our small boys were out of sorts. Paddy Lane, the government surgeon, prescribed a small glass of Guinness for each one before meals. They responded well. Paddy was a surgeon and physician of genius from County Cork. He had been a county surgeon in Ireland but soon quit – 'Couldn't stand the natives.' A strong Catholic, he was tireless in looking after his patients – African, Asian and European. His dedication was strengthened by humour.

Dining with the Skinners, I met Douglas Healey, my fellow

DO, a big, taciturn Yorkshireman. He had already benefited the Hehe by setting up a creamery co-operative that gave them much-needed cash.

Skinner took me on a tour of sub-chiefdoms in his own care. We stayed a weekend with Lord and Lady Chesham in the spacious house that our hostess had designed and built herself, directing and overseeing the baking of its bricks. It was filled with Chinese Chippendale and other treasures from the abandoned family seat near Amersham in England. Its cool, high rooms looked out on wide acres of grass. Unluckily the grass was sour, inedible by cattle, and the Cheshams were overwhelmed by debt. Lady Chesham was an American heiress of assertive character, Lord Chesham her third husband and second peer. The first, Lord Thurles, had died. I think she had divorced the second, Mr Edwards.

'Tintops!' she cried, on seeing Skinner. 'This calls for tintops!'

Servants in white kanzus and green fezzes and cummerbunds arrived with iced champagne. After a few glasses Lady Chesham said to Skinner, 'Tom, did I ever tell you about the night we buried old Thurles?'

'Indeed you did,' said the DC.

I sat with my hostess in front of a mirror while her long hair was brushed, over and over, by a cockney crone who had been with her forever. 'Tell me about yourself,' she said. I made it brief. She perked up when I asked about the night she had buried old Thurles.

After Sao Hill and the Cheshams' we drove through green tea plantations, calling at the house of Major Bowes Daley, former Master of the Galway Blazers. Mrs Trundle, with whom he had fled Ireland and its bishops, was not in evidence. The major regaled us with cherry brandy. 'I know another ex-master of the Blazers,' I said. 'Molly O'Rorke, *alias* Lady Cusack-Smith. You know her?'

The major snorted. 'Know her? The woman ruined a perfectly good pack of hounds!'

As we drove away, Skinner told me my appointment would be confirmed as soon as I passed my law exam. I would also be promoted to second-class magistrate.

Safaris in other Hehe sub-chiefdoms were rather different. I heard about the Cheshams in my office now and then. In addition to my own desk, with its antique telephone, there was another at which the resident magistrate, a Londoner named Thieman, sometimes arrived to read British motoring publications. He had an English middle-class obsession with cars. The *Bwana Jaji* was amiable enough, and when not exclaiming about Bentleys and Rovers, he talked about his efforts to keep Chesham out of bankruptcy. But Lord Chesham was in poor health and might not last the course.

I met the tribal and municipal authorities. In most matters the tribes ran themselves, under their traditional leaders, now salaried and backed by imperial might. Chief Adam Sapi was grandson of the great military leader Mkwawa, whose forces massacred a German column sent against them in the 1890s. Adam ruled through sub-chiefs and their subordinates, the *jumbes* or headmen. The town of Iringa, however, as a mixed community, was run by a *Liwali*. Ours was a sophisticated Arab, Sheikh Said Nessor bin Seth el Abri, a figure from the Arabian Nights in his gold turban and rich robes. His skin was golden, his eyes the colour of smoky topaz. After studying me for some months he said, 'Mr Dobbs,' – he was far too evolved for honorifics like *effendi* or *bwana* – 'if I may give an advice. Love everyone, that's nice, that's nice – yes, love everyone, but trust no one!'

A demanding visitor was the governor, Sir Edward Twining. I was sent to meet his car. When I opened the door, he handed me his feathered hat and struggled out. He took the hat and clapped it on his big head – a huge, sweating man with bulging eyes, buttoned tightly into a blue Windsor tailcoat covered with gold bullion, his legs in clinging trews. He believed in making a splash. 'Where's my stooge?' he said. He meant his aide-de-camp.

Now and then new responsibilities were dumped on me. Upkeep of the airstrip down the scarp from the town was one – which meant having convicts cut the grass and Public Works maintain the tiny hut. I was also to research Hehe customs by means of a questionnaire from the Secretariat. And I was to find all the war veterans of the King's African Rifles and present them with campaign medals. For the medal distribution I was given a special clerk, a former treasury clerk who had just been sprung from jail. He was said to have dipped into the cash. To Skinner's credit, he gave the man a second chance and a job. I found, however, that no one had come to his defence when he was charged. Few accused Africans received adequate defence.

While none of them enjoyed prison life, it carried no social stigma. It was sometimes referred to as Hoteli Mfalme Kingy Georgy where some lucky prisoners could learn a trade.

The clerk accompanied me on medals safaris and we became friends. I still have my report of one of these safaris. It gives a glimpse of the kind of work district officers did. In this one I started with Douglas Healey for company.

> 8 February 1951 Despite warnings that the road to Kimande was impassable, the safari left Iringa at about 10 am in the Native Treasury lorry. It consisted of Healey and myself, the medals clerk, Messenger Ayubu, the NT messenger, two game scouts and our personal boys. There were a couple of nursing mothers into the bargain, who had begged a lift. The road was neither impassable nor, I submit, a road. It is a tolerable track, made passable by Healey's bridges.
>
> En route we met David Ricardo in the middle of some cattle business with natives. He was clad in a *shuka* and a bush hat and his feet were bare. We passed the time of day. [Ricardo, a descendant of his namesake the economist, had converted to Islam and spent most of his time in the bush. He held 20,000 acres near Iringa and was a friend of Adam Sapi. He had suffered a head-wound in North Africa while serving with the King's Royal Irish Hussars. His earliest memories were of George V, who spanked him for disturbing his afternoon nap. In later life Ricardo was a loyal citizen of Tanzania. His charming wife, Lady Barbara, was home alone.]
>
> We reached Kimande at about 4 pm, only to get stuck in a patch of black cotton soil, from which we were pushed by a crowd of local inhabitants. We drank a cup of tea and set to work, Healey to his milk payments, I to my medal issues. To my disgust, only six men appeared. It may be, however, that these are really all

the ex-askaris available. I have only twenty names in my medal-roll for the whole of Pawaga.

Jumbe Shabani of Kisanga asked to have a word with me. He said that a pair of lions were doing great damage in his area, and introduced Sembambwe, who had lost a cow that very morning from his boma. The other cattle had stampeded, trampling his young maize into the earth. Learning that Kisanga was only an hour and a half away, I said I would come at once and sit over the kill. It was nearly dark, and he dissuaded me, alleging there was too much water on the way, and crocodiles in some of the irrigation ditches.

We went early to bed – I with the intention of setting out at dawn for Kisanga.

9th February 1951 (day) We were awakened at 3 am with news that the lions had returned to Sembambwe's boma, killed again and were even now on the kill. I took my Mannlicher and some ammunition. Healey borrowed Gaudenzio's 12-bore and three SSG [grape-shot] cartridges, and we set out at once with a storm lantern. It was a curious party, wading through swamps and flooded fields. There was deep, stinking mud under the water. [At one muddy irrigation furrow, Healey had himself carried over by a wiry Hehe. I remarked that he was bigger than his mount. He said he liked travelling this way. Still, there were those crocodiles …] We hoped to arrive on the kill just at dawn – the correct procedure according to George Rushby [the famous senior game-ranger, about whom more presently].

As it happened we were unlucky. The lions left about five minutes before we arrived. They had killed and begun to eat one cow (her name was Gungamwenda) and had fatally wounded a heifer by breaking both her hind legs. She was cruelly clawed. We insisted that Sembabwe put her out of pain. (He was puzzled: pain? Animals didn't feel pain!)

The boma is large – Sembambwe has at least 300 head of cattle. There's an outer enclosure surrounded by a low fence of thorn branches and an inner one similarly fenced for the calves. At the end of this smaller enclosure are the huts of Sembambwe and his family, where fires had been burning all night. Except for this clearing, the boma is surrounded by fairly thick forest.

Healey and I examined the carcasses while the men cast

about for tracks. We followed for a short time before losing the trail in thick bush. For the present, we returned to Kimande. Healey had a heavy day's work ahead at Izazi, so the lorry would have to go on with him. I decided to sit over the heifer's carcass that night and, successful or not, follow to Izazi (about 20 miles) by bicycle. I'd told Jumbe Shabani to have a hide prepared of thorn bushes about seven yards from the kill. I'd return about 4 pm with a little food for the night.

Healey set off in the lorry and I stayed behind, making three medal issues. (Total to date: 732.)

Visited the Dispensary, which was clean and tidy, and interviewed a woman who had been hauled out of bed by a hyena. [Her buttock was bitten off, a frightful wound.] The only trap which has been set so far is the trap-gun we sent them. Listlessness about such dangers could lead to another outbreak of man-eaters. [The district had suffered badly in this way, as will appear.]

I inspected the school. Kimande is one of the rare places where schoolchildren are politer than their brothers and sisters herding cattle. As this is a new school, it's not easy to assess its general efficiency, but attendance is good, retardation and wastage low, and I have good hopes for the future.

I rested for an hour or so, waking with a start at what I thought was a lion's grunt. It was a cow.

(Night) about 5 pm Set out with a guide through the swamps to Kisanga, tucking my slacks into socks for wading. To my dismay, the sky was clouded over, presaging a dark night. The thin shred of a new moon was almost set. I was cold and wet when I arrived at the boma.

The cattle were coming in from grazing, the calves and goats shut in. The tinkling of their bells was soothing. The herd boy walked to and fro calling the milk cows; each answered her name and came forward to be milked. It was a peaceful scene as darkness was falling. I pulled off my socks to dry them at the fire. I drank a cup of tea brewed in milk. The cattle were waiting to enter the boma.

Just as I was sitting down on a stool by the fire the herd stampeded. It was as if they'd all received an electric shock at the same moment. The sound was like that of a congregation rising to their feet in a cathedral. Sembambwe and his men rushed into the forest after the cattle. I ran barefoot to the kill. I was just in time to see two shadowy forms melting into the deeper shadows of the bush. The carcass was still there. I crouched in the hide with my rifle. [It was illegal to hunt with a flashlight.]

It was so dark now that I could not see the backsight of my Mannlicher, let alone the kill. After a while I heard thorns cracking, then a grunt and the sound of crunching bones. Aiming at the sound, I took a shot. Though the range was only seven yards I missed completely. I heard the lions run into the bush. The sound was heavy – like a horse in galoshes, I thought.

The lions had dragged the kill about three yards outside a gap in the thorns. I crouched inside the gap. [I was joined by an old man with a spear. He said I had a very fierce rifle.] Mosquitoes swarmed round my ankles and began biting. I stood the torture for about an hour before standing up and slapping my legs. At once I heard the lions from just outside the gap, bolting away with that curiously heavy sound. First one, then a grunt. Then the other. I fired from the hip at the sound, again without success. I was somewhat shaken to find the lions had been stalking *me*. Next morning we found they had been just one yard away, had crept along outside the thorns and stopped at the gap.

[The lions carried the carcass into the thick bush. I knew they were there. I could hear them scrunching the meat, snarling at the hyenas who were whooping around.] Sembambwe gave me a plate of pilaff and beef and we told stories. I nursed my poor feet and ankles.

10th February 1951 At first light I followed the drag into the forest, scared rigid because the undergrowth was too thick to see much. After a while a *kwali* (red-necked francolin) flew cackling out of a tree about twenty yards ahead. That meant the lions were on the move. Shortly afterwards I came on the kill under a great tangled thicket. Only the hide, some of the chest cavity and the head remained. I followed the spoor for a while, but soon gave up. I had to get back to Kimande and on to Izazi by bicycle. Once there I'd tell the game scouts to follow up.

With some difficulty I found an unpunctured bike. An old Hehe lady insisted on giving me breakfast of rice-porridge and tea brewed in milk, several others gave me eggs. I was ashamed not to have succeeded. I took about four hours peddalling through the bush and sand-drifts to reach Izazi and arrange for the return of the bike.

I reported the incident to Senior Game Ranger George Rushby on his next visit. He laughed and said I was just unlucky. ['When it's dark, fire from the left shoulder,' he advised. He said the lions obviously disliked my smell.] He has gone to Kimande himself to try his luck.

I had reported this incident in detail for good reason. The Iringa and Mjombe districts had been terrorized by man-eating lions between the early 1930s and 40s. More than a thousand Africans had been killed and eaten. The episode was reported in *The Guinness Book of Records*. Finding and killing the man-eaters had been complicated by dread of witchcraft, so that the people were afraid to report every incident. George Rushby and the only two of his game-scouts who were immune to superstition had stalked and killed the eighteen man-eaters from three prides in different parts of the district. It took many months of dangerous work. Rushby was determined to destroy any predators that had lost their fear of man.

We had also had man-eating hyenas. Most of them were trapped by game scouts. Again, the people were listless and fatalistic, believing that witchcraft was involved.

George Rushby, Senior Game Ranger of the Southern Highlands Province, was one of the most interesting men I met in Africa. His peers would have been the legendary hunters Frederick Selous and P.J. Pretorius, and in India my father's friend Jim Corbett.

A stocky figure, his battered face was kindly, the nose somewhat reconstructed. In his forties, he wore bush-jacket and shorts, a scarf at his neck. As a boy he had poached trout and game on the Duke of Portland's estate at Welbeck Abbey in Nottinghamshire, before training as an electrical engineer. He'd broken his nose fighting all comers at country fairs in England. In East Africa since 1921, he had been a gold prospector, farmer, white hunter, barman, bouncer, forester and above all a legendary ivory poacher. He'd twice survived blackwater fever and once an attack by an elephant. The authorities had wanted desperately to catch him. One district commissioner vowed to arrest Rushby and put an end to his ivory capers. George responded by shooting a big tusker within a mile of the man's *boma*. The DC had a nervous breakdown.

Some clever mandarin had a great idea. Set a thief to catch a thief – recruit George for the Game Department. There are no better conservationists than hunters. As a game ranger he was a resounding success. He showed his mettle during the terrifying outbreak of man-eaters in the Iringa and Njombe districts during the 1940s – more than a thousand persons devoured. The lions were in sleek condition. George killed all three prides of them.

He was a wonderful storyteller, and discussed elephants and their conservation with me over sundowners in the Iringa Hotel. He said his game scouts were under strict instructions not to shoot big tuskers on crop protection. It was important to protect this strain. The small number shot on licence did not signify.

The months of stalking man-eaters had taken its toll on him. 'It got personal,' he said. In one place, lions had devoured a woman, leaving her eight-year-old daughter. A year later there was another kill in the same place. On his way there George filled his pockets with sweets for the little girl. All that was left of her when he arrived was the top of her skull.

He had also investigated an occurrence of lion-men or were-lions in the nearby district of Singida. These persons, mental defectives in the power of a sorceror, had been crippled in childhood to make them walk on all fours. Dressed in lion skins and armed with knives, they murdered designated victims for a fee of thirty shillings, paid to their keeper. Their crimes caused a reign of terror similar to that caused by real man-eating lions.

For me there was plenty to do in the town as well as in the bush. Most of my cases were about wilful and unlawful neglect to pay poll tax. Offenders could be sent to jail for up to three months. I didn't think it sensible to impose the maximum penalty and so gave them two, not realizing that Skinner and Healey always gave them three.

Every week I'd inspect the jail. It was run by a starched Sikh chief warder. And once I was required to witness corporal punishment. Thieman had ordered six strokes of the cane for an industrial teacher convicted of buggery. The horror seemed to go on forever as the man gasped and sighed at our feet, Chief Warder Singh barking out the numbers, the grim askari wielding the rattan. Not long after that, I learned that if capital punishment were imposed, I would be in charge. I read instructions on how to build a scaffold with a trap, how to indent for a special rope from the Crown Agents and to what vote it should be charged, and finally a table of weights and drops. The whole thing made me feel sick.

So this, I thought, was what imperial rule came down to, the whole system based on cruelty. Worse, brutality of this kind must be what all government was based on.

I thought about it as I walked in the bush. I looked into the clear sky, not a cloud in sight. But nearby men were slaughtering a steer and silently the heavy vultures appear, to circle over the death. The death-birds were always there. Knowing the imperial secret was like that. The daylight world looked calm and rational but there was private agony hidden within it. I told myself that it couldn't be helped; laws and magistrates were needed to avert chaos.

I stopped thinking about it. But the seed of disillusion had been planted. 'The sleep of reason begets monsters.'

There was plenty of distraction. Years later I discovered from letters my father filed and kept that I founded an arts society in Iringa. An arts society! I have no memory of it at all.

I was preparing for an official foot-safari into country never visited by Europeans. By regulation, I was to take forty porters, a treasury clerk, a game scout and messengers. With the forestry officer, Maxwell, we were to find a route for a new road and decide if there was enough commercial timber in the mountains to justify the project.

It was a clear morning, the heat made bearable by a cool breeze. Bulbuls were singing. Maxwell and I, with the clerks and messengers, rode the treasury lorry down to Mahenge. The road was only one lane wide, along the sides of precipices. Every quarter-mile there was a passing bay.

'What if we meet elephants?' Maxwell said.

At Mahenge we greeted the sub-chief and elders. Porters were assembled to carry tent and camp furniture in addition to food for everyone. The journey through the mountains was going to take at least three weeks. The sub-chief told us the pay rates agreed on with the porters.

I gave the word. The head messenger barked, *'Haya! Tuende!'* (Let's go!) and we crossed the road into the wild country, Maxwell and I heading a long procession in single file, Game Scout Barnabas with his heavy Vickers .404 just behind us. For the first few miles a path had been cleared through grass and scrub. We came to a rickety bridge over a mountain torrent. On the far side our route lay through virgin bush.

On the first day we marched about fifteen miles. Tribal women met us with shrill ululation. The mountain air was fresh and sweet. Maxwell and I drank brandy and water while our tent was pitched under a spreading acacia. The African clerk drank with us. Maxwell was a quiet man who had studied forestry in Scotland. He had also completed a hotel-management course in London, and taught his own cook. We dined well.

The porters sat around fires talking drowsily. We slept soundly in our government tent, on the ground with a couple of blankets.

It was the start of twenty-two days of long marches through the mountains. On the third day the route lay through speargrass. Sharp leaves cut my legs through my slacks and the scratches became infected. We began to see wildlife. Hunting dogs crossed our path. We saw roan antelope on the slope above us, their long horns swept back like scimitars. We trudged through elephant grass higher than our heads, hearing elephants rumble and squeal somewhere upwind. Mounting a termite hill, we saw trunks rising out of the grass like periscopes, testing the wind. Barnabas stood guard beside our column until all the men had passed, then caught up with us at the van. In the forest we saw those red colobus, high up in the trees.

We had been on the move about a week when we sighted two

Cape buffaloes. They were ambling along a *karonga* below us. A big old bull with heavy horns was followed by a younger bull. Since no one had eaten meat for a couple of days, I decided to shoot the younger animal. The buffalo came to a patch of papyrus-swamp. They turned to face the wind. This tactic was what made buffalo dangerous. Alert to pursuit, they took up station for ambush.

We had seen them first, though. With a guide, who carried a kind of halberd, an S-shaped steel blade at the end of a wooden staff, I made a circle to approach from downwind. We stalked them through cover of leafy saplings. Soon I was in place for a clear shot, aiming for the shoulder of the younger bull. I saw the hit, a spurt of dust. The buffalo staggered and fell. The big bull galloped off the way he'd come.

I gave my rifle to the guide to hold, taking his halberd to poke the buffalo. I was about five yards away when he struggled to his feet. He lurched toward me. I dodged behind a sapling. I was bracing for his charge when he toppled over again, dead this time. When the bull was butchered, we found the bullet had gone clear through his heart.

Everyone had plenty of meat that night, the men singing and smacking their lips. Maxwell and I, with our African companions, relished the sirloin in a rich stew.

Maxwell was happy with the timber he'd seen. We talked about a road. My infected scratches were bothering me, and painful boils were breaking out on my jaws. I was full of aspirin, my head buzzing. We were coming into country where the narrow path ran along steep slopes. The country was swarming with elephants.

I shot a tusker on my licence and, with Barnabas, a *budi* or tuskless bull that was threatening a field of maize. The damage elephants can do to crops is devastating, which is why they cannot survive near humans. Tribesmen from a few scattered homesteads carried off the meat, to dry it over fires.

About ten days out, we camped in woodland. We dined on soup. A couple of porters approached, despite the rebukes of the head messenger. They demanded more pay. I reminded them that they had agreed in front of witnesses on the rate they were getting. It was not enough, they said; they'd just down their loads and go home unless they got the increase. The whole crowd of carriers, forty strong, was now all around us. The messengers were silent, not wanting to be in the middle. I stupidly made a joke, saying anyone who deserted would get the *kiboko* (hippo-hide whip). The men laughed, knowing this was not true. They turned toward the bush.

This was bad. We could be stranded with no one to carry water or government property, including the treasury chest with the money we had collected in poll tax along the route. I had to do something convincing, and fast.

There was a paper on the table with some notes I'd been making. I jumped onto a termite hill, brandishing the paper. 'Look at this!' I shouted. 'All your names are written here!' The porters stopped, turning to listen. 'If you don't return to work, I'll give this list to the sub-chief. He'll deal with you. But if you just continue the safari, nothing more will be said.' There was a bit of palaver, but they gave in. They were mortally scared of their sub-chief. My head was aching.

The head messenger was in a rage. 'Those *washenzi*, those savages! You should punish them anyway, *bwana mkubwa*, when you get back.' I confessed that in fact I had no list of names.

From then on I found the going hard. At one place we saw a bull elephant coming towards us down the narrow path. We had to turn him away. I moved ahead a few paces and fired a shot over him. The recoil of the rifle against my infected cheek was painful. The elephant immediately spread his ears and raised himself, seeming to grow even bigger, then charged with trunk curled. I fired again, but missed, the rifle-butt against the boil on my cheek a stab of pain. Barnabas ran forward, took aim and fired. The elephant rocked back and fell, killed instantly by a brain shot. The game scout had saved my life.

I have confused impressions of the last ten days of our safari. We skirted a lofty mountain called Lohomeru. We met elephants, too often where they were threatening the tribesmen's scanty crops.

Barnabas would move in and shoot one or two.

I remember fording a wide river, up to my waist in the middle, holding the rifle over my head. For a while the cool water brought relief. I had a fever by this time. Maxwell and Onesmo helped me along the way.

When we came out of the bush at the road, the treasury lorry was waiting. I spent the next two weeks in hospital being treated for general infection.

Thanks to Paddy Lane, I was soon back in my office, dealing with a stack of files. I made a fair copy of answers I'd collected to a Secretariat questionnaire about tribal customs. I read anthropological studies of the Hehe by one G. Gordon Brown of Toronto. Skinner was surprisingly ignorant of the tribal culture.

I resumed monthly safaris. Still plagued by boils, I came down with amoebic dysentery. It grumbled on for a full three months, after which Paddy Lane prescribed Emetine injections.

We were preparing the Hehe for a new policy on local government. The first step was to explain the separation of the judicial and the executive functions of government and why the distinction was desirable. It was not easy for tribesmen to see the point. Chiefs and sub-chiefs had always been judges.

At a series of *barazas* in my sub-chiefdoms, I tried to explain the new ideas. They were well understood, though not accepted. Sub-chiefs did not care for the prospect of rival authorities in their jurisdictions. More generally, the people feared that they would not be heard. They saw that in the higher courts, presided over by white, wigged judges in red *kanzus,* only a small group of witnesses and assessors was heard. In the sub-chiefs' village trials, elders and the whole community joined in.

Meanwhile I was studying for my law exam, poring over the Penal Code, modelled on Lord Macaulay's Indian code, and the Indian Law of Evidence, in force in Tanganyika. I also made good progress with gruesomely illustrated manuals on forensic medicine and volumes of leading cases, but my Swahili was still weak.

White officials had become disgruntled by the gap between salaries and soaring inflation. I had been in difficulty myself, compounded by incompetence with money. The administration was waiting for an excuse to bring in increases.

I was entitled to a second elephant on my current game licence. If I could bring down a half-decent tusker, my finances would be easier. I asked Barnabas to send word if he came across a bull with heavy ivory. I'd go wherever he happened to be, to try my luck. But it wasn't just for the ivory. I also needed the freedom of the bush, to be on my own for a time with African friends, away from power. And perhaps I also craved the adrenalin rush of moving close to dangerous wild animals, though I was growing out of that.

The district accountant, Stuart, had a car and liked to take me for drives in the bush to watch wildlife. A Scot who in an RAF aircrew had survived more than his share of operations, he was a slim, wiry man about my age who had been a champion sprinter. He invited me to come with him as backup on an elephant hunt. We camped in the savanna toward Mahenge and hired a guide and tracker. The next day we found the fresh spoor of a big bull, not too far ahead of us. Broken branches by his tracks bore fresh leaves. A pile of his dung was still warm.

When we came up on the bull, his flank was across the trail upwind from us, a fine tusker. The revenue officer took lengthy aim and fired. With frightful speed the elephant turned and charged us, crashing through the brush. My friend was off like the wind, the bull in pursuit. I knew he could not outrun the elephant. I dodged to one side and as the huge beast passed close by, fired two shots into him. The shock turned him, crashing away into the bush. The revenue officer stood trembling and sweating. 'Oh Cheesus,' he gasped. 'I just lost my fucking nairve!'

'We have to follow up,' I told him. After a pause he came with me and the tracker. We followed the trail all that day and the next without finding the wounded bull. Time ran out; we had to go back to work. I left word with the sub-chief to have a game scout continue the pursuit, though I knew it was hopeless.

One day Stuart asked a favour. He'd shot a giraffe (why? I wondered) without a licence. Could I claim to have shot it on my game licence. I did what he asked.

My health was not improving. I had new boils and was dizzy with fever. After work I went home to lie down for a while.

Onesmo said Barnabas wanted to speak to me. I thought he must have news of a big tusker. Fever or not, I'd take a week off to go after it. But that was not what he told me.

Later that day I was chatting with Stuart outside his office while he told the game scout, Barnabas, the weight of some ivory he had brought in. I said I'd asked Barnabas to report any big tusker he saw, so that I could go after it. 'Or better still,' *Bwana Fedha* (Mr Money) joked in English, 'just bring the tusks to the *Bwana Shauri*'s house!'

Barnabas saluted and left. I said, 'That's amazing. Because he just did that! Brought two big tusks to my house. Says he'll get the sack if he brings them to your office – Rushby told him not to shoot any more big ivory.'

'Well—'

'I owe him one; he saved my life … I know it's irregular, breach of the Game Ordinance and all that, but—'

Stuart looked unhappy, doubtless remembering that I had saved *his* life, and not only that, but had taken responsibility for his stupid giraffe. 'Not the first time we've bent the rules, you mean – well, all right. But don't bring the tusks in for a few days. Let Barnabas get out of the way.'

We parted on that.

The tusks, about eighty pounds each, were in my storeroom.

Over the next few days my fever grew worse. I had come home from the *boma* and gone to bed. At the weekend I just stayed there. Everyone but myself was out at the Club. A voice called, '*Hodi*! Anyone there?' And there was a grizzled Englishman in the room, the Provincial Commissioner himself. He didn't seem particularly friendly, but then he never did. He was staying with Skinner.

'Just thought I'd look in and see how you were,' he said. He asked about my plans for home leave. I had a feeling there was something else on his mind, something he did not want to talk about. After a few minutes of awkward conversation, he turned to leave.

'Well, I'm extremely impressed,' he said over his shoulder, 'by your *debility*.'

A very different kind of official from Tim Revington, I thought. Revington had just retired as a provincial commissioner and taken up work as executive officer of The Bukoba Native Coffee Board.

What I did not know was that Stuart, the day after he had agreed to my plan, had blurted out the whole thing over a game of snooker with the police superintendent. Mitchell had warned him not to say a word to me. Meanwhile he took the matter to Skinner. Skinner had a plan. It was important not to spook me, so that I'd be sure to commit the offence. In all that followed, nothing puzzled me more than Skinner's determination that I not be hindered from committing a crime.

As Ralph Elwell-Sutton put it in a letter to my father, 'For reasons which I can only say are between him and his conscience, Skinner waited in silence and in practically full knowledge of what was going on, until (at last) an actual offence was committed; and then, with police support duly enlisted, pounced.'

At my next check-up with Paddy Lane, the surgeon said there was something sneaky going on. He had been asked to look at some elephant tusks. 'I don't like it at all,' he said. 'There's treachery. I wouldn't trust that DC as far as I could throw him!'

Nine

I began to realize that what I had done was grossly irregular. I confided in David McQueen, an older man whom I trusted. He told me I'd been a bloody fool. Then he advised me to go the DC and tell him the whole story. So I went to Skinner in his office and said I had something to tell him,

'I've done something wrong, and if you think I should do so, I'll resign.'

Skinner was calm. 'You need not tell me about it. Answer the questions when you're asked.'

I told McQueen how Skinner had responded. Later he wrote to my father, 'He took my advice, but I am afraid his DC is not quite the type we are used to, and would not listen to him – in fact stated that he had known all about it for many days beforehand.'

I was writing my law exam when Mitchell came into the room and asked me to come outside. I was introduced to Chief Superintendent Mackenzie, an ex-soldier of starched aspect. I was to consider myself under arrest, he told me. We walked to police headquarters where I was to be charged. I expected to be accused of an offence under the game ordinance.

Nothing of the kind. When I heard charges of 'stealing by a person in public service' and 'uttering a false document', I was shocked. So shocked that my mind went blank. I said I needed a lawyer. Mackenzie said surely not – the position was quite clear. I did know that nothing I said here could be given in evidence. The

Indian law of evidence provided that no statement made to police, or in their presence or hearing, was admissible in court. This gave me a false sense of security. There would be a report to the DC.

In accordance with what was clearly a prearranged plan, I was taken straight to the court, where Thieman was already waiting. There were no witnesses. It did not immediately strike me that this meant that pleas of guilty were going to be entered no matter what I said, the point being that there was no appeal from such pleas.

Thieman, without looking at me, read the charges. I said, 'Not guilty.' This would have required the Crown to bring witnesses. Thieman, without writing a note, asked me some questions. After hearing my answers, he said, wrongly as it happened, 'Well, that's stealing. And that's forging.' He entered guilty pleas to both charges. The police then told their story. Deeply unhappy, Thieman said, 'I must do my duty. Nine months' imprisonment with hard labour.'

Next thing I knew, I was in my own jail locked up for the night by Chief Warder Singh. The yard was crowded with prisoners I had sentenced. This was Skinner's decision. It turned out like those fairy tales in which the hero is rescued by mice he has befriended. 'My' prisoners pointed me out to their friends as the *bwana shauri* who had listened to their stories.

Skinner told Pat to vacate our house. At this news the Cypriot hotelier insisted that she move into his hotel with our sons John and Christian, now aged five and three, and stay there free of charge for as long as she liked. Paddy Lane and his wife also helped. Word of our disaster spread like wildfire. David McQueen and another senior businessman, Mr Hallam, started to raise a defence fund. Not that I knew any of this at the time.

I was to be handed over to a prison officer from Dodoma, for further disposal. It was a long drive through dry bush. I was still in shock when Mackenzie climbed into a car with me. We drove down the escarpment along the Great North Road, heading for the bridge over the Great Ruaha River. Despite tightly closed windows, red dust seeped through to coat our faces. The heat was stifling. Mackenzie sat very straight, cap square on his head. As we parted at the bridge, I thanked him for accompanying me in person. He could have sent one of the local boys.

The prison officer, a chatty fellow with auburn hair, said I'd be spending the night in maximum security in Dodoma Prison, leaving next morning for the long drive to Morogoro and the minimum security prison farm at Kingolwira. His wife would come along with a picnic.

We were now in Gogo tribal lands. The Gogo were an old-fashioned lot who loved cattle raids. Many of them, charged with taking part, claimed that they had only eaten soup at the party.

My escort seemed intimidated by my silence. What could I say? It felt strange to hear chitchat while my life was in ruins. What would become of my family? If it were not for them, I would have been glad to wreck my career. I thought of my politeness to Mackenzie – what was wrong with me? The man had just rail-roaded me.

The dry thorn bush through which we were passing, varied here and there by a baobab or a raffia palm, and everywhere by ter-mite hills, was the perfect analogue of my thoughts. I kept return-ing to the question: why did Stuart not simply refuse to register the tusks? Could he have been afraid of me, simply because I had wit-nessed his failure in the face of danger, or maybe because I had done him a favour? As for the DC, what did he have against me? It was all hard to understand. Even Barnabas was an enigma.

We arrived at Dodoma just after dark. I heard the iron doors crash shut behind me. I was taken straight to a condemned cell, the sole accommodation available for a European prisoner. It was lit by a single overhead bulb, burning all night. There was a cot, a bucket smelling of carbolic acid, a washbasin with blue soap. The steel door had a judas eye. There were ringbolts in the concrete floor. Bedsheets were stiff canvas stamped with broad arrows in black.

My escort hesitated at the door. 'I'm supposed to take away your belt,' he said, 'in case—'

'I've no intention of killing myself,' I said. I was going to go through the whole thing.

The officer left, and with him the echoes of door after steel door clanging shut. In the next cell there was an Indian debtor. We seemed to have gone back a couple of centuries. He shouted over the partition, which did not quite reach the roof, 'You are district officer? Is it? My cousin-uncle in India is collector-sahib, same like you!'

I wondered how many murderers had spent their last night in this cell.

After a sleepless night, the door banged open and an askari entered with a tray. 'Your breakfast, *bwana*. From Memsahib Portugito.'

Portugito was the superintendent in charge. On the tray was a breakfast worthy of the condemned. There was fresh pawpaw and orange, steak and eggs, toast, marmalade, and a big pot of tea.

After this, I was taken to Portugito's office. Dark-haired, neat and compact, he was a Latin from South Africa. I thanked him for his wife's kindness. He waved this aside.

'We have no facility for Europeans. Couldn't let you starve.' His accent was Afrikaner. He stared at me. 'Right! Now tell me – who has his knife into you? Is it that DC?'

'I – I think it was a fair cop. It wasn't my ivory.'

'That could've been settled in the office, man. I've never seen it done this way. No, no, someone had his knife into you.' He looked down. 'By the way, the governor's on leave. I doubt if Sir Edward would be happy with this kind of *fitina*.' *Fitina* was Swahili for backbiting and treachery.

The rest of the day was spent driving to Kingolwira with my escort and his wife. We had our picnic around noon. I don't remember much about it. I was trying to get used to my convict status, and these kindly people were trying to deny it. We drove through Morogoro, which was on the railway line from Dar es Salaam to Dodoma and beyond. All I remember about the road to the prison farm is a stand of kapok trees. Otherwise it was a waterless tangle of thorn and acacia. We saw no wildlife or humans. Nomads avoided such country.

The prison farm looked like a military camp. There was a single-storey reception building with a tin roof and a veranda, in front of it a flagpole with the Union Jack hanging limp, and an elephant skull in a circle of stones. Skull, flagpole and stones were whitewashed. I thought of the military adage 'If it moves, salute it. If it doesn't move, whitewash it.'

The superintendent was a New Zealander. He told me I'd be treated like everyone else. Well, not quite everyone. There were three classes of prisoners. First class were Europeans, which included Syrians; second class were Asians, all Indian; third were Africans. A matter of diet, the super said. I'd been just a third-class magistrate. Here I was a first-class prisoner. Each class had its own buildings, kitchen and bathhouse.

Handed over to the chief warder, a fine-looking African of keen intelligence, I was given my outfit of khaki pants and shirts, stamped with broad arrows, straw hat and heavy boots. A blunt razor blade was part of the kit. The chief gave out only one at a time. He refused to give socks, although I was entitled. 'The Poles steal them,' he said.

First-class quarters were in a small compound, lightly fenced to keep out jackals. Two dormitory huts, with cinder block walls and grass thatch, faced each other across a bare yard. At the far end was an open kitchen, a brick oven beside it, and behind it a bathhouse with shower, tub and lavatory. There were eight other prisoners: three Syrians, three Poles and two English. Conversation was in Swahili. I was shown my bed with its mosquito net and chair. I put on my prison clothes.

Outside, the whole territory was discussing the case. A Hehe tribesman was reported as saying, 'They sent him to jail for stealing? They're *all* thieves.' People of all races were indignant. McQueen was raising a defence fund. Skinner was busy rallying his friends against me. I knew nothing of this. Inside the jail my fellow-prisoners were cautious. Maybe I was a spy.

Boarding-school authorities often claim that they prepare pupils for life. And the life they prepare for is jail. The minimum-security prison farm was much like school. The food was coarse, accommodation rough. As at school, the worst punishment was loss of liberty and the unbelievably slow passage of time.

The New Zealander in charge was humane. Though smoking was prohibited, he did not enforce the rule. There were no books. He was kind enough to pass on to us his out-of-date New Zealand newspapers. The papers spoke of life outside. 'The world is wide,' said Chris, a privileged prisoner, a trusty.

Chris and his brother Martin were both long-term trusties. Syrian Christians in their thirties, they were soft-spoken in English. They had worked a small diamond mine, not far from the site where the Canadian Dr Williamson had struck it rich. The brothers had been offered gemstones under the counter. They accepted, and at once were surrounded by police. It was a trap. Chris was a slender, fine-featured man with intense dark eyes. Martin was big and plump, with an air of good nature. Their offence was really against the cartel that controlled the diamond market.

A third Syrian was a thief from the Swahili coast, a furtive man with a big nose. He spoke no English but his Swahili was beautiful. He loved the language and spent hours teaching me polite forms.

Three Poles were in for violent crimes. Only one spoke English. This was Joe, who was being held for deportation. 'I'm finish my sentence,' he said. 'Why for they keep me? Sock my bloddy blod!' Once a week he took over the bathhouse for his masturbation.

The biggest Pole was not right in his head. He had knifed a man in a quarrel. He said, 'The man got well years ago. But me – I'm still here!' And burst into tears. 'It's not fair!' The third Pole, George, my workmate on the tractor when we were ploughing a big maize field, had attempted murder. He was taciturn. I was careful with him. Like the others, he'd been in jail most of his life. First the Germans had locked them up, then the Russians, who carried them off to Siberia. A postwar amnesty and many hardships later they'd found their way to Africa, this time to fall foul of British justice.

Chris explained prison protocol. One did not ask anyone what he was in for. In time he would confide it. And of course every first-class prisoner was completely innocent, the victim of a frame-up. In my durance there were a few Englishmen, a mixed-race boy who worked at the prison bodyshop, a shame-faced settler of fifty or so in for motor manslaughter, and a charming ex-soldier who had passed bad cheques. The soldier had fantasies of a gentlemanly upbringing, governess, public school, officers' mess and so on. In fact he had been a sergeant of humble origin and, like the big Pole, was mentally ill. He would wander about singing his favourite song, 'Bye bye, blackbird'. With his neat moustache and straight back he did resemble an army officer. By degrees he was reinventing his past. Everyone liked him.

We ate together, waited on by a third-class prisoner, who also made our beds and swept the huts. No one thought it strange that convicts should have a servant. At meals we spoke Swahili.

At first everyone was cagey with me. The bed-maker said, 'Bwana Shauri is the one who puts you in jail. He doesn't go to jail. Who are you?' He himself was in for magendo, a black market offence, namely selling *bhang* (cannabis). Nothing bad, he said. What would be a real crime? I wondered. Well, go to someone's house at night, wearing a mask, or break in and hurt someone while stealing their money. That was *uchawi* (witchcraft); that was very bad. As for him, selling *bhang* was just his job. When he came out he'd want his job back.

The body-shop boy told me the superintendent did not want me to know what he was doing. But he told me anyway. The prison was running a little business on the side: cut-rate bodywork for discreet customers. The super and farm manager were partners in this magendo. Prisoners working for them were given a little money.

One day the Syrians warned us to prepare for an inspection by the health officer. Our quarters had to be clean, especially the kitchen house and bathhouse. The health officer was quite demanding.

I first saw him in the kitchen house, from his left side. A small man of slight build, he wore a white shirt and slacks and a white sun helmet. He was an Indian of fair complexion, perhaps a Brahmin. He was scolding the cook, shaking a bony forefinger at him.

When he turned to face me, I got a shock. The right side of his face was missing. In its place was a deep groove that ran from his jaw to the top of his skull. The one eye, the left one, was dark and fierce. I had thought he was one of the prison staff, but in fact he was a trusty, one of us, a long-term prisoner with a responsible job. The job had been created for him, out of pity for his misfortune. The health officer was the survivor of a suicide pact. He had shot his wife, then himself. The bullet had torn away half his head, but not his life. His punishment was to have survived. His agony had happened many years before, and many more would go by before he was free.

There were other murderers among second- and third-class prisoners. They were by far the most normal persons in the jail, and the least dishonest. I remember asking a Maasai what he had done (third-class prisoners did not mind the question) and he replied calmly: 'I killed.' After a moment, he added, 'I killed a barbarian." Meaning that his victim had been a Bantu and his offence therefore trivial.

The Maasai worked with the dairy herd, which was the pride of the farm. Though there were tsetse flies in the area, the farm tried to protect the cattle from tripanosomiasis with experimental prophylactics. The drugs were ineffectual and too expensive for commercial use. There was a shining modern dairy where the milk was strained, pasteurized and chilled. Martin, who worked there, invited me to come over and drink cold milk. It was about a quarter of a mile from our compound. My heavy boots, worn without socks, chafed my ankles. So I left them off. After a couple of weeks without boots, bare feet felt more comfortable.

At night I worried about my family. I feared the strain would be too much for Pat. I soon learned that she was valiantly working with others for an appeal. I had thought any appeal impossible, given the pleas of guilty that had been entered. But David McQueen and Mr Haslam were collecting for legal expenses. Paddy and Mary Lane helped Pat go to Dar es Salaam for legal advice. She consulted a leading barrister, Bryan O'Donovan of

Atkinson, Ainslie, Childs-Clarke and O'Donovan.

Before Acting Chief Justice Sinclair in the High Court, O'Donovan successfully argued that the magistrate had erred in entering the pleas. My admissions did not amount to guilty pleas. Counsel pointed out that only forty-five minutes had passed between my arrest and trial. My state of mind was clearly unequal to the occasion. The judge quashed the conviction, ordering a new trial before a different magistrate. Sir James Henry, solicitor general, agreed with O'Donovan that the charges were excessive, and that charges under the Game Ordinance would be more appropriate. The governor was still on leave. Sir James was overruled by the Minister for Local Government in the Executive Council, a friend of Skinner's. He claimed that reduced charges would look like a move to protect an administrative officer. The charge of uttering a false document was dropped, as bad in law, but the horrible charge of theft remained and a count under the game law was added along with a new Penal Code charge of attempting to procure registration by false pretences.

I was released at once, returning to Iringa escorted by a young policeman with pink knees. We took a train from Morogoro to Dodoma. I sat at a table with the cop. The train manager came and sat beside me. He poured me a beer, excusing himself. 'Never touch it on duty.' He told a story about a policeman who had enjoyed a marvellous local leave in Arusha with a pretty English girl. She was to let him know if she became pregnant, and he'd come at once and marry her. A year later, in Arusha again, the cop met the girl, wheeling a pram with twins in it. 'Whose?' he asked. 'Yours,' she replied. 'But I promised to come and marry you if —' The girl said, 'Yes, that's what I told my Dad. But he forbade it. Said he'd rather have two bastards in the family than one policeman.'

Public opinion, for what it was worth, seemed to be on my side. The cop and I were installed in the Iringa Hotel. The room had been gazetted as a temporary prison, an askari at the door. The cop's suitcase lay open on his bed, displaying his revolver. 'Careful with that,' I said. 'You don't want to shoot yourself.'

There was a commotion outside the door. The askari said, '*Hapana ruksa!*' (not permitted). And then repeated it a couple of times, diminuendo, till it was a sob. The door burst open. The room filled with cheering British and Greek settlers and businessmen waving champagne bottles. 'Time for sundowners!'

The cop started to protest.

'Oh, shut up!' they roared. Women were arriving to bestow lucky kisses. Someone ran to the White Horse to fetch Pat. We all got smashed. Pink Knees sat on his bed and sulked. They kept saying. 'You'll get bail tomorrow. And screw Skinner.'

I became depressed, sure the DC would return to the attack. I saw how the Crown was construing my offence. Since the ivory was brought in by a game scout, it was Crown property. In falsely claiming that I had killed the elephant, I was stealing the king's property. This time the Crown would use all its resources to make the charge stick. To compound my misery, the word from Ireland was that my father was ill with uremia but determined to support me. In London *The Times* had run a brief report, 'District Officer Jailed'. Father had been badly shocked. He wrote me a letter of encouragement and sympathy. He was determined to reimburse everyone who helped me. I knew that this would offend the Greeks, their pride in generosity being every bit as strong as Irish pride in independence. My father's illness tormented me. I felt I had caused it.

I was receiving support from surprising quarters. Sir Theodore Pike, Governor of Somaliland, wrote to tell me not to think of myself as a criminal. I had never met Sir Theodore, an Irishman. Tom Marealle, soon to be elected Paramount Chief of the Chagga, sent the kindest note offering help. My friend Adam, Chief of the Hehe, came to see me, and wrote to the governor on my behalf. The Liwali came to learn my precise name so that I could be prayed for in the Mosque. There was also a note from a leading Ismaeli in Dar es Salaam assuring me that he was with me 'whole and sole' and was petitioning the governor on my behalf. These messages helped me through the bad days, as did the staunch and affectionate support of Paddy and Mary Lane, and Joyce and David McQueen.

The Crown made sure that Bryan O'Donovan was not available for my defence. They timed my trial to coincide with a manslaughter case in Dar es Salaam in which he was involved, refusing an adjournment longer than eleven days. I tried to get the only Iringa lawyer to represent me, but he thought it would be bad for business. So I had to take the bus to Dodoma and find an Indian, Mr Dara Keeka, to defend me. (Later, a Whitehall official expressed dismay that I had briefed 'an Indian pleader'.) He had the courage to accept.

The trial went on for days before a specially appointed magistrate, Phillip Biron, who had been commissioner of rent controls in Dar. A stout north-countryman in a black alpaca jacket, he was easy and folksy on the bench, filling in silences with expressions like, 'Any old 'ow.'

The Crown prosecutor was senior superintendent Arthur Poppy, the detective who had failed to nail the killer of Lord Erroll in Kenya.

Barnabas had been charged along with me this time. He was terrified, rigid with fear, convinced the whole matter had been worked by witchcraft.

We believed the Crown had failed to make its case. And there were damaging procedural errors. All three charges were based on the same facts. Under the Penal Code, the onus of proof was on the Crown; under the Game Ordinance, on the accused. We were in an impossible position, since our silence on one charge could be used to prove us guilty of the other.

Summing up, Biron said it was a simple case. The many witnesses called to identify the tusks were not in themselves convincing, Biron thought, but they were corroborated by other evidence. (Keeka disagreed.) Found guilty on all counts, I was sentenced to three months' imprisonment with hard labour. Barnabas was bound over without other punishment. I'm glad to say he got his job back.

I said goodbye to Pat and the little boys and to a sobbing Onesmo. Taking leave of African friends was painful. I had been in so many places with Onesmo and had come to love his humour and humanity, his feeling for beauty and nature. Pat and the children were soon on their way home by air, to stay with my parents in Dublin, where they now lived. As for me, I went back to the Hoteli ya Mfalme Kingy Georgy at Kingolwira, and this time I knew exactly what to expect.

The long-term inmates were still here. I did not want to be one of them. My three months would not seem so long, with time off. I had hopes of my appeal, which O'Donovan thought he could win.

Still, I was in despair. Even if I won the appeal, my life was ruined. The question that kept nagging me was 'Why me?' A case like mine was almost unheard of. I could not see that I was so bad. True, I had done something dishonest, but was I so evil as to deserve being singled out like this? The service, with its secret reports and communications, must know something horrible about me that I did not know myself.

As I went over and over what had happened, it dawned on me that Skinner must have wanted me to commit an offence. He had all but insisted, making sure that no one stopped me. And as I thought about him and the slimy provincial commissioner, depression turned to anger. I damned them to the deepest pit in hell. At the same time I came face to face with the truth about perfidious Albion, the ease with which British bureaucrats betrayed their own.

The days were running down to my release. My spirits lifted, I could almost smell the fresh air of liberty. Christmas was coming. Chris spoke his mantra of hope, 'The world is wide, *bwana.*'

I was called to the office. I went with a light heart.

The super told me to sit down, he had bad news.

It could not have been worse. Mr Justice Clifford Knight, a crony of Skinner's, had refused to consider any points of due process. 'My court,' he said, 'is not an academy of law.' In quashing the appeal, he had also increased my sentence, though it was not at issue, to eighteen months. The Crown had not sought this. Sir James Henry was as appalled as O'Donovan, who was so shocked that he refused to bill for his services.

I felt sick – literally, because my health had deteriorated as I began the long term. I was afflicted with boils. Then I suffered the first toothache of my life. It was as if I'd turned my rage on myself. As it happened, a dentist, one of four in the whole country, was visiting Morogoro. I was taken to town in the back of a truck. Clouds were piling up, the day was growing dark.

In my broad arrows I must have looked like a cartoon convict. I was marched through a room where frightened-looking memsahibs and commercial men waited. In the surgery I was astonished to find that the dentist was a fresh-faced young woman. My eye lit nervously on the drill, driven by a pedal, but it was not needed. One of my back teeth was beyond repair and would have to come out.

While the dentist was injecting painkiller, she told me her father had been a shipmaster on Lake Victoria. She had been born and bred in the territory. Once qualified, she had to make do with primitive equipment because there was no alternative. She was not put off by my broad arrows. And then began the struggle to pull the tooth. That girl was strong. The local anaesthetic had little effect. I heard myself groaning, as forceps were discarded for hammer and chisel. The grim wrestling went on. 'The roots are crossed,' the woman grunted, hammering like a stonemason to cut the jawbone. The pain was vivid. In that pain was concentrated all my misery and humiliation.

At last it was over. Staggering through the waiting room, mouth full of blood, I was not displeased to see the green, terrified faces of the memsahibs. I had been given analgesic pills. Standing alone in the back of the truck all forty miles back to Kingolwira as rain poured relentlessly down, I screamed at the sky. Back in prison, shivering with shock, I pulled off my wet clothes and climbed into bed under the mosquito net. Water was dripping from a hole in the roof.

The focused pain helped me endure diffuse mental distress.

Meanwhile O'Donovan, helped by Sir James, moved swiftly to have the Court of Appeal for Eastern Africa convene out of term. Family and friends in the British Isles had also been consulting back and forth and Clive Salter, Kenya's most eminent counsel, had been briefed to argue a third appeal.

On 17 December 1951 I was again called to the office. I was to be released at once. The sentence of eighteen months had been struck down. (My conviction, though, was upheld.) I had gone through five trials and had been in jail about four months. Enough was enough.

A couple of hours later the District Commissioner of Morogoro came in his car to drive me to his house, an unexpected kindness. The DC was an old-fashioned gentleman in a sun helmet. He and his wife could not have been more sympathetic and I stayed the night with them. I was to board the train for Dodoma next morning and from there take the bus to Iringa.

'I'm only going to say this about your troubles,' the DC said, after dinner, 'and then we won't refer to them again. I want you to know that if you'd been in *my* district, or indeed any other district than the one you were in, none of this would have happened. You'd have been torn off a strip, then given a chance to put things right. Remember that.'

I was to spend Christmas with Joyce and David McQueen. There seemed to be no end to their kindness. Paddy and Mary Lane were no less hospitable and encouraging

The Secretariat wrote that my appointment as district officer was terminated. I had expected to be dismissed. Instead, I was given five months' leave with pay and back pay, and free air passage to Britain. I was to leave the country as soon as possible. The governor, on his return, had done what he could for me. Soon there was other evidence of his intervention. Thieman was transferred to Malaya, Skinner to the High Commission in Kenya, Stuart's appointment terminated. Later I heard that other members of the Skinner gang had been dispersed.

In addition, there had just been a significant increase of pay for government employees. I benefited from this. I have come to believe that Skinner's motive in dealing with me as he did was to produce an example of an official desperate for money. This would give an excuse for an increase of pay. Fifty-five years ago my feelings were different. Perhaps other convicts feel as I did, that they are scapegoats, that each who suffers bears the guilt of all. This may be the root of the thieves' psychology which sees everyone as a crook, and the convict just the one who got caught.

In the McQueens' comfortable house I had a couple of weeks to think about such matters. While David and Joyce were both out at work, I spent the time trying to write about my ordeal. I was also trying to bring to order my notes on Hehe culture, based on the government anthropologist's questionnaire. Skinner had had the gall to send me a message in jail that he needed these notes urgently. There was no chance that I would oblige him in any way. All I wanted to do was put him out of my mind forever.

Joyce was able to explain to me, in the nicest way, that I had no talent for business.She herself was highly skilled in commerce, analyzing her sales every month, and now busy with Christmas trade. A grace note of this Christmas season was the presence of Joyce's twenty-one-year-old sister Barbara. She too went out to work every day, and in the evenings set forth on a round of sundowners and parties. She had graduated recently in English and had a bright and original mind. Barbara was a charming girl, and we became easy friends. She seemed incredibly young. At twenty-eight I felt as old as yonder elm. I was sorry to leave her. I was sorry to leave them all. I never saw them again.

All I recall of Christmas itself was a longish drive after dark with Paddy and Mary Lane to the Catholic Mission at Tosamaganga, where the Italian fathers were singing Mass with gorgeous pomp in their big cathedral. The swelling music, the blaze of candles and rich fabrics, the blue smoke of incense, the mysterious Latin and jangling bells carried a powerful emotion. The Mass was a sacrifice in which the victim suffered for the sins of humankind. I felt an affinity. When the Mass was over, a new one began. The Lanes urged me to stay and hear it again. I knew how they loved the wonderful pageant, but it was too much for me. I murmured an excuse and went out into the cool night. Paddy was angry with me, mistaking my flight for Protestant bigotry, though it was nothing of the kind.

Ten

The world had changed since my arrival in Africa by sea. In January 1952 I returned to London by air: a light aircraft from the Iringa strip to Dar es Salaam, and from there a BOAC four-engined airliner. There was a short stopover in Nairobi and others in Khartoum and Cairo.

Pat and the boys were staying at my parents' house in Temple Road, Dublin, where there was plenty of room. I joined them for a visit before going to London to seek work, and continue the hopeless quest for rehabilitation.

My father was happy to have his grandsons with him. And every day at teatime, one or more of his friends would drop in to visit, old, honourable Dubliners who had spent their lives doing the world's work. There was T.S.C. Dagg, who was president of the Royal Irish Academy of Music. My mother would invite him to sing, and accompany him on the piano while he warbled, in his fading voice, such favourites as 'Come into the garden, Maud.' There was Dawson, late of the Indian Railways, benefactor of Christ Church cathedral. Joseph Hone had been reader for Maunsel, James Joyce's first publisher, and his editor for *Dubliners* and *Chamber Music*. He had written biographies of W.B.Yeats and George Berkeley. Major General Sir Charles Gwynn was author of the standard work on policing the empire. And there were others.

I had to look for work in London. The only job I could find was supply teacher in secondary modern schools. I thought of Dr

Fagan, the headmaster in Evelyn Waugh's *Decline and Fall,* who said of the teaching profession, 'Nobody enters it unless he has a very good reason which he is anxious to conceal.'

Tim Revington, now retired from government and working as executive officer of the Bukoba Native Coffee Board, wanted me for the post of secretary to the board. It was a job that called for tact in dealing with African growers and firmness in the face of political obstruction. In March 1952 Revington wrote to say that the government had opposed my appointment. I was a prohibited immigrant. 'I am very sorry,' he added, 'as you are just what I wanted.'

There was a prejudice in England against persons who had been employed in imperial or colonial business – never mind the criminal record. My depression often turned into anger. I made up my mind to emigrate, to Australia, the US or Canada. I wanted to begin my life again. I knew that Pat felt the same way.

The climate was getting me down. I missed tropical light and colour. I was stupid enough to opt for Canada and Toronto, where the climate can be as dismal as Britain's.

It happened that I knew people in Toronto. The Reverend Cedric Sowby, formerly Warden of St Columba's, was now principal of Upper Canada College, a famous private school in the city. He had offered help if I came his way. I was ready for any help from any quarter. Provost Cosgrave of Trinity College, Toronto, once a pupil of Grandpa Bernard, promised to provide introductions.

That summer Esmonde Robertson was in London and did his best for me. He had become fat and Toryish and ran with the kind of crowd his butler Dennis would have approved of. He introduced me to a young man who said, 'I am the Honourable James Mitford and my father is Lord Redesdale.' I wondered why he wanted me to know this right away. I found that, hearing only my Christian name, he thought I was someone else. When I explained that I was not the Marquess of Kildare, he dropped me like a hot potato.

The Cold War was simmering in press and radio and intellectual life. In 1952 the US tested a hydrogen bomb, many times more destructive than the Hiroshima one.

I began to prepare for emigration to Canada, booking steerage with Cunard for the voyage from Cobh, County Cork, to Halifax, Nova Scotia, and the colonist-class train from there to Toronto. I had just enough money for my own fares. Pat and the boys would have to wait until I had saved enough to send for them.

At the chalet, I said goodbye to wife and children. My father, heaving theatrical sighs, put on one of his tragic scenes. 'I suppose I'll never see you again!' he said. I laughed. 'I'll be back!' I told him.

I spent the last couple of days with Kitty and my brother-in-law Paul Hamilton at Durrow in County Laois. Moyne was looking its beautiful best, the avenue of lime trees humming with bees, peacocks displaying on the lawns and uttering harsh cries, the Laois Hounds in residence in the kennels. Kitty had just redecorated the house. Paul was wonderful company, a retired captain of the Royal Irish Fusiliers. He had wanted to give me a loan to bring my family with me and tactfully tried to clear it with my father. I did not know this at the time. Father's reaction was characteristic. He believed the proposal had been hatched by the women of his family. 'I have a poor opinion of the reasonableness or judgment of most women in money matters, young or old,' he wrote, 'and even if most estimable and irreproachable in other ways, they are like a great many parsons in matters of money; and the Church, the children, or even sometimes their own necessities seem to them to be an excuse for procedures which to the ordinary honest layman are irregular.' (It is curious that he compares the clergy with women of his family, whom he calls 'the female soviet'.) Noting that I was already in debt to himself he added, 'Kildare has had a terrible time. In my opinion he has been treated infamously; a National Service private with a Labour MP behind him would have had more consideration. But having done all that can be done in that matter, we have now to apply common sense to existing problems.'

Paul bought me a raincoat as a parting gift. I kept it for years. At Cobh (simply the Irish form of 'Cove') I boarded a tender that carried me out to the SS *Amnesia*, the big old Cunarder that was taking on passengers in the bay. (I really do forget the name.)

Most of my fellow-passengers from Cobh were Canadian-Irish on their way home from a holiday in the old country. I was struck by the outlandish cut of their suits, factory-made in Canada no doubt. They all wore wide-brimmed hats with a bit of feather stuck in the band.

I was shown to my inside cabin deep in the bowels of the vessel, sharing it with four others. I was full of hope.

Aboard ship I had time to think. I realized that in Africa I had learned as much about human kindness as about treachery. I resolved not to look back or become embittered. Maybe this forgetting of the past would make me seem ungrateful to the friends who had helped me, the McQueens, Elwell-Suttons and Lanes, along with all the others, since they seemed to have vanished in this act of oblivion. I did not keep up with them or correspond. The weight of gratitude, perhaps, was too much for me. My father, I knew, thought me ungrateful, and to him perhaps I was. I had seen his anxiety to compensate people who helped me, to the point where some of them were offended. He wanted to keep me in his debt, and in his alone. I loved my father but had to be free of his control.

I arrived at Halifax in June 1952 in one of the last batches of immigrants to travel steerage in a Cunarder. A brass band on the wharf blared a welcome. Smiling ladies dispensed free coffee and cookies. Even the immigration and customs officers smiled as they stamped my papers.

I was almost twenty-nine, with an unjustified sense that the worst of my life was over. With a few dollars in cash and fifty more in travellers' cheques, I vowed to take the first job offered, no matter what. Later I would look for work as a teacher, though I did not intend to do it for long.

Colonist-class coaches had wooden seats like park benches. I sat next to an old Russian whose life had been spent in harness racing. We talked in French. He was heading far west, I forget where, suffering all the way, his old bones bruised by the wooden slats. I dozed, exhilarated despite the dreary miles of spruce-budworm forest we were passing with moaning whistle. At long last we hissed to a stop in Levis, over the wide St Lawrence from Quebec City, a stronghold looming out of morning mists, rocky crags, roofs and steeples and towers.

I thought of that fateful day nearly two centuries earlier, the Highlanders tense in the boats as muffled oars dipped and dripped, the sentinel's '*Qui vive?*', the scramble up the cliffs. Then the bugle calls, the sergeants' cries, the shots in the clear morning, the rattle of drums, the tumult of battle in which both Wolfe and Montcalm fell, enemies united in death.

I lugged my bags into the lofty hall of Toronto's Union Station, a heroic space celebrating the romance of steam from coast to coast. The coffee shop and cloakroom where I checked my trunk were squalid in comparison.

A porter with a nasty sense of humour told me I could find cheap lodgings at the intersection of Jarvis and Dundas streets. I could not know that the neighbourhood was infested with whores, junkies and deadbeats. I did not care for the look of the Warwick Hotel where you could take a room by the hour. But I found a cheap room soon enough, though there was no lock on my door. Stashing my wallet under the pillow, I tried to read a newspaper. I could not concentrate and, what was worse, the light flickered incessantly, so that everything looked like a bad movie. Toronto electric power was then on a twenty-five-cycle alternating current, rather than sixty-cycle as elsewhere in the world. You'll get used to it, I was told. But in 1954 Ontario Hydro changed to sixty-cycle and within six months or so had replaced, free of charge, every electric motor on the old frequency.

For the moment I knew only that I had arrived. The room smelled queer, but I fell asleep with a sense that the next day something wonderful was going to happen.

And sure enough, first thing next morning I found my wallet was gone. Someone had sneaked in and swiped it from under my sleeping head. My dismay passed quickly. So I had come to a country of thieves. Well, there was no use fretting about it. The police, when I made my report, were unhelpful – what did I expect in that neighbourhood? All was not lost, though. In my hip-pocket was a paper on which I had written the serial numbers of the missing travellers' cheques. I alerted American Express, which was then downtown. Next, I applied to an employment office and lucked into my first job – an order clerk at Heintz warehouse on Dupont Street at 53¢ an hour, then the minimum wage. Back at American Express, I was told I would have to swear an affidavit about my loss before a refund could be made. There was a lawyer's office in the same building, where I was interviewed by a Mr Young.

'You'll need a job,' he said while the document was being typed. 'What education have you had?'

I told him, adding, 'but I've got a job already, sir, thanks all the same'. When I gave him the details, Mr Young radiated pleasure and benevolence. Why, I was just the kind of immigrant Canada needed, a college man willing to take blue-collar work. He refused to take a fee. 'I'm going to call a friend of mine to advise you. Good luck to you!'

My first Sunday I visited the Royal Ontario Museum. In a display of African artefacts I was amazed to see a basket-woven drinking vessel, a *kinyamkonyi* as made by the Hehe. The donor's name was Professor G.Gordon Brown, whose publications on the tribe I had read attentively. Amazed, I pointed it out to a guard. He too was amazed. He said Professor Brown worked here and was even now in the building. He led me to Brown's office.

'*Kamweni!*' I called, the kiHehe greeting.

Gordon Brown stood up, astonished, a big man with a moustache over snaggle-teeth. We would have gone for a drink had it not been the Toronto Sabbath. Instead, Gordon Brown fetched his attractive colleague Margaret Pirie and we went for coffee. It was my lucky day. Peg Pirie found me a room, in Victoria College for seven dollars a week (just for the vacation) and invited me to dinner with her and her husband, who was the swimming instructor at the YMCA. Later they divorced and Peg went to teach at Yale.

Gordon Brown liked to drink. He took my notes on the Hehe

and read them. He said they were not bad for an amateur. I found him a delightful man; his stories of the Hehe fascinated me. And then he lost all my notes, the work of many months.

I decided that, after all, it didn't matter. It was a reminder that I had left that African life behind me and was beginning again. Like the loss of my valuables in India, it taught me that there was always something new to be faced in life.

I got myself hired as a high-school teacher in Florence, Ontario. The town was a tiny hamlet with two general stores, primary and high schools and two churches and that was about it. It had been named by a man who admired Florence Nightingale. No one had heard of an *Eye*-talian city of that name. The Lambton-Kent high school was here for the time being. The chairman of the school board owned a small hotel with a restaurant in nearby Chatham. On the restaurant wall was a sign that said, 'Dinning Room' [*sic*]. He gave me a talk on education, 'When we wuz kids,' he said, 'we wuz learned the *syllables*. We wuz teached *good*.'

In due course my family arrived and we were found a tumble-down house with the mod cons of outhouse and hand-pump. This was hard on Pat. We were sick a lot. And I was teaching again, which I detested.

Our first excitement was the Fall Fair. Along with ferris wheel, roundabouts, swings and other rides, every institution in the county ran its exhibit, including the high school. Teachers' names and qualifications were displayed on a big board. I saw my own name there, 'Kildare Dobbs MA (Cantab)'. The 'Cantab' just means 'Cambridge' but I was hoping it could be taken for a contraction of *Cantabile* which might suggest that I got the degree for a song (whereas in fact it cost me five pounds).

Among the crowds cruising the fair ground were the county librarian and his wife. They had visited England and were intrigued to see a Cantabridgian in this setting. Albert Bowron introduced himself and his wife Margaret, who resembled Botticelli's Venus. We became friends.

Albert helped me make sense of my new country, recommending books. It was from him and Margaret that I first heard of Northrop Frye and Marshall McLuhan, two great minds of the University of Toronto, and in time I would come to know them too. Albert, wide-eyed and athletic, was given to argument and when he got his teeth into an opinion would not let go. Later on, when I saw what Albert could do in libraries, I admired his diverse talents; he was highly organized and open to new ideas.

One evening we were expecting the Bowrons for dinner when a storm blew up, with heavy rain, thunder and lightning. Long after dinner time, an exhausted Albert sent a telephone message *via* the Anglican rectory. The hurricane had lifted the roof off the hotel where they had stopped for a drink, and dropped it on their car. There had been other disasters. They were lucky to be alive.

Over in Petrolia, where the first oil wells in the country had generated ephemeral wealth, the Bowrons had an apartment. They lived in the big old firehouse, a brick building with a tall belfry. The bell had been needed to muster volunteer firemen. It was an ideal place for the New Year party the Bowrons gave on the eve of 1953. There were house guests from Toronto as well as ourselves, big city sophisticates, European immigrants, and artists including the fabulously gifted photographer Lutz Dille.

One of the sophisticates was a blonde Hungarian who really knew how to party. We were all pretty well bagged by midnight, when there was loud knocking at the door. Bang bang bang! Who could it be? The blonde went to open the door. On the doorstep stood three or four weather-beaten men in farmers' overalls and peaked caps. 'We've come to ring the bell for midnight. It's kinda like, y'know, a tradition here.'

The blonde opened the door wide. 'Come on in and fuck somebody,' she said.

I was tormented by the idea that for the rest of my life I'd be stuck in a job I hated. The desire to escape became urgent.

I wrote letters applying for work in publishing. I was lucky enough to be taken on by the Macmillan Company of Canada, a branch of the well-known London firm, Macmillan & Company.

John Morgan Gray was president, a man of square features and gestures, of ruddy complexion and consummate politeness. He wore well-cut suits and kept his handkerchief in his sleeve like an Englishman. But in fact he was a strong Canadian patriot, proud of his country. He spoke of his interest in history and the need for books that would explain the country to its people. In the war he had been a major in the Intelligence Corps, veteran of the gruelling thrust from Normandy to the Low Countries in which Canadians had defeated elite German troops, liberating Holland and Belgium. Easy in his manner, he had a wicked sense of humour. It was because of him that I stayed so long at Macmillan's.

I told him about my African fiasco. Gray laughed it off, saying, 'They won't hear about it from *me!*'

In the early 1950s Toronto was a dismal place. Capital of Ontario, it was the seat of provincial government, possessing a large university and a polytechnical school. It was the centre of the nation's English-language communications, book and magazine publishing, radio, television and telephone networks; and, together with Montreal, was also a powerful financial centre with mighty banks and insurance companies and busy stock exchange. An army of accountants gave the tone. With all this it was the butt of recycled Philadelphia jokes – 'First prize – One week in Toronto; Second prize – Two weeks in Toronto.' Canadians from other centres called it 'Hog Town' or 'Toronto the Good'. Calvinist misery reigned. The liquor laws were wretched. To buy wine and spirits from the Provincial Liquor Commission (sole vendor), you needed a permit on which every purchase was noted.

Everyone went to church on Sunday in a hierarchy of religions: Anglican, United and Catholic. Together with the Lord's Day Observance Society, the Protestants made Toronto Sunday a penitential day. The churches themselves, with few exceptions, were the ugliest I had ever seen. Catholics, so long as they attended Mass, were in theory allowed to have fun, but even for them it was a challenge, with bars, theatres and shops shut. One summer in the fifties on the beaches of Toronto Island a man was arrested for not wearing a shirt as he stepped onto the path. Another was charged with drinking beer in his own backyard.

The friends I made after work were the vanguard of a new Toronto which European civilization would enrich with the arts of the good life. Albert Bowron's friend Martin Landman came from a family of German Jews who had escaped Hitler with their fine collection of paintings, especially German Expressionists. Martin was generous, driving us to Niagara to see the Falls and the site of the Battle of Queenston Heights in which British and Canadian troops, with the help of aboriginal warriors, drove Americans from our soil.

I became friends with Harold Towne and other members of Painters Eleven, the liveliest spirits in Ontario art at that time. Soon Towne ranked as a national figure, approaching the Quebec eminences, Borduas and Riopelle. Before he grew whiskers, he looked like Tenniel's Mad Hatter. He was a fascinating man whose conversation was full of surprises.

Lutz Dille I already knew. He had the German stereotypical characteristics but all injected the right way. The anal-compulsive trait made him a perfectionist in art, the arrogance made him pursue his own path, the thoroughness made him technically a master. In the early fifties he was living with a tiny brunette called Vera in a studio with a kind of shelf over the door, to which the couple climbed by a ladder at bedtime.

At Macmillan's I was happy doing work I enjoyed, with people I respected. I became senior editor with a voice in acquisitions. Editors there were not executives. Decisions were made by John Gray with his sidekick Frank Upjohn. The meat-and-potato element was the education department, grinding out schoolbooks under the astute Gladys Neale. Gray himself had come up through education.

One Macmillanite who had hoped to head the Canadian company was Horatio Lovat Dickson, who worked in London. 'Rache' had left Canada to found his own company in London. He had published Grey Owl's books and daringly issued Radclyffe Hall's *The Well of Loneliness*, the first lesbian novel. Although the Canadian house was a branch plant and agent for the parent company and some others (including Viking Press of New York and a handful of small houses in London), John Gray was given a more or less free hand, which he used like a good patriot. Our policy was to seek out Canadian books that were not just publishable but seemed to us among the best of their kind.

When I first joined Macmillan we would receive the laconic opinions of 'Mr Daniel', Harold Macmillan's elder brother. He always took time to write brief letters, seldom more than three or four sentences, ending in verdicts such as, 'I'm afraid it won't do.' Not that these judgments always prevailed, because even if our London house did not want to take copies of a book, we could usually find another publisher who did.

I imagined Macmillan in London with high desks and stools, and clerks scratching away with quill pens. In fact, editors and publicists tended to be underpaid ladies of good families. Publishing was still thought of as an occupation for gentlefolk who were too well bred to do anything so coarse as ask for money. Under Gray, the Canadian branch was so successful that Mr Daniel soon left us alone. In the eight years I worked for Macmillan we won seven Governor General's Awards in the adult categories and six in the juvenile category.

We were strong in Canadian history, with heavyweights like Donald Creighton, Maurice Careless and Charles Stacey. We often wished for less academic books, though we couldn't fault Creighton's romantic prose. He was a patriot long before the generation of nationalists who were to denounce 'continentalism' in the sixties. Creighton told me that these authors had discovered Canada at just about the time they became PhDs.

As importers, Macmillan's emphasis was on sales. The sales manager was an ambitious man who had come up from the warehouse – Jack Stoddart. He left the firm to start a successful company of his own. He felt, like all sales managers, that publishing decisions should be based on experience in sales. It seemed to me, though, that salesmen always wanted the book that had been successful last year. They were not in touch with the *zeitgeist* or the new.

In the warehouse at Macmillan's there were men who remembered *Gone with the Wind*. They'd worked shipping copies till they dropped. But John Gray was not looking for bestsellers, though he always hoped for profit as well as contribution to overheads. He told me how his boss in the thirties, the ebullient Hugh Eayrs, had read a manuscipt which he thought would probably sell like Margaret Mitchell. He also thought it was trash that Macmillan would be ashamed to publish. The book was *The Robe,* a novel about Jesus Christ, which in another publisher's hands became a huge money-spinner. Eayrs never regretted declining it, convinced it could not have succeeded with his firm.

Gray's suspicion that an editor was an unjustified luxury in a business focused on marketing and sales made him assign me to a few trade accounts in the city, notably Britnell's and Tyrrell's book-shops on Yonge Street. Roy Britnell, sandy-haired, soft-spoken and wearing spats, was known as the inventor of the one-book order. My job was to jump whenever he ordered and bring him the books, one at a time. These excursions cut into my reading and editing time. More agreeable were calls at Tyrrell's, where Miss Atwood presided, a lady assisted by other ladies catering to the carriage trade. Phyllis Atwood and I decided that we were distant cousins, connected by an Upper Canadian worthy, the architect Kivas Tully. I was fond of Miss Atwood and of her children's book specialist, Miss Catharine Brichta.

When our western representative resigned to found Duthie's bookstores in Vancouver, I became a travelling salesman *usque ad mare.*

Twice I made the long excursion across Canada by rail, stopping in Fort William, Winnipeg, Regina, Sakatoon, Medicine Hat, High River, Lethbridge, Calgary, Edmonton and Vancouver. This list of place-names, or something like it, was chanted over loud-speakers in heroic railway stations that still remembered the age of steam. Northrop Frye thought the list like the mighty roll-call of ships in the *Iliad*. I loved the trains, the private roomette, the dining-car with dazzling white linen and gleaming silverware and glass, the observation-car from which you could view the majestic country as it wheeled by, the drawing-room car where you sat in an easy chair that swivelled to face anyone you wanted to face as you sipped your whiskey. And there was dignified, attentive service from black attendants and grave, responsible conductors who knew more about the country we traversed than any geographer. By day we saw it unfurling through windows, forests, lakes, prairies, immense mountains and more forests; as evening closed in, windows became mirrors showing only our own faces – and this memory too was shared by Northop Frye.

I liked the railway hotels, the great commercial castles that arose in the wilderness before other public buildings in their cities and towns. The age of steam was romantic, and the great chateaux of the CPR and CNR sprouted towers, gables and spires. Oh the joys of room service! The table rolled into the room laden with dishes under covers – the only snag being the business with buyers that came with it. My reports were mostly complaints about these social ordeals, which scandalized the sales-people at Macmillan. I did not do too badly on the bottom line, however, considering how utterly unsuitable a rep. I was.

Eleven

Our stressful life in Africa and Ontario had all been too much for Pat. She wanted desperately to be free to find herself. With the advice of her psychiatrist I agreed to a divorce. In the early fifties divorce in Ontario was a hideous ordeal, involving a conspiracy. I was given custody of the boys, though Pat would see them whenever she wished and have them stay with her most weekends.

We were living on Lawton Boulevard, in the upper storey of an old house. The landlady, a librarian, had been brought up in China by missionary parents. I decided to share the apartment with some like-minded person, and as it happened a recent immigrant from England, *via* the University of Indiana, was looking for reasonable accommodation. Arthur Hammond at the time worked for Macmillan as an editor in the Education Department.

We got along well and the boys loved him. Tall, with the head of a Roman patrician, he was a romantic figure. He came from Battersea, across the Thames from the City of London and, as a child during the war, had been evacuated to a seaside resort in Wales. He knew the other side of the story told by Evelyn Waugh in *Put Out More Flags,* in which the British upper crust are afflicted by the arrival of tough city children. Arthur knew how to entertain little boys, making skilful use of a whoopie cushion, to them the funniest thing on earth. His good nature made for a peaceful existence, doubly welcome after the brawling of a bad marriage. He left Macmillan to become editor of *Quill & Quire,* a publication for the book trade.

During the Suez Crisis of 1956 both of us felt anxiety and cha-grin at the folly of Anglo-French collusion with Israel in the attack on Egypt after Nasser had nationalized the Suez Canal. Night after night we sat by the radio as the story unfolded. The adventure was contrary to the interests of the United States, which quickly moved to end the imperial bullying. Henceforth the only imperial bullies were to be American and Russian, as gradually the chill of their Cold War imposed an icy standoff. The Suez adventure incidentally provided a distraction that allowed the Soviets to send their tanks into Hungary, and suppress the freedom-fighters. Toronto bene-fited from an influx of talented refugees. Leaders of the anti-com-munist rising had been members of the intelligentsia – university graduates, doctors, writers, artists and musicians. An earlier wave of Hungarian immigrants had been dispossessed nobles.

I had been daunted at first to find myself a single parent, not that the subject had yet been taken up and worried to death in the media. I had to get the boys up early each morning, give them breakfast and take them to a day-school downtown before begin-ning work at 9 am. On winter mornings they would be crying with the cold.

One morning when the ordeal had been especially hard on them, I had a meeting in my office with the poet Anne Wilkinson. I was her editor on a volume Macmillan hoped to publish but had not yet decided upon. My job was to encourage and support her in revising the collection. We had become friends as well as collabora-tors in this work. Anne took one look at me and said, 'You're very pale – what's the matter?'

When I told her, she was full of womanly sympathy. She offered to 'help me' through it. Anne was an attractive woman. I felt I should come clean. I told her I was not contemplating marriage. She found this hilarious. 'Don't give it a thought,' she said, laugh-ing. 'My intentions are scrupulously dishonest!'

For a while she did help me get used to my situation, with kindness and distraction, entertaining us in her Rosedale house with roast beef and other treats.

Macmillan were less interested in her poetry than in another project, a memoir of her mother's family, the Oslers. Her great-uncles were distinguished men: Sir William Osler, the founder of modern medical education, who reigned at McGill, Oxford and Johns Hopkins; and Sir Edmund Osler, a Toronto financier. Together with a large clan of well-heeled Canadian Oslers, they descended from the Reverend Featherstone Osler, who had begun his career as a naval surgeon in the early 1800s. In those days a naval surgeon was a warrant officer; technically surgeons were still barbers who could give you a shave and a haircut – and cut you for the stone if that was what you needed. But by turning your collar around, you could become a priest and a gentleman.

Maybe this is the place to say what I thought an editor should try to do. I disliked the idea of the Great Editor, the hotshot who schools writers in their craft. Worse is the one who tries to make an author write exactly the book the editor envisions, or to obtrude an ideology. Which is not to say that writers should not be challenged to defend their vision or expression. The editor's function is to help the author deliver the *author's* book – the way he/she imagines it. The function is obstetrical. The editor is a judicious friend, who offers support, encouragement and advice. He represents the author to the publisher and the publisher to the author, knows what is valuable in his author and is able to sell his book to the sales force. (For 'he' I should probably have written 'she', since women are so often the best editors, and easier to underpay.) True, these are counsels of perfection. No one has perfect wisdom and patience, and there are times when an author's petulance, megalomania or insecurity gets on the editor's nerves.

I became a writer by way of broadcasting. It happened in a curious way.

In 1954 Macmillan had accepted a novel I had found by an American scriptwriter. He'd come to Toronto from Hollywood, where he was blacklisted after suing a studio for plagiarism. The writer was Charles Israel, a cultivated southerner; the novel, *How*

Many Angels, the first of several he published with Macmillan.

How Many Angels was going through the press in 1954 when we were visited by the writer and mandarin C.P. Snow, later Lord Snow, and his novelist wife, Pamela Hansford Johnson. Snow was interested in Charles and his novel. He amused himself by wondering whether Israel should change his name. His felt that anti-Semitism was pervasive enough to make it advisable. Gray said we were not publishing for bigots. There was no question of asking Israel to change his name – although, come to think of it, the biblical Israel had changed *his.*

Charles gave me undeserved credit for helping to get his book published. He asked me if I had any work of my own that he could show CBC producers. It happened that someone had left a recording machine in my office. I'd use it to tape a long poem of mine. I played it for Charles, who listened intently. At the end he said, 'Remarkable!'

I'm never sure what to make of this comment. Remarkable for what? But Charles said he was going to talk to a couple of men in CBC Radio. Israel was a respected scriptwriter with many credits in radio drama and documentaries. Thanks to him I was invited to play my tape for Robert Weaver and Ted Pope, respectively programmer and producer of CBC *Anthology*, a broadcast literary programme.

Weaver had persuaded the CBC that, in the absence of any print medium devoted to Canadian literature, broadcasting should fill the gap. He was already making his name as a talent-spotter of extraordinary acuity. Looking back on his discoveries I think it amazing that any editor should be so prescient, so open to talent. Genial and unpretentious, he was a pipe-smoker from the Niagara Peninsula who loved hockey and poetry. He also enjoyed paperback crime novels, and in those days would cross the border to Buffalo, New York, to stock up with the latest thrillers.

Ted Pope was a dashing figure, a poet with a passion for ski-jumping and motor racing. Unlike Weaver, who loved to gossip and tell stories about writers, Ted was taciturn and dreamy. Women were attracted to him. I have a vivid mental image of his squatting to listen to the recording.

That word 'Remarkable!' launched my thirty-year career in broadcasting with a recital of my poems on CBC *Anthology*. One thing led to another, and presently I was one of the group that launched *The Tamarack Review*, a literary quarterly, and a member of the editorial board of *The Canadian Forum*, a left-wing monthly journal of literature and opinions. I wrote for both publications, poetry and essays. I tended, though, to prefer broadcasting, because it paid. With rents so high in Toronto, it was hard to make ends meet. I had legal expenses. I was trying to repay loans my father had made me, but so slowly that he accused me of being casual about the debt. He was probably right, and perhaps I was still angry with him for paying off friends who had helped me in Africa. That money had been spent for his pride. On the other hand, he had managed to come to terms with my divorce. He wrote Pat a very kind letter.

Tamarack was a print version of CBC *Anthology*, Bob Weaver being the moving spirit and most active talent scout. But he was also a seasoned team player, so that everyone had his say.

One of my social duties for Macmillan, with John Gray, was to visit the novelist Mazo de la Roche and her friend Caroline Clement on Christmas Eve in her Forest Hill mansion. The rambling house was tudored up with black four-by-twos fastened in white stucco.

The trouble was I couldn't read Mazo's novels, and luckily I didn't have to. Her editors, who did have to read them, were in Boston. The French took Mazo's work, *Les Jalnas* with great seriousness. They had their own view of English letters, and at that time had made Charles Morgan, another Macmillan author, an immortal of l'Académie Française. Who remembers him now?

I was able to tell my hostess that her books had been read and treasured in the Irish house where I grew up. I admired Mazo's spirit. She had invented herself as well as her fictional world. She entertained me by showing photographs of the Macmillan family. 'That's Daniel, there's Harold, and this is Lady Dorothy. The young man here is Maurice, just elected to the Commons.' And one

Christmas when she asked about her Canadian sales, she declared, 'An author needs a public.'

Mazo submitted a short story to *Tamarack*. The theme was incest and the narrative salacious in a furtive way. The editors voted against it. It was my unhappy task to decline it. Mazo hit back at once. I've lost her note but I remember it much as follows: 'I'm sorry the editors did not like my story. I don't like it much myself but, as I have never liked any of the stories in your review, I thought it might do very well.'

Because she made such a mystery of herself, Mazo de la Roche attracted rumours. For example, that she had borne a child to Harold Macmillan. She was supposed to have done this when she was in her fifties, and hardly a *femme fatale*.

Another celebrity in our Canadian list was Morley Callaghan, friend of Hemingway and Scott Fitzgerald. A New York publisher told me that Callaghan was a novelist who had not fulfilled his promise. But Morley wrote gamely on, obsessed with his reputation – the subject of his novel, *The Many-Coloured Coat*. I admired Callaghan's poetic sense, though in attempting realism he was writing against his grain.

Callaghan was good company, often witty, and took literature seriously. He performed every week in a CBC radio quiz called *Now I Ask You*. The MC was Hamish McGeachie and there were four panellists – Ralph Allen (editor of *Macleans* magazine), James Bannerman, a cultural broadcaster, Morley Callaghan, and Callaghan's guest. Now and then I was the guest.

Programmes were recorded at 10 am in the hope that McGeachie would be sober at that hour. Not that it mattered – his Churchillian manner blurring the distinction between drunk and sober. Callaghan was knowledgeable about New York, Paris and Balzac, his favourite novelist; Allen was the expert at Canadian history and sport; Bannerman knew all about opera and drama and what he didn't know, he faked confidently. I remember a question: What did the following sovereigns have in common: Catherine the Great, Wilhelm II of Germany and the Shah of Iran? (The answer was that all their titles – Tsar, Kaiser, Shah – derived from Caesar.)

Bannerman said, 'They all had a withered arm.'

McGeachie weighed in, 'But my dear sir, my dear sir – what can you be thinking of? Catherine the Great did not have a withered arm!'

'She has now,' said Bannerman. And later in the show, when the name of Anita Ekberg came up, the blonde who figured massively in Fellini's *La Dolce Vita* and had recently died, Bannerman put in, 'And now *she* has a withered arm too.'

Twelve

My African trauma had stung me to ambition. I weighed in with reviews in the *Canadian Forum*, which quickly earned me the enmity of a revered Montreal poet and his friends. But worse than that, I had been thinking about my work at Macmillan – scrabbling around for signs of talent. The one-book writer was still the prevailing type. In an essay for *Tamarack*, I mocked my own enterprise. The idea came from a poem by F.R. Scott called 'Miss Crotchett's Muse'. Frank Scott was a great and famous Canadian, libertarian, constitutional lawyer and a founder of the CCF, later New Democrat, political party. He was also a poet and wit. In the poem in question he was satirizing the pretensions of the untalented. But when I made fun of the same people, and myself for chasing after them, Scott was outraged. How dare some outsider come onto his turf and scoff.

Some years later, when a search committee at McGill University was thinking of hiring me to set up a university press, Scott – who had seldom attended this committee – came out of the woodwork to ensure that I would never be given a place at his university.

There was room for guests in my apartment. In 1957 we were joined for three or four months by Mordecai Richler, the novelist and *enfant terrible* of Canadian letters. He was still married to his first wife, Cathy Boudreau, then in London, with whom he had long telephone conversations that left him agitated. He contributed to the rent without being asked and paid for his long-distance calls.

'Hey, we're like, all in the same boat,' he said.

Mordecai was trying to drum up television work to finance more time in Paris.

He lodged in the sunroom off the kitchen, where he hung a sausage on the door handle and managed to sleep despite the early-morning light. He was writing a story with the revealing title 'It's harder to be anyone', a variant on the saying, 'It's hard to be a Jew.' He was trying to shake off the constrictions of his origin in the Jewish underclass of Montreal. Many a rabbi denounced him as anti-Semitic, a sad misunderstanding of a man whose grandfather had been a famous Hasidic rabbi. It was true, though, that he tended to be a scold in his portraits of Jews. He knew them better than *goyim*. At that time he reminded me of *What Makes Sammy Run* – a *macher*, a Jewboy on the make. He had not yet found his true voice. That was to come with *The Apprenticeship of Duddy Kravitz* – which was about a Jewboy on the make.

At a CBC party we attended together the action was in a space a few stairs below the entrance. We were looking down into a room full of CBC programmers and producers, many of them women. We could not help noticing that the more attractive producers and broadcasters were absent. Mordecai, whom a sister-in-law described as a 'social zombie', wore his usual party grimace of fear and loathing. In a bitter tone he said, 'I do like a woman you can talk to.'

After one of his phone calls to his wife he seemed flushed and unsteady. Arthur and I both took his pulse, which was unusually rapid. We made him promise to see a doctor. After his divorce, his health greatly improved. Some years later I met Cathy Boudreau, an Indian-looking woman of vital presence, involved with a Buddhist cult. In time she became, so she said, the first Buddhist nun in Canada.

When Mordecai was not being sardonic, he was sentimental, but always serious about literature. He admired Isaac Babel's *Tales of the Red Cavalry* and *Zuleika Dobson* by Max Beerbohm, works of completely different character. He had travelled to Cambridge, he told me, to pay respects to E.M. Forster, a Fellow of King's, and revered author of half a dozen novels. Mordecai admired Evelyn Waugh's work, and perhaps also his feats of bad behaviour in which the admirer was to equal him. Despite his wit, Mordecai was not a conversationalist, but he enjoyed badinage or kibitzing in a Rotarian kind of way. Something should be said about his sartorial aspect. No matter how new or old his clothes, they hung on him like a kaftan. He liked to joke that his grandfather, a rag-and-bone man, had been in the recycling business. I'm not sure whether or not this was the same grandfather who had been a famous rabbi. Pious Jews visited his grave in Montreal to pray. Mordecai remembered his grandfather spitting and chuckling whenever he saw a Christian funeral. 'Good! Another of them dead!'

He enjoyed the stories told by Patrick Lyndon, at that time teaching at Upper Canada College. Patrick had been a musical prodigy and at nine years old gave piano recitals with his brother at London's Wigmore Hall. He had abandoned piano in his teens, read English at Oxford and served for one day at the front in Korea. On the voyage out, the troopship called at Singapore. Patrick stayed on board reading. He did not bother to go ashore with his brother-officers because he knew what it would be like. His stories about all this were masterpieces of self-deprecation. Mordecai called him Happy Pat Lyndon.

Some years later, Patrick was appointed Dean of Communications at the new Simon Fraser University in Burnaby, British Columbia. Some of the English faculty wanted a visit from Mordecai Richler, which Patrick arranged, not without difficulty. Mordecai was brought from London, housed and feted by the professors. He detested them, returning to London to jeer in *The Spectator*, where he made his name by catering to the unshakeable British belief that Canadians are always boring. The piece was deeply resented by some of the faculty, which made Patrick's relations with them unpleasant. In his own mind, Mordecai was just being honest. His honesty was often like that – someone had to suffer for it. Years later, when I mentioned Lyndon to Mordecai, he said,

'Patrick! – Hey, give him my love.' He'd long forgotten that he'd given offence.

During the Suez crisis, when Britain and France joined Israel in an attack on Egypt, we had a discussion. I wanted to make the point that enemies should listen to each other in order to avoid war. I quoted a line from W.H. Auden, 'We must love one another or die.'

I'll never forget the look of infinite contempt that Mordecai gave me. I cringed. To Mordecai the remark betrayed Christian hypocrisy. Auden himself had deleted it from later versions of his poem.

On my visits to London in the 1960s, Mordecai introduced me to his agent and his editor at the *Sunday Times* supplement. Nothing came of these contacts, but the mutual-help books had been balanced. With Jewish friends I often found that a score would be kept and a favour returned. It was a pleasing custom.

Still, it caused me trouble with the redoubtable theatre critic Nathan Cohen. He let me know that he had recommended me as a CBC film critic. Soon after this, he submitted to Macmillan a collection of his theatre columns from *The Toronto Star*. After several adverse opinions from readers, repelled by Cohen's graceless prose, it fell to me to decline the collection, which I did as tactfully as possible. This earned me Cohen's enmity. As he saw it, I had failed to return a favour.

Although Mordecai's early novels – before *Duddy Kravitz* – did not seem to me fully achieved, they were bursting with vitality. It is a tribute to Diana Athill, London editor for publisher André Deutsch, that she saw this quality in his very first effort, *The Acrobats*, a bad novel fulminating with promise. And it is a tribute to Mordecai's character that he learned from his failure, and remade himself as a writer. I don't believe he could have done it without the support of his second wife, Florence.

To her he was devoted, making little shows of protecting her from annoying attentions to which her beauty sometimes exposed her. She guarded his privacy and working hours, edited and typed his copy, and shielded him from bores. I think I may have been one of these when I tried to tell Mordecai a story. He'd stop me in mid-sentence, saying something like, 'Excuse me a minute – Florence, did the postman come yet?' And once I was launched again, Florence would come in with, 'Oh Mordecai – sorry Kildare – have you opened the letter from —?' It was a masterly *pas de deux*, silencing the visitor and exposing him as one of those boring Canadians Mordecai liked to skewer in the posh weeklies.

Being Mordecai's friend was not always easy. Early in the history of TV Ontario I was commissioned to interview Mordecai on camera. I thought I should challenge him with a couple of tough questions. I don't believe I was impelled by malice. My challenge went to his careerism in choosing where to place his articles. He was seriously annoyed. 'I don't claim to be virtuous,' he said. Off camera, he demanded a glass of Remy Martin. The producer said it was not permitted. Mordecai poured out his anger on the producer – anger that was really for me.

In the Lawton Boulevard apartment the sculptor and print-maker George Wallace was with us for a while. Newly arrived from England, he was looking for a job and accommodation where his wife Margaret could join him. George had been my senior at St Columba's. He had already been an artist then, a serious boy who dyed his pants red and wanted to take Holy Orders. But in the Divinity School at Trinity College Dublin, he had decided the truth was not in them, leaving to combine teaching with art and art scholarship. He continued in Ontario schools until he became the first Professor of Fine Art at McMaster University and a founder of the Hamilton art gallery. His work as print-maker and sculptor was daring and profound, though he made no effort to promote himself. He seldom took praise seriously. He would ask in a lofty way how a non-artist would know whether his work was good or not. Determined to be free of the Vanity Fair of dealers and critics and art guff, he was the best of company.

I had already made friends with Brian Moore, then living in Montreal with his first wife, the journalist Jacqueline Sirois. I had read his first acknowledged novel, *The Lonely Passion of Judith Hearne*

(1955), just published by André Deutsch, excited by the emergence of a major new Irish and Canadian writer. Visiting Montreal, I telephoned to convey this, explaining that I was a Macmillan editor, but not looking to seduce him from his publisher. 'Where are you?' he said.

'Here, right here in Montreal.'

'Come on over for a drink. We're home.'

I found them in a beautifully appointed house in Westmount, its white walls hung with abstract paintings. It did not occur to me to wonder how the author of a first novel could afford such comfort. I had not known that Jackie was a talented staff writer at *Weekend* magazine or that Brian had published five profitable paperback mysteries under various names. Both were smallish, plump figures of vivid personality. Jackie was carelessly dressed for a Montrealer, Brian almost a dandy. Even his jeans, I learned later, were tailormade in London and he was never otherwise than elegantly shod. He was an Ulsterman in his speech and in his toughness in making room for his work. His family was part of a Belfast minority of Catholic professionals, his father a respected surgeon, an uncle, James MacNeill, one of the founders of the Gaelic League and second Governor General of the Irish Free State. Like me, Brian had grown up with sisters. One was a nun, another a nurse, and his brother a pathologist at McMaster University. His early view of life and love, it seemed to me, was detached and clinical, a surgeon's view, coloured with Catholic guilt. Over time his work was to grow in warmth and imaginative scope. The Moores told me they had a young son, Michael, although I was not to meet him.

Brian was above all competent, capable in every way, and as a writer the complete master. At twenty, serving with the Ministry of Transport, Brian had been assistant port officer of Naples, after it fell to the Allies in World War II. His own city had endured the Nazi onslaught in air raids. He himself was a Joycean, struggling to be free of the British empire and the Catholic Church. Yet he created Catholic characters with cool objectivity. One of his most resonant works, *Catholics* (1972), a novella, reflected the anxieties of traditionalists facing the reforms of Vatican II.

Brian, like others who lose their religious faith, had not shed its prejudices. He himself resented liturgical innovation.

I remember a literary evening at the house of Robert Weaver, where Morley Callaghan met Moore for the first time. Morley characteristically buttonholed Brian to set him right about the Church. There was nothing in Moore's fiction, Callaghan told him, in any way contrary to Catholic doctrine. Moore spoke through his Ulster teeth. 'What d'you have to *do* then, brother Callaghan?'

His sensibility is shot through not just with Catholic imagery, but with purely local forms of it prevailing in Ireland, the factory-made plaster saints and sacred hearts, the stock apparitions of the Virgin, the anxieties about sex. Yet out of this unpromising material he makes some of the most significant fiction of the twentieth century. Critics scolded Moore for *not* repeating himself. Every new work was a new test of his imaginative powers. Critics were left behind. When Moore came out with *The Great Victorian Collection* in 1975 even the most respectable Canadian reviewers were baffled. What was this – fantasy? A man wakes up in a Californian motel and finds the parking lot full of a priceless collection of Victoriana. Somehow he knows that the whole thing belongs to him. How could a Canadian of sound mind believe such stuff?

Canada had inherited a powerful tradition of literal documentary. The founders of the Hudson's Bay Company had instructed their servants, 'You are to keep exact records.' Jesuits contributed their *Relations*, factual narratives designed to win support for their missions. The National Film Board continued the tradition. Yet Moore had delivered the real toad in the imaginary garden, the essence of poetry and magic realism. *The Great Victorian Collection* was an allegory about the nature of fiction itself, rigorously imagined and realized.

While no antiquarian in love with Victorian objects, he could invent the whole collection in detail after reading, say, a few pages of the catalogue of the Great Exhibition of 1851. Readers who thought of fiction as a form of reporting with names changed were puzzled. Moore's was the supreme case of the disappearing author – who and what was he?

That evening in Westmount was the first in many years of friendship, not only with Brian but with Jackie too, even during the aftermath of their painful divorce.

The divorce took place not long after the success of *Judith Hearne*, published in 1955, when the Moores shared a house in Long Island with another writer, Franklin Russell, and his wife Jean. Frank, a New Zealander, wrote eloquently about nature, Jean was an actress from Nova Scotia of great charm and elegance. I remember her as especially dazzling that summer. Brian was writing and rewriting a stage version of *Judith Hearne*, financed by options. The play was never produced. As the season went on Brian and Jean fell passionately in love, Brian seeing in her the woman who would be his lifelong companion and supporter. They flew to California, abandoning their spouses and little Michael.

Many of Jackie's friends were appalled by this ruthless act, taking sides and condemning Brian *ex parte*. Knowing that there's more than one side to every story, I stayed friends with all of them. When I saw her in New York, Jackie would say, 'Whatever happened to forever after?' Knowing that he had hurt Frank and Jackie, Brian would say of Jean, 'Was she not worth it?' With her he was happy for the rest of his life, and she with him. Life was calm in their house above the beach in Malibu, and later in their second home in Nova Scotia.

Before long, the abandoned couple, Frank and Jackie, married each other and stayed together till her untimely death.

I think the divorce was more than a change of partners. Moore was changing his whole life. No more journalism or schlock fiction. Perhaps influenced by Mordecai's example, he had confronted his vocation as a serious writer. There may even have been the sense that if Mordecai Richler could do it, he could do it better, a subtext I find in *An Answer from Limbo*. The respectful reception of *Judith Hearne* assured him of his talent. He had now to reinvent himself and his life. He did his best to suppress any mention of his genre fiction. With Jean as muse and protector, he found an ideal work-place in his house above the beach at Malibu, California. It was isolated enough to prevent distraction, yet connected with an intellectual centre of global influence. In one of our many conver-sations, he told me that he thought Flann O'Brien would have been a much more influential writer had he not worked in the obscurity of wartime Dublin.

Brian conducted a small class in creative writing at the Uni-verstiy of California in Los Angeles. He selected some fifteen stu-dents and worked with them as editor, the object being to get them into print.

He discussed his work in general terms. Occasionally, we would sit side by side with our drinks and talk on his patio above the long white beach. Sometimes we walked south along the white sand. He had friends down that way, Joan Didion being one of them. She suffered from migraines. On one of these southward walks he told me a story about the actress Barbara Bel Geddes. He thought it could make a novel, but talking about it must have spooked it, since he never did write that particular story. On another walk he told me of a long and distressful dream he'd had about Jackie, his first wife. We stopped to watch sea lions sunning themselves on some rocks offshore.

He had finished *Black Robe* when he told me about it. He had been profoundly impressed by the great American historian William Prescott. He remarked on the fact that the Indians of early days were very different from their modern descendants, who tended to affect a kind of New Age religion of nature. At one point, when he was coming to Ontario, Brian asked me if I could get the Ontario government to help him visit the shrine of the Jesuit mar-tyrs whose story he was telling in *Black Robe*, published in 1985. At the time, my friend Bernard Ostry was a deputy minister in the provincial government. He gave enthusiastic support, easing the writer's way.

When the book was made into a film, a Toronto critic couldn't wait to tell its author what was wrong with it. Brian said, 'There was no way I could listen to that joker. How could he imagine that I'd be interested in his opinion? I'd just put years of work into that project.'

Though he was a Canadian citizen and two of his novels won Governor General's Awards and three were nominated for the Booker Prize, Moore was never honoured with the Order of Canada. A letter he wrote to me in February 1978 may cast light on this curious fact. 'I was thinking of you last week in Calgary,' he wrote, 'when I was suddenly exposed to a large cloud of Can Lit blowing up a storm called "the 100 (or ten) significant Canadian novels". Mordecai, Bill Weintraub and a very high-floating Jack McClelland were among the gathered alumni, along with such *fleurs de mal* as Earle Birney [elder poet], a demented coprophiliac called — [female novelist's name omitted], Margaret Laurence & others, including Malcolm Ross [Can Lit academic], who tried to console me for not making the best ten with my oeuvre by telling me that for Canadians my lack of residence qualification is final.'

This qualification is overlooked, I notice, in some Hollywood actors of Canadian origin who are officers of the Order.

Brian continued by recalling a conversation with a Canada Council officer called Naim Kattan. Kattan was a talented writer, a Jew from Baghdad who had been taken up by the French in colonial days. 'I did discuss you with N. Kattan who said, surprisingly, that you were a "bohemian". I wonder would your ancestor the Bishop agree? I think that Kattan, a bureaucrat's bureaucrat, must have been quietly pondering all the plummy jobs he thinks you passed up in your day.'

Thirteen

At the *Canadian Forum* I came to know Stefan Stykolt. Born Polish, Stefan had been taken to France as a child, then to Canada where he was schooled at Upper Canada College. He became an economist and authority on restrictive trade practices. Like many professors of the Dismal Science he enjoyed the good life, which was beginning to be possible for university professors. Both he and my friend Alan Brown, a CBC programmer who gave me work, fed my growing longing for European travel. My war years and time in Africa had kept me out of touch with Western culture. Stykolt and Brown were immersed in it. Alan had been decorated in the RCAF and after the war made a living playing guitar and singing ballads in Parisian nightclubs and in Spain. A linguist, he later became a translator, mostly from French. Among his CBC appointments were head of the Canadian Forces Radio and of the CBC International Service.

Stefan visited Alan at Metz, where he was running the Forces Radio. On his return Stefan told me, 'We have to get Alan away from those marshmallow German girls and have him sharpen his teeth on the hard girls of France!'

Stykolt was one day younger than me. When I heard he was in hospital, I went to visit. He told me he'd become ill at his summer cottage. 'I met up with a surgeon,' he said, 'who slit me from gullet to crotch, narrowly missed making a girl of me. I should not like to enter that very competitive field at my time of life.' He said he had three months to live. He flew to Paris to deliver a learned paper, then to Spain to enjoy his last weeks. He left his affairs in perfect order.

During the fifties listeners could tolerate a nine-minute radio talk. I gave a good many in the form of sketches, stories and brief memoirs. I wrote similar pieces for magazines, including the excellent American journal *The Reporter*, which proved hospitable to my writings. The magazine was the favourite project of its owner Max Ascoli, and, when he died, it died with him. And so did my budding career in American journalism.

When Ivon Owen suggested there was a book in my short pieces, I began to put together the text of my first book, *Running to Paradise*. I was still fully occupied with publishing. On my westward sales trips for Macmillan, I tried to meet as many authors as I could. In High River, Alberta, W.O. Mitchell, author of the prairie classic *Who Has Seen the Wind?* showed me the orchids he was growing and regaled me with his stories of *Maclean's* magazine and its editors. I made my number with young Alice Munro and older Ethel Wilson on the Pacific coast, both charming women and serious writers.

Ethel Wilson was a novelist on the Macmillan list with a budding reputation in Britain. A big-boned lady of Scots origin, born in South Africa, she spoke in a high, light voice and wrote with graceful ease. Her husband, Wallace Wilson, was a physician and president of the Canadian Medical Association. He confessed, chuckling, that he never read his wife's books until they were in print.

When I met Ethel, her most recent novel was *Love and Salt Water*, in which the heroine was said to be based on Mary McAlpine, a lively journalist with the *Vancouver Sun*; she was also contributing fiction to *Tamarack*. I looked her up as a possible author. The McAlpine family was well known in Vancouver and when I met Mary and eventually proposed marriage, her mother had me 'investigated'. I survived this, and never lost my affection for the McAlpines, especially Mary's brother John and his wife Sarah. Unluckily a gossip of Ethel's, an Ulsterwoman I never met, gave a lurid account of me as a jailbird. Greatly agitated, Ethel Wilson wrote me a long letter demanding an explanation. With despair, I had to defend myself all over again. This too I survived, perhaps because Ethel believed, as she put it, that 'I had the goods.' She was not so sure about Mary, despite her outstanding prowess as a newspaperwoman. Mary had just finished a thirty-day tour of Europe during which she had filed no fewer than twenty-nine interviews with figures like Beaverbrook and Archbishop Makarios.

We were married in Vancouver in March 1961 and began our thirteen years together on Lawton Boulevard, while Arthur found his own apartment. He left an inscription on the wall: 'On this spot, sacred to the Muses, were deposited the bones of Arthur Hammond.' After a couple of moves and the birth of our two daughters, Lucinda and Sarah, we managed to buy a house on Duplex Avenue, where we spent the rest of our married life. All went merrily for about ten years, my sons becoming protective friends with our two little girls, who would accompany us on our travels to Spain, Morocco, France and Mexico.

In 1959 my father was very ill. I scraped together enough money to make my first trip back to Ireland. He lay in an old-fashioned Dublin nursing home in Hatch Street. The Georgian house had floors of brown battleship linoleum. There was a fire in the room; the patient was charged for coal. I saw with a pang how wasted he had become, his great bones showing, though he was not in any way dismayed. He criticized me for being overweight – 'a portly literary gent' as he put it. Irritated, I told him that if I were a general or a bishop he'd say I was 'light on my feet'. But we enjoyed our talks together. He wanted to know what contemporary writers I admired. I spoke of Louis MacNeice. 'Son of the Bishop of Down and Connor,' he said. 'Who else?' Well, Robert Graves. 'Grandson of the Bishop of Limerick.' And when he asked if there was a Canadian writer he might enjoy I thought of Roderick Haig-Brown, who wrote about fishing. 'I think his grandfather was Headmaster of Charterhouse.'

His physician warned me Father would probably not recover, and that he knew it. The family gathering around him gave more than a hint.

I was with him one day when his brother-in-law Robert Grove-

White came in. The big news that morning was that the flamboyant entertainer Liberace had succeeded in a libel suit against the columnist 'Cassandra' in the *Daily Mail*. Cassandra had reeled off a string of nasty epithets suggesting that Liberace was homosexual – which he was, of course, while not admitting it. At that time such a charge, if unproven, was libellous. Father was delighted that Liberace had won. He hated yellow journalism. In India he had threatened the editor of *The Pioneer* with prosecution for sedition. Uncle Robert, a barrister, argued fiercely for freedom of the press. The lawyer in Father was aroused and the two old men joined issue, going at it with great heat, eyes flashing.

The last time I saw my father he was telling Cousin Avice Swan, a trim maiden-lady in her eighties, how to vote in the Irish presidential election and in the referendum on proportional representation. 'Now listen, Avice – and Kildare, let you remind her at the booth – it doesn't matter whether you choose Dev or the Blacksmith, both good enough men, but when it comes to proportional representation you *must* vote to continue it, otherwise those blackguards will be all over us!'

The election turned out the way he wanted. As far as I could see, Ireland was still struggling with poverty and clerical repression. The villages were still grey and dilapidated, and in Dublin, where I walked in the Liberties, the bells of St Patrick's and Christ Church pealed over ruined streets. In the North, trouble was brewing over social injustice. Conversation was furtive, and the common phrase 'mind you, I said nothing' gave Honor Tracy a title for one of her books.

Father died a few months after my visit, on 13 September 1959, the 200th anniversary of the Battle of the Plains of Abraham. Father had told me that my grandfather Joseph was fond of the story of General Wolfe's death in the hour of victory. I had no funds to cross the Atlantic again for the funeral but was glad to have seen him while he was still full of life. By the time I visited his grave years later in Castlecomer churchyard, the lead fillings of the lettering on his tombstone had been pried away, probably by boys seeking pellets for their catapults. The inscription was almost unreadable.

Our family has two plots in the pleasant green cemetery, I'm told because grandmother Dobbs quarrelled with her in-laws and did not wish to be resurrected in their company. One plot is grouped around great-grandfather Kildare Dobbs; the other – at a distance – around grandfather Joseph.

Years later I wrote an elegy, 'Memorial', to honour my father's memory. It appears in my first volume of poetry, *The Eleventh Hour*.

> The day of Queen Victoria's funeral,
> in the sad ranks behold my Irish father
> resting on his arms reversed with a downcast
> mournful gaze, as the royal corpse expected …
>
> Conscience, his mother's sour milk, choked ambition;
> he retired early, side-stepping the insults,
> the tripwires of power, or art or action,
> a conspicuous man afraid of notice—
> yes, even his tombstone is illegible.
> Yet I, a son whose birth he hailed with fireworks,
> honouring my sire as per the fifth commandment,
> tune up my strings to mourn his ruined wishes.
>
> *Princes and powers fall to the blade of time,*
> *their garlands withered and the last servant dead*
> *My father lies in Castlecomer churchyard*
> *with Queen Victoria's coffin in his head.*

Two events in 1960 taught me that I had no talent for political action. I had kept in touch with affairs in Africa, exchanging a letter now and then with my friends Chiefs Tom Marrealle on Kilimanjaro and Adam Sapi Mkwawa in the Iringa district. I had also subscribed to a South African journal, the voice of Jan Hoffmeyer's anti-apartheid liberals. In March came the horrific news of the Sharpeville massacre. A number of black Africans in the town of Sharpeville had refused to carry identity passes, an act of civil disobedience, accompanied by peaceful demonstrations. The police lost their heads and fired on the crowd, killing 69 persons and wounding 187 others.

Distressed by this appalling act, and the continuing injustice of apartheid – a measure that turned the clock back in African history – I was complaining to Arthur Hammond and a political science student called Bogdan Kipling that I felt sick and powerless. Bogdan's elder brother had been a fighter-pilot in the Battle of Britain, a Pole who had changed his name to Kipling in honour of his British comrades. Bogdan himself was capable of decisive action. He said, 'Well, we *can* do something about it!' and picked up the phone. He hired Massey Hall for a meeting at an alarmingly close date.

In a short time we had formed the Committee of Concern for South Africa, raised seed money and invited Archbishop Trevor Huddlestone (Archbishop Tutu's English-born predecessor) to come and address a mass meeting in Massey Hall and raise funds for the relief of Sharpeville victims' families. We rounded up the usual suspects: Rabbi Feinberg, author Pierre Berton, broadcaster Max Ferguson and others to form the committee and sit on the platform. At the meetings to plan the event, I was surprised to find that the main object was to keep communists out. If communists took part, I was told, no one would give money. I also learned that it was important to keep Ukrainian nationalists out of the hall – they could demonstrate on the street outside.

It happened, the hall was crowded. Rabbi Feinberg delivered an oration of ringing scorn for tyrants, Archbishop Trevor Huddlestone spoke from the heart, money poured in. Pierre Berton in *The Toronto Star* remarked that the event was unprecedented. Toronto had come of age. (It was to come of age again a few more times in his writings.) There were other meetings, one of them addressed by Alan Paton (*Cry the Beloved Country*), a small, angry author of scarlet complexion.

After that, I realized that I was not qualified to do anything useful about African injustice. I put it behind me. Henceforth I would think of Africa only when there were headlines about famine, genocide or tyranny. All I could do was boycott South African wine and refuse free trips to the Dark Continent, plainly intended to generate good news in Canadian travel pages to offset front-page horrors.

The other event where I felt out of place was the Liberal Thinkers' Conference at Queen's University, Kingston, Ontario, an attempt by the Pearson government to acquire new ideas. I spoke on government and culture. I suggested that the party had convened the Conference as a blanket to hide its nakedness. I had puzzled myself by reading T.S. Eliot's *Notes Toward a Definition of Culture*. The Canada Council was already in existence and my message was (and still is): Just give us the money. I warned the politicians, 'You're feeding the hand that bites you.' Lester Pearson signed a letter congratulating me on a 'brilliant' speech. I think every speaker got one.

One aim of the conference was to woo certain French-Canadian leaders. Pearson did succeed in bringing Pierre Trudeau, Gerard Pelletier and Jean Marchand into the Liberal fold, to the benefit of Canada. In the men's room I found myself next to Paul Martin the elder, a seasoned Cabinet Minister. He was telling his neighbour on the other side that it was good to have all these guys express themselves so long as one ignored their advice. The most amiable politician was Lester Pearson himself, who gave off a glow of geniality and the illusion of being interested in anyone who talked to him.

Economists were thick on the ground. Considering their subject, it was amazing what good company they were. My friend Stefan Stykolt had put it like this: 'Economics is an art, but an art without aesthetic rewards. The financial rewards, however, can be great – which explains why there are so many corrupt economists.'

I noticed some odd things about economists. They were listened to devoutly, as though they held the secret of the universe. They were almost always wrong, yet no one held them to blame. They were never ashamed.

At nearly forty, it was time for my midlife crisis, change of job and, I should confess, the *demon de midi*. I had come as far as I could at Macmillan. John Gray did not want me as an executive. I had noticed that my friend did not care to have possible successors close to him. Several of his staff were potential chief executives, but he favoured none of them.

It was my good luck to work on different occasions with several talented editors, notably Janice Tyrwhitt, who left us to write almost full time for *Reader's Digest*. I tried to learn her great patience with authors. She only once remarked on a swollen ego. That was when Hugh MacLennan had submitted his novel *The Watch that Ends the Night*, claiming to have created a new kind of fiction. 'So he's invented the psychological novel!' Janice mused, as she read his long, excited letter. 'I do wish he'd invent the detective story – I love a good mystery.' The *Digest* paid big bucks. Janice had a family to support, and Macmillan salaries were not generous.

Near the end of my years with the company, John Gray told me to find a qualified woman to take a departing editor's place. Just then we received a very funny, interesting letter from a recent graduate from the Ryerson Polytechnical Institute (now a university). He wanted to work in publishing. When John Gray met Richard B. Wright, he was charmed. This was exactly the kind of young man we needed in publishing, he said, lively, articulate, eager – a hockey fan! And with a sense of humour. We took him on, unaware that we were hiring a future novelist, who would win all the major prizes in fiction that Canada offers. It was already clear that he was somebody who would be heard from.

He pitched into the work and was soon the hottest Lothario in the house, up to all sorts of fun with girls in the accounting department. In the end he married Phyllis, the smartest of them. And as he became a novelist, she made herself over as a librarian at Brock University nearby. But all of that came later in their lives, when Wright took up teaching at an expensive private school, rising at 5 am to write his daily stint of fiction.

I had been able to commission a few good books in addition to regular submissions. I had noticed, for example, a newspaper report which said that the Soviet ambassador to the United Nations had attacked NATO for 'monstrous instructions' in publishing a how-to-do-it essay on the *coup d'état* by a Canadian officer, Major D.J. Goodspeed (later Colonel, then Professor). He did not need much prompting to expand his essay into a monograph, *The Conspirators*, deriving the theory of the *coup d'état* from six historical examples. He believed that in an era when full-scale war risked nuclear exchanges, political objectives might more safely be attained by the limited violence of the *coup*. The book we published became the standard text on its subject. Since that subject was violence in the service of policy, Goodspeed had to recommend a safe way to deal with defeated leaders. He favoured killing them, since there seemed to be no secure alternative. (It had not yet been discovered that, if exiled to the United Nations fleshpots in New York, they would never come home.) The text was used in almost every subsequent *coup*, mostly in Africa. In some countries it proved cheaper in blood and money than a general election.

Goodspeed worked in the Historical Section at Defence Head-quarters, Ottawa, a regular nest of singing birds writing official accounts of Canadian wars. The section was headed by Colonel Herbert Wood, and he too became a Macmillan author.

The soldier-writers may have been a bit mad, but they were tremendous fun.

I think the commissioned book in which I took most pride was by the poet and scholar Jay Macpherson. *The Four Ages of Man* (1962) was a succinct volume of mythology, at that time a subject in the Ontario schools' curriculum. I had greatly admired her book of poetry, *The Boatman*, and knew that she had worked in the house-hold of Robert Graves in Ibiza and studied myth with Northrop Frye. Graves was a mythopoeic poet of wide knowledge and Frye a leading authority on myth and the Bible. The book Jay delivered surpassed expectations, arranging the classical stories in an order that parallels the biblical canon, starting with the Creation and Deucalion's Flood. She told the stories in lucid and graceful prose.

Before I left Macmillan I was assigned to oversee publication of a book of speeches by the Right Hon.Vincent Massey C.H., the first native-born Canadian to be appointed Governor General, rep-resenting the sovereign in Canada. It was Massey's ambition to be as vice-regal as any of the Grand Ornamentals who were his noble predecessors. He wore the hand-me-down Windsor uniform of

Lord Tweedsmuir, *alias* John Buchan, which included tight trews, a tail-coat blazing with gold bullion and a cocked hat with feathers. He came from the Toronto family which had grown rich by selling Massey-Harris farm machinery and had shared the wealth with the city and the University of Toronto.

I first met Vincent Massey with John Gray when we called on him in the vice-regal railway car, backed onto a siding at Union Station, Toronto.

We had other meetings, at Rideau Hall in Ottawa, and at Massey's country house near Port Hope. I think the Governor General just liked to have someone to talk to him about his literary plans. I did not edit his books. Dinner at Rideau Hall was excellent. There was a rack of lamb, I recall, and other good things. We toasted Her Majesty in port. After that, I went with Massey to his study to talk and drink beer. At Port Hope in later years we talked over lunch. Vincent Massey was fond of this place, which was as much like an English country house as he could make it.

On my last visit, long after I left publishing for journalism, and Massey had retired from office, I broached a project of my own. I had visited St-Malo in Brittany and the farmhouse Manoir Limoilou, birthplace and home of the discoverer Jacques Cartier. In a sense, I argued, this was Canada's cradle. My idea was that Ottawa could acquire the manor and estate, install a museum of discoveries, and run it as an annex of our French embassy. It would be an 'attraction' for St-Malo, a compliment to France and a symbol of integration for Canada. Massey was interested (there was nothing on paper as yet) and promised to give the proposal thought. Before anything could be done, in December 1967, Vincent Massey died.

I recall that he had been fretful. 'The Queen', he told me in lugubrious tones, 'wanted me to have the Garter. It would have been a great honour for Canada.' The Garter, the world's oldest order of chivalry, was coveted by many heads of state. 'Diefenbaker would not allow it,' Massey went on. 'Claimed that no Canadian could accept it.' The Queen was disappointed. She gave Massey the

Royal Victorian Chain, another high honour, but so exclusive that no one knew what it was.

I began a new life as a journalist when *Maclean's* magazine assigned me to write a profile of the playwright Ted Allan. Ted, an unrepentant communist, had plays running in the West End of London and Paris at the same time. He was a full-blown 'character', so that everyone I interviewed about him had a story to tell. Since I had never before written anything of the kind, I faked the journalese. It was a success. The editors asked for more. This time I suggested a profile of Marshall McLuhan, then an English professor known for his fascinating book *The Mechanical Bride*. There had been a couple of columns about him in the newspapers, but so far no magazine profile. The editors said, 'Okay. If you can understand him!'

After interviews with McLuhan and many of the people in his intellectual life, I wrote what I thought was a lively piece. It was rejected on the ground that 'even with a talented midwife in attendance', the man was incomprehensible. It was the fashion for journalists to be baffled by McLuhan's paradoxes, and I had taken notice of this. I immediately took the article to *The Star Weekly* magazine, at that time the most widely distributed and read Canadian publication. They accepted it with enthusiasm. Then they offered me a job as staff writer.

Once again I began a new career.

Like all general magazines in the early sixties, *The Star Weekly* was in decline, its advertising leaking away to the new medium of television. Ignorant of this, I plunged into the work with zeal and hope. It was wonderful to be paid a living wage for doing what I liked best – writing. The magazine was an excellent read, with something for everyone and lots of pictures.

I arrived early in 1962 with eight proposals for articles. 'Very interesting,' I was told, 'but first we have some assignments for you.' I never did get to write my own articles.

The *Weekly* was published by the *Toronto Daily Star*. It seemed that everyone from Ernest Hemingway to the lowest hack had worked at the *Star*. The newspaper was then housed in a skyscraper on King Street West with a grand lobby. Later, during the erectile frenzy of downtown moneymen, the whole building was bulldozed to make room for taller bank towers. The *Star* built a new Tower of Babel at number 1 Yonge Street, with a city room carpetted in purple.

Staff writers of the *Weekly* had desks in a big, open hall. At the back a couple of ladies were busy shortening light novels for the fiction section. Overlooking King Street and Lake Ontario, the grander editors worked in offices with glass-panelled doors and partitions. The editor was John Clare, a former war correspondent, who had also been – somewhat incongruously for so macho a personality – editor of *Chatelaine*, a Maclean-Hunter magazine for Canadian farm wives with genteel longings. A big, handsome man who smoked a pipe, Clare possessed – in the words of his friend Jack Harris, Canada's first crime novelist – 'all the affability of a wounded grizzly bear'. This was true only in the mornings, when he was hungover. He could not stand his publisher or the proprietor's ever-present son-in-law, so that as soon as he could, he would anaesthetize himself with vodka. 'Keeping just under the Plimsoll line,' as he put it

About three weeks after I joined, Clare invited me to lunch. We walked over to Yonge Street, into the bar of the Victoria Hotel. Clare ordered a double screwdriver and invited me to name my drink. Mine was beer. We were on our fourth round when I began to grow hungry. Clare had downed eight vodkas. Calling for his bill, he told the barman to give me mine. And left. That was lunch with the editor.

At dinner in his grand house in Forest Hill, he later told me, 'No one comes through that door that I don't like.' When I botched an assignment, he said, 'God damn it, Dobbs, you let me down!' But after I had written some nonsense about information technology in Chicago, he growled, 'Thanks, Dobbs, you got me off the hook. Appreciate that.'

It was said that the publisher thought one picture was worth a thousand words – so there had to be a thousand words with every picture, and that he demanded what he called 'human-interest antidotes'. The publisher was an evolved Amish from small-town Ontario. He believed in clean living and clean desks. It was true that he called for something red in every photograph. The director of the Royal Ontario Museum was astonished when a *Star* photographer arrived carrying a scarlet sweater for him to wear.

There was talk of putting me with the pilot in a jet fighter-plane for a defence story. I was sent instead to NORAD headquarters in Colorado to write about North American air defences under the command of the Canadian air marshal Guy Slemmon. With me was my friend Kryn Taconis, an associate of Cartier-Bresson and Capa in the Magnum agency. Veteran of the Dutch Resistance, Kryn had been imprisoned and tortured by the Gestapo. From Denver we rode a US air-force bus out to the NORAD site, a huge concrete egg mounted on colossal springs inside a mountain. A corporal stood guard at the entrance, so rare a specimen they had put him in a glass case. Inside, colonels and generals sat on green leather chairs facing a vast, glimmering iconorama. It displayed a map of the Soviet Union and North America.

An attack with nuclear weapons was simulated. A light came on in Siberia. Then a sign saying: 'Minutes to next impact – ten, nine, eight —.' At zero, loops of light surrounded Chicago and New York, both cities vapourized. One of the generals left his chair to get a Coke from a slot machine. Senior officers were becoming inured to the idea of a nuclear attack. They would survive in their concrete egg, while the rest of us were incinerated.

I had just seen the movie *Dr Strangelove* and it all seemed idiotic. I thought I could have captured and scrambled their egg with a troop of boy scouts armed with toasting forks. But I did not tell Air-Marshal Slemmon this. He was aggressive, beating back questions with counter-questions. Wielding the nuclear big stick must have been a heady experience for a Canadian.

Taconis spent a couple of weeks taking a perfect photograph

of the iconorama and overseeing the processing of his film in the local lab. Back in Toronto I wrote an ironic piece. An editor whose name I forget was a strong cold warrior. He cut the story to a few lines accompanying Kryn's fascinating image of the iconorama, and sat on it for a couple of years, by which time any resonance with *Dr Strangelove* was lost. It was now a gee-whizz story about American technology.

Kryn was with me on a couple of other, less controversial assignments. I enjoyed witnessing his professional pride, and his beautiful, haunting images. Like other Magnum photographers, he had worked for *Life* and *ParisMatch*. The *Weekly* must have seemed a comedown, but this decline of photo-journalism affected all the major photographers, thanks to television.

Kryn and his wife Tess became great friends of my daughters. The girls loved Kryn because he could make a tree out of a news-paper and, at Christmas, a house of cookies and cakes; and Tess they loved because she let them wear her high-heeled shoes.

On one assignment in Vancouver, Kryn and I dined with Helen McAlpine, my then mother-in-law. The housekeeper brought out linen napkins instead of the usual paper ones. I told Kryn that the linen was in his honour. He must have done some Calvinist brooding on this remark for, some weeks later, he said solemnly that such a comment was evidence of 'snobbism'.

Colleagues at the *Weekly* were among the best journalists in Canada. The women included Jeannine Locke, who progressed to television, where she made important docu-dramas. She had a sense of fun and a short fuse, and one of the pleasures of the work-place was hearing her yell at editors behind the glass partitions. Once, when we were both in Montreal on assignments, we dined together and got stoned. That was the start of a lasting friendship.

In 1962 I was assigned to write an article describing what would happen if an atom bomb should fall. Since two American atom bombs had already destroyed the Japanese cities of Hiroshima and Nagasaki, I felt there would be more point in telling the story of what actually did happen. I found a Hiroshima survivor in Toronto, a young woman named Emiko, and told her story, punctuated with excerpts from the diaries of crewmen in the bomber *Enola Gay*. The resulting article has been reprinted many times over the years, beginning with the *Catholic Digest* and progressing to successive editions of *The Norton Reader*, in addition to other textbooks.

I was at the *Weekly* when my first book, *Running to Paradise,* was published by Oxford University Press. I was still there when it won a Governor General's Award. The newspaper headlined 'Star man wins award'. It may have been the first time the paper put culture on the front page. I described the awards ceremony in a second edition of *Running to Paradise.*

Part of the charm was the tall, genial presence of Marshall McLuhan as brother laureate. He and his wife Corinne stayed in the room next to ours in the Château Laurier. He summoned Mary and myself to join him and Corinne before breakfast and drink a bottle of iced champagne. I was still poor and had no dressing gown, so I wore my shabby old raincoat.

The award came with a little money, enough for a trip to Ireland. By this time transatlantic travel was by air. We flew in a four-engined propeller aircraft to Shannon, stopping at Gander, Newfoundland, on the way. And climbed out of the plane to find ourselves deep in the dark green fields of rural Ireland.

The place had once been so familiar as to be invisible. Now I could *see* it, a land making the best of hard times. The country villages were still grey and depressing, especially during winter. In Belfast, where I went to visit my sister Joan, a new wave of civic violence had begun. My brother-in-law Gibbon FitzGibbon made light of it – all hokum worked up by the media, he insisted. But blood had already been shed.

I wanted no part of it. It seemed senseless. In Ontario everyone got along pretty well together, Orange and Green. Why couldn't the homeland Irish be more like us?

Mother was living in an apartment at Wilton Place, near the Grand Canal in Dublin. The man in the apartment below hers had made friends with her in the lift. 'Are you the lady who plays the piano?' he asked. Mother began to apologize; yes, it was she. But he said, 'I wish you would play more Bach, you do it so well.' He was Frank O'Connor, one of the greatest living writers. His American wife Harriet Sheeny and he became fond of Mother, visiting back and forth.

When I met him, he told me that he could teach students to write only if they had not yet been published. O'Connor was as pig-headed in his opinions as any other Irishman. He believed, for example, that the so-called *Black Diaries* of Sir Roger Casement were forged by the British to smear the doomed patriot. These diaries, if genuine, reveal their author as a promiscuous homosexual with a preference for rough trade. Such proclivities, to men like O'Connor, seemed incompatible with lofty ideals. When I read them, I saw no reason to doubt their authenticity. It did not strike me as incredible that a generous patriot should have coarse sexual appetites. What was shocking was that the British had shown the diaries to opinion-leaders to discourage agitation for a repeal of Casement's death sentence.

Mother had many old friends in Dublin, with grandchildren and music to beguile her solitude. She did not possess a record-player, but made her own music on the piano. She could read any score at sight and did a lot of exploring. I remember her delight at discovering Bach's aria *'Bist du bei mir'*. Later she was joined by her granddaughter Caroline Fitzgerald who cared for her. Caroline, like many of the young Fitzgeralds, was to be involved in theatre all her life. During the inevitable 'rests' she cooked lunches for company directors for a living.

Mother's stories, I noticed, had improved since Father's death, especially the ghost stories, which could be spoiled by a sceptical listener. She was relishing her independence. O'Connor was not the only intelligent man whose company she enjoyed. There was also Dean Seaver of Ossory, who had written several biographies, including a popular one of Albert Schweitzer. 'Such a good-looking man,' Mother sighed. And then, after a pause, 'A pity he has no sense of humour.'

Fourteen

Spain was where I longed to be. Alan Brown played the recording he had made of *cante jondo* performed by El Niño de Ronda in Andalusia. I was also inspired by John Simmonds, who introduced me to the poetry of Federico García Lorca. Simmonds taught Spanish at Upper Canada College. I'll never forget his brilliant explication of the 'Lament for Ignacio Sánchez Mejías' with its refrain tolling like a passing bell, *'a las cinco de la tarde'*.

I felt a strong call to get away and come to grips with the African novel which was sprawling out of control. I applied successfully for a grant from the new Canada Council. I felt sure I could do the work. We set sail from Jersey City in a small, smelly passenger steamer. It was spring 1964. I had taken leave of absence from the *Star*. We had let our house in Toronto.

Disembarking at last in Bilbao, we found our way by train to Ronda, a hill town of Andalusia, 'the cracked pearl of the sierras' as Alan Brown called it. It was a place to dream about, perched on top of crags, white houses scribbled over with wrought-iron grilles and balconies. The town was split down the centre by a deep gorge. You could look from the New Bridge (a couple of centuries old) and see kestrels chasing pigeons far below. We took an apartment in a seventeenth-century house beside the big church, originally a mosque built by the Moors. This was the old side of the gorge. On the far side were the eighteenth-century bullring – the oldest in Spain – the Town Hall and Casino, and the Hotel Reina Victoria.

Days began early with the cracked church bells from the minaret next door. Next came the harsh cries of *arrieros*, driving trains of mules from the coast near Gibraltar. Many were smuggling Scotch whisky and American cigarettes. The braying of mules and asses increased the din. Another early arrival was the man who sold lime for whitewash, yelling, *'Cal! Cal!'* The knife-grinder made pleasanter sounds, blowing panpipes. But most noise-makers were ordinary citizens having ordinary conversations, right under my window. I began to rise earlier and earlier to find a quiet hour or two. Soon I was at my typewriter by 5 am when the town was still dark.

I complained of drowsiness. 'You should do what we do,' a Spanish friend advised. 'Take a shot of cognac and light up a cigar.' I bought Canary Island *puros* and lit up, choking down a brandy. It did get me started. I wrote John Gray and told him. 'I can understand your starting,' he replied, 'but how the hell do you stop?' In fact I stopped about 9 am. Then I would go out to buy fresh *churros*, long ropes of doughnut fried in deep fat, and bring them home to dunk in coffee. The girls loved them.

The breadman would arrive with his donkey. Worried that my daughters were acquiring Andaluz accents, he'd call up the stairs, enunciating with great clarity in Castilian, sounding the esses, 'Buenos días, señoritas. ¿Qué tal?' It was fascinating to watch the children learn Spanish from their playmates. They began by mimicking the sounds. Within a month they were chattering in Andaluz and singing the skipping songs, counting out songs and nursery rhymes. When it was time for the Fiesta, neighbours carried them off, dressed them as gypsies, with their blonde locks in spit-curls. A caballero took them on his horse to ride through the streets.

I spent the days like an idle *señorito*. After breakfast, to the barber to be shaved; then the café about 10 am for an espresso with a second cognac. I read the *Herald Tribune* while the bootblack worked. Often a friend would join me. Adolfo, the *maestro* who made cabinets and carved wood, would sit down for a Nescafé with cognac. Carmelo, who made fine guitars, was younger. There were a few foreigners living in the town or nearby. Alistair Boyd, the future Baron Kilmarnock, kept a language school for young people, often Etonians or Wykehamists. Alistair, a fascinating man who wrote a couple of delightful books about Spain and Andalusia, was in love with the country. He had rented the Casa Mondragon, a Moorish palace with patios, horseshoe arches and sixteenth-century tiles. Built in 1498, it was too big and too expensive for most Spaniards at that time. Today, inevitably, it's a tourist attraction. In two apartments in our own building were other foreigners. Next door was Ward Just, an American writer, with his wife and two young girls. Ward had just left *Newsweek* to try his hand at short stories. He had yet to write the political novels that would make his name. Another American on the same floor was the painter Richard Sergeant with his wife. Dick Sergeant had done almost as many covers for the *Saturday Evening Post* as Norman Rockwell. He was now painting luscious figurative canvases. His wife was homesick for Westchester County.

After an hour or so of desultory chat with the *maestro* or one of these expatriates, it was time to go to a bar and play liar-dice with the regulars. This would be accompanied by small glasses of *fino* or Montilla. Two o'clock and it was time for lunch at home with *vino corriente*. I'd buy wine by the carboy for a couple of dollars from the vintner in his dark shop, its tall earthenware jars resembling the vessels in which Ali Baba's forty thieves hid. And after lunch the siesta, sleeping through the hot afternoons of summer. In this way one could achieve two hangovers a day.

After 5 pm there were more rounds to make, including the *paseo* or promenade, for which we dressed up and strolled about the streets bowing to the neighbours. The little girls, ours and Ward's, were favourites. They went to the convent school in their white pinafores and played in the cobbled street with little friends. Every-one in Andalusia loves children and protects them. The girls could not skip a hundred yards without being kissed and complimented. The confidence gained in one year would last their lives.

For myself, everything around me became vivid and real, colours more saturated, sounds more resonant.

The sense of renewal did not extend to my work, which was going badly. I realized I had a long way to go before I could see life steadily and whole. Voices in my head were endlessly pleading and arguing. I realized that my African story would have to be in some measure political, and the politics of post-colonial Africa were hideously depressing. I could hardly bring myself to think about it – and indeed I had lost touch. The news from Africa, like the news from Ireland, was too depressing to think about. I had another problem, which was how to render the words and actions of preliterate tribesmen without making them sound like suburbanites or idiots. I had been on intimate terms with men and women who believed in magic and a vital spirit in everything, living or inanimate. Their very ontology was different from ours. I could not hear them speaking like modernized workers or college boys, or like Old Testament heroes the way some writers did.

Ward Just complained of something different. He had been working as a journalist and knew how to do that to perfection. He had grown up in a newspaper family, his father the proprietor of a small paper in Illinois. Now he was trying to write short stories and finding it hard. We shared a number of adventures.

Peter Richmond lived in a farmhouse just out of town with Nora Richmond. They were neither married nor related, but just happened to have the same surname. Expressionist painters, they were pupils of David Bomberg, who had worked in Ronda for years. I later found his work in the Tate Gallery.

The ruins of Roman Ronda, *Ronda la Vieja*, were about seven kilometres from the present town on a hill that could be reached only on foot. Ward and I wanted to see them. Peter joined us, along with a visitor from Toronto. We brought red wine, bread and stopped at a farm to buy *chorizo* and bacon. The day was hot and dry.

At last we arrived at the ruined theatre, a few columns and tumbled stones. Surrounded by ruins, a swineherd sat in the shade of an ilex oak. He was playing a straight flute, his pigs rooting for acorns. A boy of about twelve, he had been alone and silent so long he could hardly speak.

In this place, with its air of classical myth, we gathered wood for a fire, and toasted our *tocino* and *chorizo* on long sticks. We talked very little, savouring the wine, the bread and meat, the antiquity of the scene. After resting a while, we cleaned up the site and walked back to Ronda.

Another friend during that year in Spain was Ian Cochrane, who had been invalided out of the Royal Navy, disabled by arthritis. A submariner, he was the first nuclear chief engineer in the RN. Ian had been told that if he lived in a dry climate he might find some relief from arthritis. He made a complete recovery in Benoajaz, a small hill *pueblo* not far from Ronda. Ian stayed with us in Ronda and we did the rounds of the bars together.

We decided to follow our Spanish year with a trip in Morocco. Ian volunteered to come with us. Our Spanish friends were alarmed. '¡No son civilizados!' my bootblack told me. And it was true that there had been a lot of killing in Morocco just before independence.

We found the country fascinating, a flashback to the *Thousand Nights and One Nights*, especially in Fez and Marrakech. The people, now living under home-grown tyranny, were friendly. The highlight of the trip was our encounter in the Sahara with the explorer Wilfred Thesiger and his fascinating mother, Mrs Astley, then in her nineties. Mrs Astley, a famous beauty in youth, was born a Vigors (rhymes with tigers) of Burgage, about five miles from Viewmount in County Carlow. Thesiger was a cousin of The O'Grady of Kilballyowen and had met some of my family at Holloden, Esther Vigors O'Grady's home near Bagenalstown.

Thesiger was the man who had crossed the Empty Quarter of Arabia twice. The story is told in his classic *Arabian Sands*. Later he spent some years in the Euphrates delta, a time he recalled in his book *The Marsh Arabs*. He had also figured as a leader of irregulars in the British campaign against the Italians in Abyssinia, which won him a DSO. He was a tall, powerful man with a long face that seemed cut from granite. Friendly and polite, his opinions were romantic and reactionary, even kinky. He was proud of his amateur skill at surgery, remarking that he had once circumcised scores of Arab boys in a single day. He had not enjoyed Ireland much – it was too green. The landscapes he loved were tawny and sunburnt.

We were about to set out for M'Hamid at the end of the road in the Draa Valley, when my car, a decrepit Dauphine, failed to start. I stayed to have it fixed by the village mechanic.

My family went ahead with Ian, following Thesiger's car. I'd catch up when I could. Repairs took a while, but at last I was on the road again, crossing the *hammad*, or hard desert. I had passed a small kasbah and left it ten kilometres behind me when the car broke down again. I looked into the engine and saw a hole in the carburettor. I sat on the stony ground and thought about it. I watched an ant picking its busy way among the pebbles.

After a longish time I saw a plume of dust on the horizon. It was a jeep coming my way. At last it stopped beside me.

The driver was a veterinary officer, the passenger an army captain. They told me to come with them to the kasbah for help. There I talked with the Khaid in command, who called an NCO to escort us. 'We can't leave your car there,' the Khaid said. *'Les bergers – ils font des bêtises!'*

Les bergers were desert nomads, Tuareg tribesmen who carried off anything that was not nailed down, the sort of people Thesiger adored.

We drove back to my car. The NCO took a short stick from his pocket, sharpened it like a pencil, and used it to plug the hole in the carburettor. The Dauphine started without trouble. Now I was able to drive back to Zagora, the jeep following in case of further snags.

At the hotel I invited the two Moroccans in for a drink. Thesiger and the others were in the lobby. They had returned by a different route. Thesiger joined us for a few minutes to drink a coffee, then excused himself. Next morning he apologized. 'Nothing to say to them,' he explained. 'Once they get socks on, they're no good.'

I came home to Canada with a sense of failure. I had achieved nothing in my work. On the other hand I had found that travel allowed me to see more clearly, both with my eyes and with my mind. I had learned a good deal and made some progress toward catching up with 'culture' which I had missed during four years of war and three years in Africa. And I had given my daughters an informal education.

Fifteen

Back in Toronto I met John Polanyi when we were both writing songs for *Clap Hands*, a musical revue. Our words were set to music by John's wife Sue. John was a chemistry professor at the University of Toronto and an FRS. He could not explain in lay terms what he did in his lab, except that it had to do with tracking molecular motions. His discoveries led to the invention of lasers and many years later won him a Nobel prize.

Another friend of whom I was in awe was Northrop Frye, principal of Victoria College, author of the magisterial *Anatomy of Criticism* (1957) and, later, *The Great Code: The Bible and Literature* (1982). Frye's presence was distinctive, especially his silences. In conversation – if that's the word – he spoke only to answer questions. His silence was a brooding benevolence; he had no small talk. After a question there would be a slight pause, while the wheels and cogs of cerebration engaged, when the professor would speak in clear, beautifully ordered sentences. It was disconcerting to talk without the normal comforts of friendly blather and stroking. The Frye method, though, did seem to carry immense authority. Once, when we met on a flight to Ottawa, he told me that the government seemed to have an inexhaustible appetite for Great Thoughts, and that he was on his way to deliver a few. This happened during the Trudeau years, when mental activity was actually in demand.

I once sat beside Frye at a dinner and saw his notes as he made an eloquent fifteen-minute speech. There were about four lines written on a card. I asked Helen, his first wife, a small, pert ex-journalist, how he was able to do it. She said, 'Norrie is really a Methodist circuit-rider, a minister who began his career as an itinerant preacher. He learned to be ready with his words.'

Frye's view of the Bible was also traditional and Methodist. He was not much interested, if at all, in textual inquiries. What he valued was the canon of the Bible formed by tradition, with its medieval theory of types and antitypes. In scripture he found a sequence that contained the whole of literature from the Creation to the Apocalypse. For him the Bible was not merely literature but *kerygma* or proclamation socially affirmed. He made distinctions that allowed him to be at once rational and imaginative. There were different modes of truth. In some respects his views were almost Jungian.

I found Frye's thought inspiring. He was, it's true, an almost compulsive constructor of systems. His mental *structures* (as he called them, a spacial metaphor) were always symmetrical. Marshall McLuhan called him the Great Classifier. Frye, for his part, could be condescending about McLuhan. Rivals in fame, no doubt. But this was nothing like the spiteful way the novelist-turned-academic Robertson Davies spoke about his famous colleagues. I enjoyed Davies' early books, but was put off by a remark I heard him make about Frye. With an epicene snigger, he said to a friend, 'When Norrie was born, they threw away the wrong part!'

Davies was intensely theatrical, though he had failed both as actor and playwright. He cultivated presence, with snow-white beard and a trick English accent. He disliked me because I had said in a review that his values were rooted in snobbery, as when he remarked that it was very common to make love with your clothes on. McLuhan once let slip that when he caught the eye of Davies during a committee meeting, he saw the calculating glance of an Ontario farmer.

McLuhan was tall, with a fine open face. His professorial tweeds were not quite rumpled. A media prophet, he liked to speak in oracles, using his special vocabulary. His major thesis – that media exerted an effect on the mind distinct from the messages they conveyed – was expressed in the paradox 'The medium is the message.' He found this idea, as he often acknowledged, in the later work of Harold Innis, who in turn found the seed of it in the Irish historian W.E.H. Lecky. Lecky had noticed that the electric telegraph led to the rise of local newspapers, ending the metropolitan advantage of priority of information.

McLuhan's academic expertise was in Renaissance rhetoric. With that interest in view, I had described him in my *Weekly* profile as 'a grammarian reading the Book of Nature'. Donald Theall, a scholar to whom I put this formulation in an interview, later claimed it for his own. Marshall expressed his speculations as dogmas, without much interest in proof. And as he developed it, his system became an ideology, a closed myth that explained everything. Ideologies cannot question the dogmas on which they rest. Just as Catholics who raised objections were 'heretics', dissident Freudians 'neurotics' and unconvinced communists 'bourgeois', so McLuhanites who needed proofs were 'linear thinkers'.

McLuhan had an idea for a musical, on which he wanted me to collaborate. It was to be a life of Tom Moore of *Moore's Irish Melodies*. 'The songs are already written,' he said, 'and his life is fascinating. His friend Byron would be an important character; we could find stuff in his letters.' Somehow we never got around to it.

While I was learning from spirits like these, *Saturday Night* was collapsing. One Mr Moneybags was selling it to another, who fronted for a group of right-wing enthusiasts in the prairies. There was a day when Arnold called in a long line of employees, including some who had worked at the magazine for years. Each staggered out of his office, white-faced and shocked, men and women with families who had given their best years to the magazine. They had all been fired. But when Herb McManus, the veteran managing editor, was told his services were no longer required, he said to Arnold, as he informed me, 'You can't fire me – *you're* the one who should be fired!' And he came back to the office every day and sat in the library, the ghost of Christmas past.

Arnold summoned the survivors. 'We're being taken over by a

man who's going to use the magazine to promote Social Credit.' This was a right-wing party based on the queer economics that drove Ezra Pound mad. 'I'm putting out a release that we're all resigning.' He repeats this assertion in his autobiography.

'*I'm* not quitting', I told him. 'We have a verbal contract. I'd rather be fired.'

'Contract? There's nothing in writing,' Arnold said. 'I'd make a bad witness.'

My lawyer advised that Arnold would make an excellent witness.

I called Mary Lowrey Ross, a contributor for thirty years, and gave her the bad news. 'Don't worry,' she said. 'I've been down with the ship so often, I don't even get seasick any more.'

I sat at my desk waiting to be fired. McManus sat in the library waiting for his second coming.

To my great relief I was fired by the end of the week. Herb McManus was back in his old office. My lawyer prepared a suit on my behalf for wrongful dismissal. As it happened, there was no need to raise the issue of a contract. Without embarrassing Arnold, we settled for a couple of months severance pay. I began immediately to earn fairly good money freelance. My lawyer said I was ruining my case for damages.

I gave a series of broadcasts in the CBC programme *Ideas*, and rewrote them for a book I called *Reading the Time*. It included a number of travel essays, my first efforts in a genre that became my favourite. The book was a survey of the era we lived in, from the changing points of view of an observer on the move through time and place. The series was repeated in the US over public radio. Thirty years later the broadcast on the Beat movement was repeated. I was given a tiny fee.

A vivid memory of those years is of an evening with Kathleen Coburn and her guests in her house on Willcocks Avenue. Professor Coburn was pre-eminent in the study of S.T. Coleridge, general editor of the great Böllengen Princeton edition of the poet. She told me how she came to her subject, more or less as she was to tell the story in her fascinating book *In Pursuit of Coleridge*.

Professor Coburn described her career as a series of lucky accidents. Dublin was where she had wanted to do postgraduate studies – but they took women only as undergraduates. So she went to Oxford. Had Kate not gone there, she wouldn't have met, at a party she nearly missed, the woman who introduced her to Lord Coleridge, owner of the poet's notebooks. And so on. But to meet her was to realize that all doors could be opened by her charm.

Now Professor Emeritus at Victoria College in the University of Toronto, her guest of honour was I.A. Richards, to me a figure of legendary eminence. I had missed him at Cambridge, though I'd read his books on practical criticism and found them useful as an editor. I also admired his part in devising Basic English, a system by which one could say everything with 800 English words. It could have made a fine lingua franca.

He told me a story about Ludwig Wittgenstein. It seemed that the German philosopher (thought by many to be the greatest thinker of the twentieth century) wanted to take a PhD at the university. No one knew why. It was a degree commonly taken by Americans as a kind of union-card for academic employment. Wittgenstein would need a supervisor, not so much to direct his studies as to discuss what he was up to and give support and encouragement. But who was qualified to work with so subtle a thinker? Richards was a member of a committee to find a solution. Their first thought, naturally, was Bertrand Russell. He, however, declined, protesting that his views differed too much from the candidate's to be objective. Other eminences were considered and rejected for one reason or another. What was needed was someone with enough German to converse easily about the work, and enough Greek and Greek philosophy to keep up with the candidate's own classical learning. Where could such a person be found? It happened that one of the dons had a son at the Perse School, an elite secondary institution in Cambridge, whose German was fluent and idiomatic and whose Greek and philosophy were excellent. So the schoolboy was appointed supervisor to the great Wittgenstein. The arrangement worked perfectly. The candidate was happy and in due course took his degree. 'You couldn't have a solution like that today,' Richards said. 'Cambridge has become much more rigid.'

Kathleen Coburn had enjoyed 'a wonderfully enriching relationship' with my own Cambridge supervisor, A.P. Rossiter. He had introduced himself by letter as 'a Cambridge don and rock-climber' who was interested in STC on mountains. His friendship with Coburn ended only with his death in a road accident in 1956.

A very strange accident, as it happened. Some months before his death, Rossiter had set out from Cambridge to ride his motorbike north to his home. Along the road he had had a frightful crash that hospitalized him for weeks. As soon as he felt strong enough, he mounted his bike once more and set out on the same route. Again there was an accident — at the same spot where he had crashed before. This time it was fatal.

I thought about Coburn and Frye and other scholars who devoted their whole career to one author. Thanks to their single-minded labours, one could be sure about the text and the life. Slogging away at one author was not something the common reader, or even the common writer, could endure. Frye's belief was that the chosen author, fully understood, could open the way to all literature. For him it was William Blake. Yet these one-author scholars tended to be receptive to new experiences of all kinds. Knowing everything about someone did not prevent their knowing something about everyone.

The prairie investors called their magazine *The Canadian* and quickly sank it, losing their social credit money. Arnold had the satisfaction of rustling up financial support so that he could buy it back. Maclean-Hunter wanted to keep it going and there was still magic in the name *Saturday Night*. In his first signed editorial of the revived magazine, Arnold borrowed a ploy from Fray Luis de León, the Salamanca monk whose lecture was interrupted for some years by the Inquisition. 'As I was saying,' Arnold wrote, 'before I was interrupted by *The Canadian* …'

The office moved to York Street, next to the Royal York Hotel. Staff was cut to the bone. On the editorial side David Levy, a Russian linguist, was managing editor, and the illustrator Trevor Hutchings part-time art director. The magazine relied on freelancers writing for minimal fees. Levy soon left to become CBC correspondent in Moscow, and was replaced by a *Maclean's* staffer, the talented Harry Bruce.

In 1966, when Harry decided to remove himself and family from the big city, Arnold invited me to be managing editor. I accepted gladly. At first I wondered just what was I managing. The editorial staff consisted of Trevor Hutchings, now full-time art director, Arnold, his secretary and myself. The budget per issue was tiny. The situation was ideal for getting things done. Arnold was mostly out of the office promoting and trouble-shooting. Trevor and I could get on with the job, without time-wasting meetings, except the monthly conference on where to put the colour pages.

Harry had added several columnists moonlighting under pen-names. Since they were among the best journalists in Canada, I would just mark up their copy and send it to the printer. Academics who could write were treated the same way. Those who were dull or illiterate I rewrote. Copy-editing was quick and dirty.

For the main features I had to find bright spirits with ideas and talent. The mid-sixties was a time of rapid social change. The contraceptive pill was altering relations between the sexes. Feminism was returning with renewed force. Trudeau was turning Ottawa into an intellectual centre where the brooding on human destiny normally done in academe was being undertaken by government. In Quebec separatism was coming into vogue.

Writers who came to us with ideas gave the magazine a new direction, responsive to trends and social change. Ideas are always in the air. We were not first in finding them but we could act on them first, sometimes as much as three months before the powerful American competition. We put out special issues on 'The New New Woman', 'Love' and 'The Peacock Male'. Under cover of such vanities we raised and discussed issues that mattered to everyone. We also tried to show the human side of politics, especially in Ottawa. The writers who gave us direction were Wendy Michener (whose father was Governor General), Helen Wilson (a high-flyer in the public service), Joan Fox (a film critic), and the American correspondent whom Arnold had found in *The Village Voice*, David McReynolds.

Arnold hired an advertising agency to promote the magazine. The squibs devised by BBD&O featured caricatures of Arnold himself. To raise our profile we collaborated in a TV show called *Telepol*. I did not think much of it – the audience was polled to find out what it thought about current issues, a reflexive method that pretended to lead opinion by following it. There were heavy meetings with everyone concerned. I liked the producer, a world-weary New York Jew with seven Emmys under his belt and the ribbon of the Légion d'honneur in his lapel. He found the Canadian aversion to bigshots incomprehensible. When Pierre Berton's name came up, the Canadians groaned. 'Pu-lease! The man is too well known, he's a cliché!' And when the central bank governor Coyne was proposed as 'man of the year', Ross Maclean, for CTV, said, 'I happen to know he won't accept.' The producer fetched up a sigh from his many chins. 'Just *esk* the man. Okay? Just *esk*.' Coyne accepted. The BBD&O man demanded more exposure for *Saturday Night*. Arnold's time on camera was increased.

These ploys made Arnold better known than the magazine and helped him raise money. Arnold was always on; if he had nothing to say, he'd say it anyway. Or he'd pick up a book or a magazine and read to you. Once, he picked a paper from my desk and said, 'Listen to this, it's rather good.' And I have to say it did seem good. It was my own article for the next issue.

With Trevor's approval I was able to promote some of my artist friends. We ran a sequence of photographs by Lutz Dille. We also showcased the art of Gershon Iskowitz, an Auschwitz survivor, who had painted naïve images of fellow-sufferers in the death camp. Somehow he'd kept these heart-rending pictures hidden from the guards. Gershon worked and lived in a loft on Spadina Avenue, south of College Street. His talk was exclusively about himself and his work. He had to be solitary, a kind of anchorite. Experience had taught him not to trust anyone. As a living witness to the worst episode in history, he was precious.

Our women writers were noticing changes in the nature of love. It was no longer a matter of horny men pursuing reluctant women. Liberated by the pill, horny women were now pursuing startled men. We wanted to present these ideas in a playful format. Trevor Hutchings had left and the new art director, Anton, was enthusiastic about the scheme I had in mind. We had Harold Towne collaborate in art direction by painting on the lovely body of a French Canadian blonde named Mireille Matthieu – no relation of the renowned French chanteuse. No bimbo either – Mireille was to become a CBC radio producer before heading north with a teacher to raise a family at Igloolik in the Arctic. John Reeves took the photographs. Payments were negligible.

Arnold insisted on taking the slides home, to look at with his wife and decide which could decently be used. Next day he gave his selection to Anton. The art director was in despair. He did not see how he could work with this selection. I said, 'Give me the slides – all of them.' I shuffled the lot, then gave them back to Anton. 'You're the art director. Make your own choice.'

When the issue hit the stands, Arnold was proud of his magazine. And Canada could be proud of Mireille.

For an issue on the 'New New Woman' we used photographs of a Barbie doll, then a new toy. In these special issues we were catching ideas that were blowing in the wind. Other journals caught them too. They were not copying us. An advertising man told us Canadians could not believe anything that did not come first from the US – it was a mistake to be in the vanguard. With misgivings of this kind, Canadians chose to take second place.

In my first year as managing editor, Ralph Allen, now managing editor of *The Toronto Star*, twice took me to lunch and urged me to accept the job of entertainment editor at his paper. I knew the *Star*'s habit of admiring an editor or writer until they hired him/her, when they'd despise her/him as just another employee. I did not need that kind of grief. I was having too much fun doing a softshoe number with Arnold.

People walked into my office with ideas. One day Harry Bruce came in with a young woman who, he said, had written a funny piece on sniffing bad breath. It was about a scientific way of testing the effects of mouthwash. The writer's husband was a dentist. Harry was right – the piece was funny, avoiding coarseness. We published it. This was Barbara Frum's first break in journalism. She went on to become a major star of radio and television and a national heroine.

I assigned her a column on television, an interest of hers. After about three columns of interesting and accurate reporting, I told Barbara that it was not forbidden to express opinions. 'Oh, I don't know if I can do that!' she said. But she quickly developed into the opinionated hostess of *As It Happens*, a CBC news show.

Later on, her husband, after making megabucks in real estate, became one of the most generous benefactors of the magazine. It still needed benefactions. A journal of this kind was no longer commercially feasible in Canada. It stumbled from crisis to crisis.

Since I could see what was happening, despite all our efforts through a couple of years, I decided to focus on my own writing. I enjoyed journalism, though my view of it differed from the prevailing doctrine. What I wanted to do was raise issues and ask questions. I wanted to have the first word – get it wrong maybe, but get it out.

The Calvinist temperament wanted articles that *answered* all the questions. When Robert Fulford became editor, he did his honest best to have the last word on absolutely everything. He mastered his subjects before uttering a word. He became Canada's most able and best-informed commentator, impressing readers with exhaustive pieces that closed their subjects. Year after year the magazine carried off National Magazine Awards. I learn, however, from *The New Yorker*, of a category of articles that Dave Barry thought should be labelled 'Caution! Journalism Prize Entry! Do not read!'

And perhaps too many *SN* pieces were in that class. On the other hand, one seldom finished them anyway.

Saturday Night acquired fact-checkers, interns and a veritable college of editors. Office politics flourished in an increasingly expensive operation. Parkinson's law prevailed as busywork expanded to fill the time available for its completion. The more the busywork, the more the court of editors felt they were understaffed. They developed a corporate culture in which it was not cool to return calls, answer letters or queries from writers.

I did not foresee any of this. I did see that being an editor was making me drift toward power and self-importance again. I did not agree with Lionel Trilling that power was what everyone wanted. My African experience taught me more about power and responsibility than a New York critic could know. I did not want it. I wanted to be an outsider – and my nemesis was that I became one.

I passed the torch to Jack Batten, a sound professional who could balance Arnold's impulsiveness. In time Arnold became tired, letting himself be elbowed aside by Fulford, who needed a national platform for his opinions.

Sixteen

I have mentioned the *demon de midi* that caught me in the late nineteen-sixties, that restless spirit that besets some of us in middle years. As will be seen, I had lost faith in marriage to Mary. I drifted away emotionally and began to have affairs. I was not very good at being a husband. One example of my propensity for farce demonstrates my incompetence.

Assigned to attend a conference on city planning in New York's Central Park, I invited a dear friend from Quebec to join me the second day in my hotel. On the first day, a company of players put on an open-air performance of political theatre. William Hoving of the Metropolitan Museum spoke. Then the whole circus was rained out, drenching us. I ran for cover toward Madison Avenue, along with two young art students and a civil servant from Ottawa, who kept reminding the girls that I was old and going bald. This aroused their interest.

We found a warm tavern and ordered hot toddy. While we chatted, one of the art students, a girl from Montreal, slipped me a piece of paper with her phone number. I took the hint, and later in the day called her to meet me for dinner. The evening ended in her bedroom. She talked about her art and her admiration for an Irish celebrity who had taken part in freedom marches, calling him Conor 'Cruiser' O'Brien. I was interested in her as a young person who marched in protests for the hell of it. She was interested in me as a specimen of a species that wore gilt cufflinks, which I happened for once to be wearing. In the morning, I excused myself, alleging I had to meet an aunt from Chatham, Ontario.

It was the turn of the beautiful friend, also from Montreal, and a francophone. This was different. I could have been in love with her. At the same time, I was afraid of love. I thought myself clever to have neutralized emotion with a double ploy. It happened that both these young Montrealers were having it off (as the Brits say) with the same man in their home-town. In the novels of Dickens I relished coincidence. In life it was not enjoyable at all. The women talked. The boyfriend – who by a further coincidence was Irish and knew me by name – was kind enough to tell each about the other's New York adventure. I was not so clever after all.

And since I had turned away from Mary, because of her callous indifference to sickness, I became open to love. Busy with other things, I did not pursue it very strenuously. It would be easy now, from the perspective of old age, to dismiss it all as folly. The wisdom of age is a chimera, the result of fading desire or more simply failure of nerve. Love may be madness but it is real, pre-empting common sense and calculation.

I don't believe in confession – there's a danger that one will confess something really disgraceful. Perhaps I've already done so. If I speak of love, I do so because in any lived life it is a powerful influence.

I think back over many years to a time when I was more than once shaken by that reality. I think of a young woman opposite me at a dinner table, radiant with her fair skin, her daffodil hair in a single plait, meeting my glance with the steady gaze of sapphire blue eyes. It was a gaze of desire, yet also a display of power. We were in company. There was nothing I could do or say at the time. It was many months before we found ourselves together. I knew it was a fleeting love, that this splendid girl was not going to throw herself away on someone like me, married with children, and without the glamour that money brings. Still, she was sensuous enough to risk an adventure, and came bravely to it. One night with her was worth the sense of loss that followed, softened by friendship.

The delights of the one-night stand are often underestimated: the isolation of the impersonal hotel room, the drawn curtains, the comfort of room service delivering the sacramental club sandwich, the beer or wine, the thermos of coffee; the luxury of the gleaming bathroom, the hot shower taken together; the frisson of danger when the phone rings by mistake, the intense intimacy, the sense that the world of work and duty locked out, leaving two souls with their secret.

For a short time I was besotted by a blonde ex-gymnast from the Baltic region. We spent a couple of evenings together while I furtively admired her splendid body. It helped me to turn a deaf ear to her New Age sermons. After an evening's entertainment − I think it was dinner and a movie − when I escorted her to her door, she invited me to come up to her apartment for a drink. Now, I thought, we're getting somewhere!

My hostess settled me in an armchair with a Scotch on the rocks, dimmed the light and excused herself. 'I vant to get into somezing more comfortable.' This traditional line would have seemed more promising if I hadn't heard it before from another Baltic blonde. That young woman had really meant it. She had returned from her bedroom in a heavy Irish sweater and thick trousers. Still, one could always hope.

This gymnast made her re-entry stark naked, a dazzling sight. I choked on my Scotch. There was a marvellous harmony in the relationship between her smooth neck, proud breasts, small waist and round buttocks. I could see a hint of golden fuzz on her long thighs.

'We have a wonderful spiritual relationship,' she breathed. 'We were meant for zis. We must not spoil it by getting physical.'

I believe that was the moment from which I should trace my loathing of the word 'spiritual'. She passed so close that one of her breasts brushed my burning cheek. Groaning, I gulped down my whisky. Within minutes I was on my way home to my lonely pad. I was almost asleep when the phone rang. It was the impossible she. 'I can feel your unhappy vibes all the way across the city.' 'Damn right,' I said, and hung up. I took the phone off the hook.

Another lovely woman who stooped to folly with me had a couple of others in tow. After years of marriage she had left her husband temporarily to see whether screwing around was any better. She had enlisted the usual suspects: a television producer who could promise a future in show-business and an Irish journalist of genuine charm. Both men had restored the self-esteem of several fine women.

She was tall and slim with blue eyes, put in, as the saying goes, with a sooty finger. She had a delightful sense of humour and was adventurous, if not downright kinky in the sack. On the other hand, she was none too considerate of the partner's feelings. Splendidly naked beside me, she would talk on the phone for hours in low breathy tones to her alternates. And one day she insisted on showing me a letter from her husband, begging her to come home. It was a letter of such pure affection and kindness that I felt the way Adam did after he had eaten the apple. I felt an overwhelming impulse to reach for the fig leaves. Lust withered. I told her, 'The guy loves you. You don't know how lucky you are. You must be crazy.'

I was happy when she went back to him.

That was one kind of affair. But there was also the drawn-out agony of obsessive love. One woman ... I will call her Louise. I was drawn to her for her dark beauty and vital mind and imagination – not least for her anarchic humour. She was ready for an affair, since her husband neglected her, taking long trips with his mistress. So what if I was just an instrument of revenge – for me she was the promised land. We struggled frantically in her bed, on her sofa or whatever plain surface was nearest, hardly taking the time to tear off our clothes. We travelled to Mexico together, to Zihuatanejo. She was nervous, mocking my enthusiasm for exotic birds and wildlife. In a little while, though, she calmed down and surrendered to the adventure and the charm of the place.

Her husband asked for a divorce, so that he could move in with his mistress. She changed, seeing me as unprofitable. She wanted to find another husband. I was not quite ready for another divorce. Nor was she quite ready to let me go. She told me in detail about her new affairs. This was torture, though I knew why she was doing it.

Then came my own divorce, after which Mary took our daughters away with her to Vancouver. They were now out of reach, though the court had granted 'reasonable access'.

A couple of years later Louise and I were both free, and set up house together. It was not to be a happy ending. Something about me aroused her anger. I truly loved her, though our history had made me distrustful and reserved. She attacked me for my 'bourgeois' origins, herself being of the worthy working class. There was nothing I could do to change my origins. Raised a Catholic, she was convinced that Protestants did not believe people had souls, that they were emotionally cold and callous, unlike the warm and caring Catholics.

In the end I was alone again, this time with at least two women furiously angry with me. Mary forbade me to attend the wedding of our daughter Sarah, threatening dire consequences. Her letter had been typed so violently, there were holes in the paper. The wretchedly sad thing is that some years later, poor Mary died suddenly in Vancouver of a cerebral aneurism. She had been on the point of leaving for an African safari.

After I left Louise, the phone would often ring around 4 am and her voice would whisper, 'Die, you bastard.' Sometimes I would find my car vandalized in the underground garage, with the paint scratched or windshield wipers torn off. After months of violent anger, she simmered down to marry a nice man who was comfortably off. She had sworn to blacken my reputation, which I think she did quite successfully in Toronto.

This ill repute saved me from entanglements with a couple of nasty women, and made me interesting to others who were merely naughty.

The Hudson's Bay Company was preparing to celebrate its third centennial, to take place in 1970. In Winnipeg in 1967, Barbara Kilvert, their publicist, had an idea for a special project. The company's story was an important part of Canadian history. Scholars had worked on this connection. There had even been a popular history.

Something different was needed. Kilvert thought it should be a nonsense history, of the kind Sellar and Yeatman had done for British history in *1066 and All That*. She decided to put together one of the greatest living illustrators with a Canadian who could provide a lighthearted text. This was how Ronald Searle and I came to collaborate on the book. We called it *The Great Fur Opera*. It is a travesty of corporate history.

McClelland & Stewart were the Canadian publishers, in Toronto, where I lived. Searle was in Paris with Monica, his second wife. Operational headquarters of the Hudson's Bay Company, now a chain of Canadian department stores known as 'The Bay', were in Winnipeg, Manitoba. Overall direction was from offices in the City of London. Beaver Hall was near St Paul's, housing the archives of the 300-year-old chartered corporation. (After the tercentennial, head office and archives were moved to Winnipeg, where the records are preserved with the provincial archives.)

We met in Winnipeg. Searle, a trim figure with a Van Dyck beard, was courteous and witty. He had grown up in Cambridge, begun his career in London and, after joining the army during World War II, had suffered as a prisoner of the Japanese in Singapore. The drawings he made in secret, recording unspeakable cruelty, are exquisite and heart-breaking. After marrying Monica, he had migrated to Paris, where they lived in a rent-controlled apartment off rue Monsieur le Prince.

I needed to know the true history before I could make fun of it. A problem was that Canadians did not agree on a single national story, even if they knew it, which could be taken for granted. I went to London to look into the archives.

Beaver Hall was close to St James Garlickhythe. A column in the church is inscribed, 'Sir / Chris.Wren / Hee builded / this church.' Wren was one of the original 'Adventurers of England tradeing into Hudson Bay'. An early entry in a book of minutes noted that he had been ordered to make locks for the warehouse where the furs were kept. Searle depicted Wren dreaming of St Paul's cathedral, the dome flaunting a flag saying 'Shoppe at ye Baye'.

Another founding adventurer was Robert Boyle of Boyle's Law, 'the father of pneumatical philosophy and the brother of the Earl of Cork'.

London was splendid for research. In addition to the archives, I was able to read calendar rolls in the Guildhall Library and pamphlets in the Friends Library, including several by Charles Baily, the Company's first governor in Canada.

My fancy was that Charles II had set up a chain of department stores across Rupertsland, which included most of what is now north-west Canada, as well as a sizable chunk of the USA.

Searle's illustrations are beautiful and funny, his line sensuous and lively. As for my text, I tried to give a sense of time passing by parody, and to mix fact and fantasy in such a way that readers could not tell which was which. We worked well together, thanks to the artist's forbearance. The book was published in 1970 and fairly well reviewed. In London the governor, Lord Emery, hated the book, even though I had removed a joke to please him. (I'd noted that there was only one letter to distinguish 'viscount' from 'discount'. I had refrained from calling him Lord Haemorrhoid.)

I visited the Searles in Paris. They started evenings with champagne in their apartment. Monica did quilting, keeping squares of different materials in little chests of drawers. On display was Searle's collection of English caricatures by the best artists from Rowlandson to the Victorians and after. There were antique clockwork toys that friends and admirers had given Ronald. We would saunter out to dine in one of the many restaurants in the neighbourhood, including a couple that Searle had decorated.

Ronald Searle was a serious artist whose friends at that time included famous expatriates like Samuel Beckett. His humour, often macabre, arose from a tragic sense. However, unlike many comedians, he is not in the least morose or ill-natured. When the French Mint commissioned him to design commemorative medals, he succeeded in persuading them to let him celebrate Edward Lear, although – as he said – the French do not understand nonsense (because it doesn't make sense) and there isn't even a word for it in

French. When he suggested a medal in honour of Lord Nelson, he knew he'd gone too far.

A typical Searle episode occurred later. He had made a book of drawings called *Searle's Cats*. It included such images as 'Ugly Cat admiring Self in Mirror' and other extravagances. The proofs were sent to his German publisher. There was a letter from the Herr Direktor. 'Dear Mr Searle, In Germany are many cat-lovers, but your attitude to cats is ambiguous.' The Germans wanted a preface in the form of a love letter to cats. This was too much for Searle. 'Dear Dr Stumpf,' he wrote – or some such – 'I have never felt strongly about cats, one way or the other. As a prisoner of war, however, I found them perfectly delicious. I would be glad to send a recipe.'

When the Honourable Company moved its head office to Winnipeg in 1970, its Canadian bosses felt they need not be nice to the natives any more. They gave up their support of Canadian culture. Soon the company was bucketing around the market in the takeover frenzies of the 1970s. It was at last acquired by a newpaper magnate, the second Baron Thomson, who sold off its northern trading posts and settled down to humdrum shop-keeping.

On one of several visits to London in the sixties, I called Jack Ludwig.

He was spending a sabbatical year with his wife Leah and daughters in a rented house in Highgate. Novelist and English professor at Stoneybrook University on Long Island, Jack had been a friend since my last years at Macmillan. He had sent me chapters of his first novel, *Confusions*, as he wrote them. I had tried to get Macmillan to give him a contract. The only result of my efforts and enthusiasm was to alert our competitor Jack McClelland. He promptly snapped up book and author for his list. Although Ludwig seemed to have used me as a lever, I blamed my over-cautious principals. My great regret was that Jack had weakened his book by over-revision.

Already he was a figure in the underground history of letters. He and Saul Bellow had been close friends and rivals for the esteem of

Pascal Covici. The legendary New York editor had been a kind of literary grandfather to both of them. I had met Pat Covici at Viking – a tweedy Romanian Jew with a big nose and shaggy white hair. New York literary men tended toward the grotesque – witness the huge, silly moustache of Alfred Knopf, the froggy aspect of Bennett Cerf.

Jack and Bellow's wife Sondra fell in love and moved away together. Ludwig exerted an almost magical attraction on women. Sondra said he was a steam-roller – he said she was 'gorgeous'. His Stalinesque good looks and burning brown eyes were augmented by overpowering eloquence. In the wars of love, he could talk his way out of the tightest corner, such as a lover's discovery of an alien diaphragm in his bathroom cupboard.

Since boyhood in Winnipeg, he'd been disabled by a bone disease that left him with a drastic limp. Bellow introduced a character with this physical trait in *Herzog*, the subtly villainous Valentine who makes off with the narrator's wife. Valentine limps like a gondolier at his oar, dip and straighten, dip and straighten.

It is a hostile but distinct portrait. Missing is the lifelong physical pain that Jack stoically endured. But the character Valentine does catch the prophetic intensity of Ludwig's conversation, laced with street slang and Yiddishisms. Jack was not ashamed of the caricature nor, indeed, of the affair. He told a nosy gossip at a party, 'Do I know Saul Bellow? Hell, I'm fucking his wife!'

We spent an afternoon at the Highgate Cemetery in London, where, with Jack's daughters, we visited the grave of Karl Marx. It stands near the tomb of Herbert Spenser – an area known as Marx and Spensers. It happened to be Marx's birthday. There were flowers to soften his bearded scowl.

Jack invited me to dinner. There were three guests: myself, the critic Leslie Fiedler and Mordecai Richler, who had just been appointed writer-in-residence at Sir George Williams University (later Concordia), in Montreal. Mordecai was silent most of the time, his customary frown of social martyrdom enhanced. Obviously he was deeply troubled about something. Leah, a gentle Griselda, served a fine dinner. Ludwig and Fiedler played with academic and

New York literary gossip. I forget what else we talked about.

Mordecai came out with it at last, the thing that was eating him. 'What d'you do, y'know? What d'you do if a student in your class, like, actually has *talent*?'

Fiedler and Ludwig stared at Mordecai for a moment. They both taught creative writing at their universities. With one voice they gave their answer: 'Crush him!'

I came to enjoy the comedy of mutual disapproval between Richler and Ludwig, two Jewish writers with different habits. Jack thought it a pity that a nice Jewish boy should drink so much as Mordecai: Mordecai was scandalized that a Jewish scholar should screw around as much as Jack.

Another time I visited Mordecai at his house in Kingston-upon-Thames, a fine, roomy mansion with a spacious garden. Mordecai, who had grown up amid bricks and mortar on St Urbain's Street in Montreal, was proud of his rolling half-acre.

'See those trees?' he said. 'Know what they are?'

'Beeches.'

Mordecai was quite disappointed. He had hoped to astonish me.

On the top floor was Mordecai's spacious study, guarded from interruption or intruders by Florence, Mordecai's elegant and capable wife. At dinner, Mordecai became the patriarch, ladling out stew for his family. The peaceful scene could be disturbed, though, by a visit from Richler's mother. I was present during one of the exchanges with her in which there was an edge of exasperation in Florence's voice. Despite Florence's tact, mother and son soon stopped speaking to each other. Mordecai did not attend her funeral.

During his suburban days Mordecai was under contract to write a film script. The producers had him sleep in a London hotel near the studio. It was a time when British telephone systems were more unreliable than ever. Mordecai was wakened by his telephone ringing.

A voice said, 'Is that room service?'

'No.'

'Good. I want my breakfast now. Coffee, two poached eggs and toast. Will you see to it?'

'No.'

'*What* did you say?'

Mordecai was now wide awake. 'I said *no*, I will not send you breakfast!'

'What! How dare you. I want to speak to the manager!'

After a pause, Mordecai said, 'I am the manager. You're speaking to him.'

'Good. I have this simple request. Coffee, two poached eggs and toast. Can you manage that?'

'No. I can do no such thing! And what's more, we don't want your sort in this hotel. Just pack your bags, y'hear? And leave, this minute!'

'Why you –! I'm coming to your office and punch your nose!'

'You do that,' said Mordecai and hung up.

Another Richler feat of bad behaviour took place during a flight from London to Montreal. He was sitting at the front of the economy class and recognized a white-haired clergyman taking his seat in first class – the Archbishop of Canterbury.

When the flight attendant was bringing Richler's Remy Martin, he handed her a note and asked her to give it to the clergyman in first class. Within minutes there was a young parson at his elbow, the prelate's chaplain.

'Are you the man who sent a note to the archbishop?'

The note said, 'Would Jesus Christ travel first class?'

Richler admitted his authorship. The chaplain said, 'Well, it's most unfair. The archbishop has a free pass!'

Seventeen

Before our divorce, Mary McAlpine and I spent a winter in Ireland in 1969, staying in County Laois at Moyne in a disused wing. I was lucky enough to enjoy some time with Mother.

I drove to Belfast where she now lived in a nursing home near my eldest sister Joan. I was to bring her to Moyne for a visit of a few weeks. Once installed in her room, she was ready to tell stories. I read to her from my friend John Glassco's *Memoirs of Montparnasse*.

When she heard about Glassco's visit to George Moore, she stopped me, 'George Moore! You know, I met that man in Dublin when I was a girl. At a soirée given by Lady Thompson, a surgeon's wife.'

'What was he like?'

'George Moore? Oh, a horrid little yellow man! When I told my mother about him she was angry. She said Lady Thompson had no right to entertain that man when young ladies were present.

'Well, I went to another of the lady's evenings where I talked with a young lecturer from Trinity College. I wanted to know about the Renaissance. He told me I should read Benvenuto Cellini's diary. I asked Mother if we had the book. She was quite upset. She asked the Provost – it was Mahaffy – whether it was suitable reading for me. He rolled his eyes, lisping, "Oh, if indeed you posseth that book, Mrs Bairnard, I beg you to keep it for your own pairthonal and private peruthal!"'

There was an upright piano in our sitting room. One spring

morning, with flowery scents wafting from the open window, Mother called me. She wanted to play the piano. Mary and I carried her there. She was clutching two pieces of sheet music.

Settled at the piano, she began to play J.S. Bach's 'Sheep may safely graze'. The room was full of sunlight and heavenly counterpoint. Reading the score, her face was rapt and abstracted. Frail as she was, her touch was sure. It seemed to me that I was seeing little Maudie Bernard in the early years of the century. After the first cantata she paused. Then went on to play the whole of 'Sleepers Wake' at sight without an error.

As she played the last notes, she began to wheeze. We took her to bed, giving her oxygen from a little dispenser that my brother Bernard had found for her – but soon we had to call the doctor. She was suffering yet another attack of congestive heart failure. I looked into her room to see the doctor and nurse busy with her. She gave a quick smile between gasps.

I think she had a premonition that spring day. She said that she wanted to play Bach one more time while she could. She rallied that time and lived for another five years, managing a winter of parties in Freeport, Bahamas with Nancy, who was living there, before returning to Belfast.

Sheer love of life kept her going, despite frequent heart failure. Near the end she was troubled by the thought that she had been wrong to make her husband retire when he did. She sent for George Seaver, the very reverend friend with good looks and brains but no sense of humour. When she confided her anxieties, the dean told her that none of that mattered any more. She was comforted.

During that time at Moyne I had hoped to feel more at home in Ireland. But I sensed that the county society had become more irrelevant than ever, and the endless anger and violence in the North was insufferable.

I came down with a painful attack of cystitis and a high fever. Mary was disgusted and left me to it. A doctor came from Abbeyleix with antibiotics and painkillers. My brother-in-law brought coal for the fire. I could not understand Mary's unkindness. When I spoke of it, she said, 'You forget that I've watched two men die.' So the reason for her scorn was that I was not dying, like her father and uncle.

There had been a previous incident in Mexico, where acute colitis had made me faint. 'A vasovagal syncope,' a Toronto physician said, when I described the attack. On that occasion too Mary had been callous and scorning. She could not see that there was anything untoward in her attitude, even when she herself suffered a bad go of colitis and I took care of her.

The year 1970 was packed with incident. For seven or eight months that year, after returning from Ireland, I worked as a consultant in Ottawa. As everyone knows, a consultant is someone from out of town. Hired by my friend Bernard Ostry, I was to edit and write in the citizenship branch of the department of the Secretary of State. This made me part of a collective effort to integrate the ethnic identities of Canada.

I had known Bernard and his wife Sylvia since *Star Weekly* days, when they'd helped me with a piece I was writing about Ottawa. Then with the CBC, Bernard was now an assistant deputy minister. The Ostrys, a handsome couple with great intellectual pizzazz, had been influential in Ottawa for some years, throwing parties in their mansion in Hull, Quebec, just across the river. Trudeau, with his prejudice in favour of brains, had brought them into the public service. Sylvia was an economist of repute, and now prominent in the Department of Statistics, of which she would soon become head. It was not long before husband and wife were both deputy ministers heading departments – she of Finance, he of Communications.

I was trying to edit and correct the language in which the officials addressed one another and the public. I found that removing the bureaucratic fog made the authors unhappy. Clarity was not what they wanted.

I was also drafting a paper on citizenship and Canadian pluralism. The neighbour republic was committed to individualism, to the cowpoke with a gun. Ours was not a country that believed civic peace could be maintained by private citizens taking the law into their own hands. The Canadian West was won, not by trigger-happy gunmen, but by mounted policemen who seldom drew their weapons.

Citizens were persons, members of families and of communities. They should be assured cultural freedom. This policy was already called 'multiculturalism'. The doctrine was an obvious response to the hopes and fears of many ethnicities. It came to be accepted throughout the country. The idea was for groups to share their culture with others, not for each group to go off into a corner, turning its back on the wider community. (Later I was to write background papers for the Queen on this and other topics.)

The origins of the multicultural policy have been widely misunderstood. It was developed on the initiative of Lester Pearson, who was responding to pressure from the Canadian grassroots. The Royal Commission on Bilingualism and Biculturalism had believed Canada to be a country with two cultures, British and French. That had been true after the fall of New France, when the British had assured French Canadians that they could keep their religion and language (something denied to the Irish), their culture and even their civil law. But throughout the nineteenth and twentieth centuries immigrants had been arriving with dozens of other languages and cultures which the commissioners at first ignored. The ethnic groups that settled the West could accept the two founding languages but were not about to give up their own cultures. Canada's First Nations were also insistent on their rights. In justice, these identities had to be accommodated. The Trudeau administration worked on the details of the policy.

Ostry hoped the document would be tabled as a green paper – a document for discussion. In the event, he would have liked it to be controversial. Jules Leger advised Secretary of State Gerard Pelletier *against* tabling the paper. 'It will be obvious,' he said, 'that it is not the result of the usual consulting back and forth.' The formulations, though, were silently adopted, and I kept seeing my phrases in public speeches.

Ostry, an aesthete and master of style, was abrasive and full of ideas. The media sniped at his flawless tailoring and grand airs. He had private means, which strengthened his hand in controversy. I realized how important a financial cushion could be to a public-spirited official, especially one whose candour made enemies.

In October of that year – 1970 – the country was shaken by the crimes of the FLQ, a group of separatist terrorists in Quebec. They kidnapped the British trade commissioner, Jasper Cross, and brutally murdered a provincial Cabinet minister. I happened to be in the gallery of the House of Commons when Pierre Trudeau announced the government's response. A small, dapper figure with a pink rose in his buttonhole, he stood to invoke the War Measures Act, a draconian law that temporarily suspended civil rights. Tommy Douglas, another bantam-cock and leader of the socialist New Democrats, was on his feet with strong objections. Trudeau replied, 'The Right Honourable gentleman should ask himself what Kerensky should have done in 1917.'

Many Quebec intellectuals were arrested and held overnight. Troops patrolled the streets of Montreal and took up position at key points in Ottawa. One nervous soldier shot himself in the foot. And all over Canada the political science profs and editorial writers raised their voices in angry protest. I believe, though, that Ottawa acted wisely and with good timing. Terrorist crimes are theatre. A theatrical response was proper. Civil liberties were only briefly suspended. The government had shed no blood. Separatists renounced violence.

For me, the best thing about my Ottawa months was the cementing of my friendship with Bernard and Sylvia Ostry. In the years to come I also worked for him from time to time as editor of his speeches and publications. He continued to invite controversy.

The fact that I was consorting with high fliers in Ottawa caught the attention of Martin Goodman, one of his publisher's two Jewish henchmen on the *Star*. The other was Peter Newman, whom the publisher often addressed as Goodman and vice versa. What's the diff? he must have thought; they're both Jews, both smart and they both work for *me*. Peter had the sense to quit.

Goodman invited me to rejoin the *Star* as books columnist and literary editor, remarking that my predecessor had been okay till he started thinking. 'Then he got turgid.'

I needed a job, so I accepted. And soon found that the entertainment editor was ready with his knife – just in case I was after his job; a job I'd twice refused years ago. I stuck with the corporation for three years, quitting when they were sick of me. 'Dobbs was okay until he started thinking,' Goodman told a friend of mine. 'Then he got turgid.' I laughed when I heard this.

I had one strange experience on the paper. Reading the entertainment section one day, I came on a piece about the Stratford Festival by a new writer. Her name was unfamiliar. I thought, This is good writing, why have I not heard of this woman? And soon I had a feeling that I had seen this article before. Then it dawned on me. No wonder I liked it – it was my own work. I had written this years ago in the *Weekly*. In the library I checked it out. Yes, no question, this new writer had copied my piece word for word – and put her byline on it.

I found the plagiarist, a fine-looking girl – stacked, as they said in those days. She tried to tough it out. There had been no byline on it, she said. (The byline had been cut to make the page fit the file.) Surely she could use anything in the morgue! She was young and such an idiot that I couldn't bring myself to report her. I said, 'You owe me lunch, at least.' Her answer astonished me. 'What about your wife?'

The Japanese-Canadian reviewer, who filled my slot some time after I had left, was twice caught out in plagiarism. Paralyzed by depression, the poor man killed himself. Forest Hill girls are made of sterner stuff.

In 1971 I flew from Toronto for Mother's funeral, reaching the Hamiltons' Dublin house jetlagged, just in time to leave for St Patrick's Cathedral. I sat with Joan in the nave. There were youngish people in the congregation whom I did not know, friends Mother had made in her last years.

The service was sung by the boy-choristers: 'Sleepers Wake' and a favourite hymn of Mother's, 'O God of Bethel'. The thirty-two foot bourdon of the great Willis organ rumbled like doom. In the aisles I could see tourists with backpacks tiptoeing from monument to monument. After the service we followed the hearse all the way to Castlecomer churchyard. Countryfolk raised their hats as we passed.

Moyne was a few miles away. We met there for a reunion. It was the last time I saw Joan. Her husband had recently died, and within a year she was dead too. I still feel her loss. I like to remember her playing her violin, the haunting melody that Charles Villiers Stanford heard and transcribed from the streets of Derry, the famous 'Londonderry Air'.

It was during that visit that I attended a cocktail party in Howth, given by Brian Boydell who had been my teacher and friend in my teens. Composer and conductor, he was to become Regius Professor of Music at TCD. My former schoolmate Michael Yeats was at the party, chairman of the Irish Senate.

Brian Faulkner had just become leader of the Unionist party and Premier of Northern Ireland. I reminded Senator Yeats that he and Faulkner had been inseparable friends at St Columba's; why did he not speak to his old friend, proposing conversations to find a détente?

'Well, of course. I've been trying to do just that. He has not answered my letters or returned my phone calls. It's a bitter disappointment. And to think that I persuaded him to go into politics!'

Faulkner did not last long in office. His own party would not accept his proposals for power-sharing. And in 1972 the British suspended the Stormont parliament and imposed direct rule from Westminster. They made Faulkner a baron. In 1977 Lord Faulkner went fox-hunting and broke his neck.

At the end of my stint in Ottawa as a consultant I was assigned to draft a speech for the Sovereign to be given in Vancouver at a Citizenship Ceremony. Because I'd been involved in formulating the multicultural policy, the draft was to express that policy. The speech was a success, Her Majesty delivered it almost verbatim and the audience was moved.

For the Queen's next visit, in 1973, I was recruited again, this time to 'edit' ten speeches for various occasions. Most of them I had to rewrite completely. I remember one draft, prepared in Toronto, in which the Queen was expected to present herself as a kind of salesperson for the United Kingdom. I thought it a good idea for her to explain her constitutional role as Queen of Canada, so I wrote a new draft to that effect. She was to say she was not just Queen of the Anglos but of all Canadians, whatever their culture or origin. Reeves Haggan, my friend in the Privy Council, wrote to say that HM liked it. He added, 'Up the Republic!'

All went to plan and I was shown a long telegramme from the Queen's private secretary congratulating Ottawa on turning 'lacklustre drafts into first-rate proposals to set before Her Majesty'. Wow! In fact she delivered the speeches almost word for word as I wrote them. There was reaction from press and media. The Sovereign was actually saying something! My friend Barbara Frum, now a busy CBC broadcaster, wondered what she was up to. Was she currying favour with the ethnics? When I told Barbara how the speech got written, she was not interested. Journalists care about the myth, rather than the history.

For a few weeks I told people I had invented the phrase 'My husband and I' and that I was paid residuals whenever HM said it. The truth is, I'm ashamed to report how little I was paid for this work.

Reeves called, pleased at his cleverness in hiring me. Did I want to be presented to the Queen? I declined, saying that I was not a monarchist. (But neither was I *anti*-monarchist.) I could not believe there was any reality to such encounters.

Not long after leaving the *Star* in 1974, I was in Hollywood, commissioned by McClelland & Stewart to help an elderly Canadian actor edit his memoirs. I stayed at the Beverly Hills Hotel. The actor lived just round the corner with his third wife, a former corporation lawyer from Connecticut.

Hollywood itself is a squalid place, with decaying art-deco

buildings and bars with names like Filthy McNasty's, which live up to their names – or down. As in most US cities, violent crime flourishes. Beverly Hills has streets and streets of bizarre mansions, Spanish colonial, neo-classical, Palladian, bankers' Tudor, Frank Lloyd Wrong or whatever the fancy of a suddenly enriched 'artiste' could dream up. These streets are dangerous, or so the natives believe. Go for a walk and a police cruiser stops beside you to ask what you mean by this weird activity.

The actor, his wife and I got along well. We lunched in the Polo Lounge, under the eyes of starlets and fans. At our third consultation, he told me to call him Ray, short for Raymond, 'But I have trouble calling you Kildare,' he confessed. Dr Kildare had been played in the movies by Richard Chamberlain, while Raymond Massey, my client, had been Dr Gillespie. I did not tell him right away that his brother Vincent had also been my client. There was not much brotherly love between them. Raymond was tall, a glow of fame about him, and walked with a cane. Dorothy was small and feisty, a Yankee to her fingertips. She and Ray were unregenerate right-wing Republicans, referring to President Carter as 'the little swine'.

As we worked on the first volume, our friendship developed to the point where Dorothy Massey announced with excitement that she had a present for me.

'It's a painting,' she said. 'If you don't like it, as I strongly suspect you won't, and decide to sell, the deal is that you give half what you get to me.'

'If you want to sell a picture, why not take it to a dealer?' I said, a little stiffly, not much caring for gifts with conditions.

'Now just a minute! The other part of it is that you tell the story of the picture whenever you can.

'It shows in lurid colours – and I choose my words carefully – three big balls in a bowl against a striped background. It's not signed. Now, here's the scoop: when Ray married his first wife, daughter of the British sea lord who in 1919 watched the German fleet scuttle itself at Scapa Flow, their wedding-present from brother Vincent Massey was this picture. The first Mrs Massey didn't like it and hid it in the attic. The strange thing was that after divorcing and marrying again, Ray's wedding gift from Vincent was the same picture. Somehow he'd repossessed it. And again – surprise, surprise! – when Ray and I married, it turned up as *our* present from Vincent. The second Mrs Massey must have hidden it in the basement. And that's what I did too.

'And now I'll show it to you.'

It was a smallish canvas, almost square, a still-life of a bowl of fruit. To my disquiet it was quite obviously a Fauve work, possibly by Dérain or someone equally known. It looked valuable, a good painting, though something about it was repulsive to me. Surely this was too much for a gift. 'I'll take it to a dealer for you,' I said.

'No, no – a deal's a deal.'

The first thing I had to know was the painter's identity. One Fauve was much like another, so that it was hard to guess from style. Then I thought of something – Vincent Massey's diaries. There might be a record of the purchase there. Who would know what was in the diaries? I remembered an art scholar called David Silcox. He was making a *catalogue raisonnée* of David Milne, a painter whose early work had been collected by Vincent Massey. Silcox would know where to look in the diaries for Vincent's purchases.

I had known Silcox when I served for two years on the Advisory Arts Panel to the Canada Council, of which he was then an officer. When I showed him the painting, he became quite excited, asking to be allowed to take it home to research its provenance. After a month or so he called to say he knew who the painter was.

We met for lunch to discuss it in the Danish Food Centre, where we ordered aquavit, Tuborg lager and smorgasbord. Silcox had not brought the picture with him. Instead he showed me a letter from Sotheby's valuing the picture at $4000. It was by Sir Matthew Smith, a British Fauve who had gone mad and been knighted – or vice versa. Silcox offered to buy the painting for the sum named. Remembering that Dorothy Massey was a Yankee, I did not jump at the offer. After a lot more aquavit I said I'd sleep on it. And next day I telephoned to say Silcox could have it for, if memory serves, $5000.

He agreed and, after a leisurely pause, sent his cheque. I endorsed and sent it on to Dorothy.

Dorothy insisted on sending back half. Some of her share, she said, she was giving to the first Mrs Raymond, but not one cent to the second, 'because she was such a bitch'.

Raymond got good reviews for his first volume. This gave him confidence to resist unwelcome advice. When I tried to get him to drop his long descriptions in the second volume of constructing stage scenery, he became seriously annoyed. He was now an author. He was also a rich man used to having his way. I had liberated a monster.

Publisher Jack McClelland wrote to say that I was fired, alleging I had done a lousy job. I was not paid what was owed for the first volume, and nothing for my work on the second. Instead McClelland got me a small grant from the Ontario Arts Council. Using the grant in this way was illegal but, rather than be stiffed altogether, I accepted it.

Raymond's second volume, potentially the more saleable, was not a success.

Some years later in London in the Tate Gallery I visited the Matthew Smith/Bomberg room. And there was 'my' picture. When Dorothy heard that the painting was in the Tate, she was furious. 'I hate to be shafted like that,' she fumed. 'I'm supposed to be a corporation lawyer and a Yankee, God damn it!'

Silcox went on from strength to strength, to become a provincial deputy minister, a university gallery director and, finally, head of Sotheby's in Canada.

Eighteen

By the mid-seventies I was in a financial morass. My health was degenerating, blood pressure up. As with other freelancers, my work came in cycles. There were times when editors wanted my work and times when they did not. This was the *not* time. I did not know the editors. They were the kind of help employers bought cheaply. Editing, in the view of sales managers and publishers, was women's work. They came and went, each new relay thinking the predecessor's writers were old hat. In broadcasting there was an additional hazard. The CBC was being punished for its political impartiality with budget cuts. I was one of them, I think. I had already lost a continuing place in CBC *Anthology* as a literary essayist. The programmer Howard Engel had given me regular work. For him, among other things, I had adapted James Joyce's *Finnegans Wake* for radio, as well as *Dubliners*. When Robert Weaver resumed control of *Anthology* he dropped me in order to have more time for poetry and stories. Later on Howard Engel himself was part of a budget cut. With unerring discrimination, CBC administrators singled out their most talented staff for the axe.

I did have one small, steady gig, in the form of a new CBC quiz show called *Yes, You're Wrong*. I thought I'd been chosen because of my performances in *Now I Ask You*. But the programmers of the new quiz show had never heard of the earlier one. There was no continuity at the CBC, no corporate memory and, what was more surprising, not much interest in popularity. Programmes rose and fell because of internal struggles between executives.

The quiz show brought in a small weekly sum, though not enough to cover child-support payments. When I fell in arrears, I found my small bank account had been disembowelled by a writ of *fieri facias*, 'Fi-Fa' in thieves'/lawyers' cant.

There was a weekend when I was down to a single dollar in cash, and no credit. I was expecting a cheque on the Monday. Luckily my friend Bob Rogers, a film producer in the stand-easy mode, called to say we'd both been invited to lunch with Jack and Lorraine Herman in Kleinburg, a little north of Toronto. Bob drove us there. The Hermans are two of the finest ceramic artists in Canada and dear friends of mine and Bob's. They gave us, as always, a splendid lunch. That took care of nourishment for the time being. And when Bob left me at my door in Toronto, he leaned over and said, 'Can you lend me a dollar? Gail Singer left her dog with me for the weekend. His special food has run out. I need one more dollar to buy it.'

'All I *have* is a dollar,' I said, 'to see me through the weekend. I—'

Bob fixed me with his eye. 'It's either you or the dog.'

Since he put it that way, I gave him the dollar. Over the next couple of weeks I spread the story around. It got back to Bob. He invited me to dine with him and our friend Gail Singer, the filmmaker.

When I arrived, he led me to his basement to show a rack of overcoats. 'Bought these at the Symphony Sale at the last moment,' he said. 'I paid twenty-five cents each. Take a couple.'

I chose a sober overcoat, its former owner doubtless in his grave, and a raincoat.

I told the story to Richard Wright, whose privations as a writer had made him careful with a buck. He gave judgment. 'The way I see it,' he said, 'the man still owes you fifty cents.'

The quiz show brought new friends. There were four participants on air, and the announcer, Bob Oxley. Don Ryan was a kind of Professor Higgins who could identify and mimic dialects. Dubarry Campau, a retired newspaperwoman, was a droll lady from Grand Rapids, Michigan who had invented her name and accent. 'If you came from Grand Rapids,' she drawled, 'you would too.' Ted Roberts was a busy jazz guitar-player and showman. The programme was written by David Foote, *alias* David Drake the magician. At one time Carol Commisso was part of the act; a former Miss Canada, she was witty and smart as well as beautiful.

There were many stories about Dubarry. In my favourite, she was sitting at a sidewalk table with a friend, when a man stripped to his underpants sprinted by, a look of panic on his face. The next moment a second almost-naked man rushed past, a big black bruiser in polka-dot shorts, a kitchen-knife flashing in his hand. Dubarry's friend started up, 'I'll call the police!' he said.

'Don't bother,' Dubarry drawled. 'Sit down. They'll make up.'

Friendships outlasted the show, which ran successfully for four years. It was fun to work with live audiences. Dubarry died without revealing her age. Dave received a death sentence from an oncologist, accepting it calmly and even with humour. Ted went on broadcasting for a while, while continuing to work as a jobbing musician and a member of The Travellers, an ensemble often in demand for national occasions. His real passion was always for jazz, which he now plays every Thursday with a group of equally accomplished musicians in Sergeant Pepper's, a pub on the outskirts of Toronto.

As for me, after thirty years of broadcasting, I vanished from the air.

Now that I knew my way to Hollywood, I came back at long intervals whenever I could get a travel assigment, mainly to visit Brian and Jean Moore in Malibu. Their house was some eighty miles up the Pacific Coast Highway on sandy bluffs above the ocean. The bluffs were stabilized by a dense growth of ice-plant, a succulent that blossoms in spring. The house was a flat-roofed bungalow with big windows on the sea. After some years they enlarged it.

It was always restful to be with them. Jean was a beautiful and thoughtful hostess and Brian always entertaining. Both of them were sumptuary aesthetes, Jean quietly chic and also a brilliant cook, Brian neatly tailored and groomed. Their house was luxurious, with excellent art and appointments. They were wonderful together, as Brian worked productively to produce one masterpiece after another and Jean created an ambiance of peace and tranquillity. She would tell anthropological stories about the world of the jet-set which they visited occasionally. The last time I saw them, Brian summed up their easy-going life together. 'We're like a couple of old fags!' he said.

For a while they were troubled by an official letter declaring that their property was now part of a national park and their tenure doubtful. Their lawyer told them to ignore the notice. Meanwhile a state legislator questioned the need for immediate action. It would be unfair and expensive, he argued, to evict residents who were there for the long term, celebrities like Vincent Price, and other famous neighbours. Let them live out their lives. In the event no one was disturbed.

Sometimes I sat on the patio with the Moores, drink in hand, looking out to sea to view the long, slow procession of grey whales going south. I took lengthy walks with Brian along the beach, the heavy surf rolling in to crash on the shore. He talked about his son, and how the young man learned too much about doctors from his relations and so had qualified as a nurse. One morning, on the beach, we came near to an old sea lion dying on the sand. His fur was dry and we saw that his natural colour was reddish instead of black, as it looks when wet. His breathing was laboured. A park ranger stood near to keep surfers at a distance. 'He's entitled to die in peace,' he said. We watched the dying animal for a while without saying anything.

After breakfast Moore would disappear into his study at the back of the house. It was a large, airy room painted white. At one end was his desk with typewriter. He never did convert to word-processing. He had sold his papers to the University of Calgary for a substantial sum. He knew that scholars wanted to see successive drafts of a work, with corrections and editing.

Brian showed me his commonplace book. In his distinctive italic hand were excerpts from works that had moved him. Some entries had suggested themes for books. This too would go to Calgary. I had read Brian's early unacknowledged thrillers. He bitterly resented any reference to them. He sought to create for himself the persona of dedicated writer in the image of Flaubert and Joyce. It was as if he had taken Holy Orders and was renouncing past sins.

And yet he did learn from his work on crime novels. They were attempts, he alleged, to master the North American idiom. They were also a school of narrative. Something had to happen on every page. Moore learned to find the narrow path through a large subject, to start *in medias res*, and grip the reader's attention through the arts of the page-turner.

So, at one end of the room, the typewriter. At the other end, a large, walk-in closet where he kept his clothes. After I had been reading in the living room for a couple of hours, I saw Brian drifting out of his study with an abstracted air, his garb completely different from what he'd had on when he started. Fetching a glass of water, he disappeared again. Later, he came out, having changed his outfit once more. He did this several times, and quite unconsciously. I knew that clothes mattered to him, maybe as aspects of personality. I'd been sitting at a distance from him one morning when he looked at my feet and said, 'Are those Testoni shoes?' Testonis are made in Bologna and extremely expensive. I had bought mine cheaply in a bankrupt sale. I confessed, amazed he should recognize the brand. 'They're supposed to be the best,' he said.

We both indulged the fancy of being well dressed, though neither of us possessed the physique for it. When I first knew Brian, he was roly-poly or rather, as his first editor Diana Athill bluntly put it, fat. After his heart trouble he dieted and worked out, slimming down. Myself, I was more or less fat too. We could never come up to the standard of Sir Eddy Lindsay Hogg, or Bernard Ostry, or my school friend Peter Seale, each of them thin and leggy.

Brian had scripted Alfred Hitchcock's *Torn Curtain*, and knew it was a failure. He did not care for Hitchcock or trust him. The famous director, he said, was ashamed of his commercial origins in London, his family (Mac's Fisheries) were rich, yet not accepted by the real toffs. They would wear their grey toppers in the Royal Enclosure at Ascot and be cold-shouldered. Hitchcock took out his class resentment by hiring as script assistants nice young English ladies, and going out of his way to humiliate them. But Moore had nothing against script-writing. He would still write films based on his own novels.

One evening there was a dinner party at which I met Julia O'Faolain, daughter of Sean O'Faolain, and her Italian-born husband, an English professor. At some point I compared the status of fiction-writers and essayists. I said it was strange that a mediocre novelist should be valued above a fine essayist. This enraged the professor, who launched a personal attack on me. Brian came to my defence, saying I did not deserve reproach and that I had been a good influence on writing in Canada. Later he explained that Julia was struggling to make her mark in fiction, which made her husband hypersensitive.

I still see imaginative writing as a seamless garment. There are distinct genres, yet we need not set one above others. The only hierarchy is that of talent, imaginative reach and command of language.

On one of my visits, the Moores and I made an excursion to Rodeo Drive in Beverly Hills to shop. We went on to a reception in a grand salon with a ceiling of Tiffany glass, to promote an animated film which its producers claimed was 'Ort'. (In CBC reports this is pronounced 'Airt'.) For my entertainment Brian scanned the room for celebrities. '*Personne de connaissance!*' he said. 'Let's go.'

He was a good mimic, taking off a movie producer giving advice. 'The important thang in the motion-pitcher bidness,' he'd say in his Hollywood voice, 'is to have a gross position.'

In a conversation we had once I confessed that I was no good at marriage. My ex-wives could be right: there had to be something wrong with me. Brian dismissed this with energy. 'There's nothing wrong with you! It's just a matter of luck.'

At one point I found Brian exasperated by a phone call from

Mordecai from Los Angeles airport. Richler wanted to see him, he said. Would Brian drive down and fetch him, maybe for dinner, and drive him back? He himself did not drive, so could not rent a car. The distance was eighty miles each way. This would have put Moore to the trouble of driving 320 miles for the pleasure of Mordecai's company. He could not understand why Moore, who was far from robust at the time, would not oblige.

In a column in *Saturday Night* magazine, written after Moore's death in January 1999, and not long before his own in July 2001, Richler expressed his grief at being estranged from Brian. He had shed tears, he claimed.

In the mid-seventies I had decided to concentrate on travel journalism, partly because this ancient imaginative genre was so varied in form that I'd never have to be bored with the writing, and partly because the travel was interesting in itself – and, incidentally, could help me keep in touch with my far-flung family. I was fairly busy with it by the early eighties.

The disadvantages were obvious. The genre was not highly regarded by newspaper and magazine editors. They tended to think that just about anyone who had taken a trip could write interestingly about it. Consequently they assigned travel-pieces as rewards to friends or favourite reporters. Press tours arranged by tourism authorities in various countries were dismissed as 'junkets'. And of course hard-drinking newsmen treated them as junkets. Some publications would not take travel-pieces from writers who had accepted free passes or free anything. The same publications paid less for the article than the price of an air ticket – they did not pay expenses. In other words, they thought it only fair to have writers subsidize their travel pages.

Tourism authorities, airlines and hotels, for their part wanted something for their money. Some government tourism agencies hated to let the writers explore on their own. Often the writers would be shown 'attractions' too boring to write about, yet their hosts could still show their constituency that they had been given the chance to tell their story. Writers, for their part, knowing they could help their hosts make money by attracting tourists, often developed a sense of entitlement. Sometimes the fatigues of a press tour would get to the writer, who then became impatient and petulant.

Generally hosts simply wanted to promote tourism. Nobody has to go anywhere, so they hoped writers would show why visitors should come to their place and not somewhere else. Most writers, though, wanted to gain a true picture of a place, its people and culture; they were less interested in tourism or attractions. The conflict became acute when the host country sought to use good news in the travel pages to offset bad publicity on the front pages. Over the years of apartheid I refused three invitations to tour South Africa at the government's expense. I made the mistake of accepting a press tour of Israel, unaware that I would find it an oppressive colony. Since I genuinely liked my guide, my driver and some of the people I met, I found the experience distressing.

By degrees I caught up with my family. Bernard was a British diplomat by the seventies. I was able to visit him in London, in Italy and eventually, in 1981, in Vientiane, Laos, where he became British Ambassador. Lucinda, whose husband died after a long illness, had gone to work to support herself and small son. Like Bernard, she joined the British Foreign Office. I visited her in Suffolk in the seventies and eighties, gradually becoming aware that she was in intelligence of some sort, though she never hinted as much. Nancy and her husband were in the Bahamas in the eighties, and in Oxford, where they retired, till his death. I'd see my sisters Kitty and Sally and other relations when I came to Ireland on travel assignments, and dropped in on my sons and daughters in British Columbia on my way to Pacific destinations. They had all gone to the coast.

Travel cleared my eyes. In memory everything is simultaneous, all time eternally present so that there's no chronology, not without external checks. One sees a sequence of events as through a telescope, each image close to its predecessor. Or the scenes are perceived like speeded-up photographic exposures, as in films of an opening flower. I could see how Toronto had grown from a dismal provincial city in the fifties to a megalopolis in the seventies, teeming with ethnic variety. Canada itself, however, through those years, was losing the great place it had won after its exertions in World War II, though during the Pearson and Trudeau years it was still well respected. After the Trudeau regime ended in 1984, I lunched in Ottawa with my friend Reeves Haggan, a high civil servant and fellow Irishman. I asked him how he found the Tory regime under Brian Mulroney. A weighty man in every way, Reeves thought for a moment, remembering the rudeness and arrogance of the former prime minister: 'As you know, Pierre Trudeau was a shit. But he was an *interesting* shit. These people are not interesting. You can't talk to them.'

In Ireland I saw as a speeded-up sequence how the arrival of television had begun to modernize the land, bringing kitsch, cash and self-awareness. Press and media would soon be buzzing with 'problems'. The nomadic tinkers who moved about the country in caravans were a *problem*. People who were problems were renamed. Tinkers were reborn as 'travellers' and 'eye-tinerants'.

The process sociologists call modernization was under way. W.B.Yeats had felt its first stirrings. 'I have nothing but reason to be my guide,' he wrote, 'so am constantly in doubt about small matters.' It was a late kick from the Enlightenment, when the whole of life began to come under the scrutiny of reason. Catholics were not immune – indeed the movement had begun in Catholic France. 'Reason, God's Viceroy in me', John Donne had written, a Catholic Anglican in Jacobean times.

Reason began to question the authority of clergy. A newly vigilant fourth estate began to uncover scandals. The randy bishop whose son confronted him was a problem. He kept his rank but was spirited away to Africa. There were all sorts of other problems, many of them imitated from other countries. And it was in the nature of problems to have solutions. The positivist view prevailed.

Later, as the Republic joined Europe, I witnessed the remarkable successes in business and arts that are still transforming the country. And what was more extraordinary, in a sense it all happened without Irish people losing their easy-going ways. In the same market with anal-compulsive Germans and diligent French, they did not become early risers or lose their love of late carousing in pubs. And in Northern Ireland, a sick culture still cherished its undying angers.

As for the US, the generous country I had seen in 1942, where prosperity grew out of a lively working class, by the nineties had turned into a money-grubbing Vanity Fair. With a global economy, the blue-collar jobs were now in the Orient while at home an increasingly aggressive and militarist population dealt in the illusions called information. Large numbers were now playing the stock market. The know-nothings were rampant, in the South banning the discoveries of Darwin and his successors and claiming divine authority for world domination. Under the Bushes, America's principles were those of Franco's Spain, with gangsters and gunmen now in power, abetted by renegade academics. In a period when crime was in decline the courts crowded the jails with minor offenders, while acquitting murderers rich enough to hire clever counsel. Economists were replacing moralists in legal matters. Formerly it had been held that courts existed to administer justice. Now it seemed that their function was to defend the children of the rich.

I managed to publish my African book in 1981 by cutting it to a novella and short stories. *Pride and Fall*, as I called it, had cost me great labour and pain. The publisher, Clarke Irwin, went bankrupt shortly after the book came out. It was met either with silence or vituperation. Those who did review it had no experience of preliterate people and found my African portraits condescending. Trying to imagine such persons at all was politically incorrect. One reviewer took five pages of a little magazine to declare that Canada should not tolerate such writers as me. This would have helped sales if the magazine had had any readers.

This was profoundly discouraging. I had made enemies as a reviewer for the *Toronto Star*. I had gone through a period when persons of my age were denounced as Establishment, even though I had neither money, power nor a national platform. The hungry generations were treading me down. I could not jump on the band-wagon of Canadian nativist nationalism, though it was clear that nations were losing their power to vast transnational corporations. I knew I had no choice but to go on working.

Nineteen

For much of the eighties and nineties, I was on the move here and there around the world. Some of my travel essays appeared in *Saturday Night*, where as managing editor I had first introduced the genre in the mid-sixties. Now, encouraged by *SN*'s art director and taught by Lutz Dille, I contributed photographs to go with my words. When *SN* gave up travel, I wrote for *Toronto Calendar*, before it was swallowed by *Toronto Life*. After that, editor Jerry Tutunjian invited me to contribute regularly to *LeisureWays*, organ of the Canadian Automobile Association in Ontario. Jerry had the unusual idea that travel essays should contribute to knowledge and be a pleasure to read. In his own essays, he could turn out the good-news pieces as well as the next man. But his forte was for comic expressions of road rage, the result of his history as an Armenian, a Palestinian and a contemporary writer.

Through Tutunjian and my friend Ed Safarian, an eminent economist, and former dean of the graduate school of arts, University of Toronto, I became interested in Turkey and the story of the Armenian genocide. The result was my book *Anatolian Suite*, published in 1989. Unlike other travel books about Turkey, it included reports of the genocide denied by the Turks, and was generally disrespectful about Kemal's regime and later governments. The publisher was Little, Brown of Canada, but neither in the US nor the UK would anyone else take on the book. It was deemed unfair to confront Turks with their historical crimes, given their unblinking denials. The Turks did not like the book, but Armenians loved it. I was invited to be keynote speaker at a Toronto commemoration of the genocide. It was moving to see a row of frail old survivors, living witnesses who had escaped the slaughter when they were children. Tutunjian's father had been left for dead before he was rescued and adopted by an Arab nomad.

To go back a little, something happened before my last assignments for *Toronto Calendar*. I was about to depart on a journey that would last two months, taking me to five countries. Five essays for *Calendar* were planned. My hospitable friend Genevieve Macaulay found this an opportunity for a leaving-town party in her Toronto apartment. Like all her parties, this was a lively occasion with interesting guests. Among these was a pretty American brunette, an artist who worked as an illustrator. Of Greek and Russian ancestry, she was funny, candid and sparky. Her name was Linda Kooluris. I found her delightful, and she seemed to like me. I promised to send a postcard from Rome.

And did so a couple of days later. 'A woman as attractive as you,' I wrote, 'must have a worthless man at home. I just want you to know that I am as worthless as any man.' This was enough to catch her attention. I went on to India and to three other countries. On my return I called her and we set a date to meet.

I mistook the day and stood her up. This could have been a disaster for me. It is a measure of Linda's self-confidence that she was not offended. Why would anyone stand her up? There must be some mistake. She called, laughing, at about 10 pm to ask what had happened. A couple of days later I made the rendez-vous, and we have been together ever since. It was her self-assurance that won my heart, but we also had many interests in common – music, books, art. Her mother was an Isadora-Duncan dancer of renown, her father a successful restaurateur in New Jersey. When I met her family, I found them all fascinating. On her mother's side were painters, concert pianists and at least one cousin who was a man of letters, busy translating Latin American books. Asa Zatz became the friend to whom I dedicated my first volume of poems. The

Greek relations were full of fun and generosity: 'Come for coffee,' they'd say, and we'd arrive to find a table bent under its load of *baklava* and other good things.

My travels continued. Since Linda and I were both freelancers, we supported each other, living on hope, and before long she was able to fulfil her dream of working full-time as a fine artist, strong on formal portraiture and on watercolour landscapes. She was also an excellent teacher of art.

Her work may be classed as high realism, almost *trompe l'oeil*. In her still lifes you can almost eat the fruit, smell the flowers. She is an outstanding colourist and her compositions are strong and original. For abstract subjects she paints rusting machinery and the like. Formal portraits by her hang in the Ontario Parliament Building, Osgoode Hall and Mount Sinai Hospital. Her portrait of Brian Moore aroused interest in the National Gallery of Ireland, until the authorities realized that it was not going to be a gift. It is now on loan to the University of Texas.

For my part, with Linda as partner, I was able to find more time for work on books, though travel was still my bread and butter.

More than once I have had the strange experience of treading on my ancestral soil with the jackboot of a tourist. During one of my Irish trips I became reacquainted with a famous character I had known in my teens, the horsewoman Molly O'Rorke, long divorced from an English baronet. Lady Cusack-Smith, as she was now called, lived in Bermingham, near Tuam, Galway, seat of O'Rorke of Breffny, her historic family.

I stayed with her to write about fox-hunting. She had been Master of the Galway Blazers and now ran her own pack, the North Galway Foxhounds. The fine house and nearly everything in it, as it seemed, dated from 1760. Molly herself, a florid, imposing woman and former beauty, was too old for hunting, but still *en pleine forme* as a great lady of the west.

As MFH of the Blazers she had been hacking along between coverts when a countryman accosted her. 'Begod, Miss O'Rorke, but you're a terrible hard rider to hounds!'

She said, 'Why would you say that, Mr Reilly?'

'Will ye look at the harse, Miss, and you driving the sweat out through him!'

'And wouldn't ye sweat yerself if ye'd spent three hours between *my* thighs?'

For this, the country people admired her.

When I stayed at Bermingham, the huntsman, an ex-performer from the circus, was working up for the opening meet of the season. A bearded whipper-in, not too strong an equestrian, was cruelly derided by the huntsman. Still, Molly and I drove into Galway to buy him riding boots. He already had his livery of scarlet coat, velvet cap and white breeches.

By the time the meet opened, it appeared that the whip had run away, wounded by the huntsman's unbearable insults. 'If the bloody man told us he couldn't fucking ride, we'd have *taught* him,' Molly said. Still, hounds drew a fox with great promptness and away they all thundered. Horses in that country have to be immensely strong to cross the many bogs.

I wrote a satirical letter about it all to my daughter Sarah in Vancouver. Unfortunately I got the address slightly wrong. After I left, the letter was returned to Bermingham.

Molly opened it. She was too grand for common decencies. She showed it to my nephew Dominic Hamilton, who was visiting. She was enraged. Still, it served her right.

In the fifties the literary scene in Canada had been bleak. This was no longer true. The establishment of the Canada Council for the Arts, and provincial bodies of the kind, stimulated an extraordinary growth of talent and achievement. By the nineties, Canadian novelists and poets were among the leading writers of the English-speaking world, among them my friend and former co-worker at Macmillan's, Richard B. Wright.

Wright's interest was in radio. In the late fifties he came to books and Macmillan with a strong sense that he had everything to learn. John Morgan Gray, then president of the company, saw him as a possible future successor. But the young editor in his work and play – and he was full of fun and high jinks – was discovering that his future lay elsewhere. Writers don't always recognize their vocation at once. It's something that grows on them slowly. The fact that, although Wright's family called him *Bruce*, he chose to become *Richard* betrays an early sense of his latent ambition: literally, to *make* his name.

There was an occasion when my friend Howard Engel telephoned to invite me to his place for drinks. Howard was then a radio producer, specializing in literary programmes. He had given me a lot of work. Still married to his first wife, the novelist Marian Engel, he was not yet the respected mystery-writer he was later to become.

I told him I was entertaining Richard Wright. 'Bring him along,' Howard said. 'We'd love to see him.'

When we were all settled with drinks, Marian embarked on a long anecdote in which she spoke of Howard 'waving his funny hand'. This phrase, repeated more than once, was painfully embarrassing. First, because Howard's left hand is deformed, and his wife seemed to be mocking him. Secondly, Richard's left hand is also withered, though he's skilful at concealing it. Had Marian noticed?

She went to her kitchen for more beer. At the same moment the front door bell rang; Howard left the room to answer it. Richard turned his head to look at me. 'One more crack out of that woman,' he said, 'and she'll get the back of my funny hand across her mouth!'

It came as no surprise when the Engels were divorced.

In 2001 Richard Wright's ninth novel *Clara Callan* won the Giller Prize and the Governor General's Award as well as being acclaimed Canada's Book of the Year. The Giller citation described him well: 'Mr Wright is an understated, graceful writer who never makes a false step … a master at revealing the small dramas that unfold in what might appear to others as an unremarkable life … accomplished and utterly convincing.' His protagonists are not larger than life. There are readers who do not care to contemplate characters so nearly like themselves. Press and media are interested above all in the money aspects of art. Good novels are seldom blockbusters. The winning of big bucks is about the only way authors attract attention, short of robbing a bank or knifing the missus. Then, all of a sudden, readers see and acclaim what has been under their noses for years.

As time went by, running ever faster as it seemed, we travelled increasingly to where Linda and I had friends or relations. And still, much as I loved these trips, I longed to journey to places unknown to me and where I knew no one, for true travel is always a venture into ignorance, the traveller essentially the fool. The test is to be where you cannot read the signs, do not know the language or customs of the people, yet still can make your way and learn, reaching out for signals of shared humanity like a blind, deaf mute.

Soon after marrying Linda, I had been asked by one of her friends whether I had read Tolstoy's *War and Peace*. Of course I'd read it! 'Well then,' said this Montrealer, the dashing entrepreneur Ron McKenna, 'you'll know how to make a list of characters, so you can keep track. Linda has so many friends you're going to need it.'

It was true. And Linda's friends were not figures in a network, like the business contacts of a careerist, but people she deeply cared about. She corresponded with several, learning Spanish, Italian, Greek and Swedish to do so, in addition to the French in which she was fluent.

For my part, I had kinsfolk and friends in many places, from London to Hong Kong, Australia and New Zealand, as well as Ireland, Scotland and Iceland, many of them with fascinating stories.

I had long caught up with Esmonde Robertson's elder brother Lawrence, *dit* 'Derry', at Huntington Castle, County Carlow. He had taken Holy Orders, inherited the estate and married a rich banker's heiress. An Irish eccentric in Toronto told me of the new regime in the castle. 'Bejazus, 'tis Rommel in the kitchen and von Runstedt in the garden!' Every three months, he said, an official of the heiress's trust would arrive to sign cheques with an expression of deepest melancholy.

I had to see for myself. The house now had crenellations, added with the proceeds of a deal with the producers of Stanley Kubrick's film *Barry Lyndon*, in which the castle appears. My old friend greeted me in the drawing-room, clad in an ancient suit ingrained with soil, such as Irish ploughmen wear, and a horned helmet, his blue eyes pale with the light of religion. His sister Olivia, painter and writer, was with him. The heiress appeared at teatime. Derry, having discovered that God was a woman, had founded a cult of the goddess Isis in his castle. He had studied the subject intensively, printing his revelations in a book which he sold to me on the spot, briskly pocketing cash. The volume proved impenetrably boring.

Grandpa Bernard, tactfully declining Tractarian vestments, had celebrated Communion in the chapel for Derry's grandmother. It had been turned into a temple of the goddess. On the altar was a Celtic 'Sheelagh-na-gig', her spread genitals painted bright red. Other props included a witch's cauldron. A number of busty young women in bare feet and dirndl skirts, many from California, had taken up residence to serve the goddess. Derry had assumed the title of High Priest of Isis and Olivia that of High Priestess. I had the feeling that Olivia's imagination was the driving force of the enterprise, underpinned by Derry's obsessive research.

Derry had acquired, with heraldic blessing prompted by lawyers, the Scots title of Baron Strathloch. At some point he had undergone a long conversation with the Bishop of Leighlin, whose charitable heart found the gentle laird harmless. I'm told that Esmonde thought the whole enterprise scandalous, though, given his pride of pedigree, he could hardly have minded his son being pronounced the heir, and Master of Strathloch.

The cult of Isis proved timely and successful. Outlandish faith was softened by the good nature of Irish gentlefolk. After Esmonde and Derry had died, I learn, there were 40,000 members of the Order of Isis around the world. As for God, she still moves in a mysterious way.

In my first years as a Canadian immigrant I had avoided people from Ireland. I did not want to become an 'ethnic' or allow nostalgia to hinder my efforts to become a useful citizen. But once I was safely integrated, after a fashion, I began to feel the tug of lost Inisfail. Something within me remains irredeemably alien.

In the eighties, I took part in a wonderful conference of Irish writers and scholars convened by Desmond Maxwell, Master of Winter's College of York University in greater Tononto. Des is from Northern Ireland, where he's now retired in Belfast. He was (and is) a scholar of delightful ebullience and wit. Many Irish poets, authors and men of letters are happy to keep him company, the sea-divided Gael coming together to feast and indulge in learned blather. I had the honour of giving the postprandial address. I suggested that we Irish were not all of one tradition or of unmixed descent in religion. I cited my great-grandfather William Harte, a Roman Catholic county surveyor from Ballymena who had turned Protestant, then, 'perhaps under the influence of Geology', as my father wrote, 'became indifferent to religion'. My feeling was that Ireland could use some of that indifference in order to counter bigotry. I said that Canada had a great deal of geology, which we would gladly give Ireland if we could.

Seamus Heaney rose to declare, 'We never took the soup!' There's a widespread belief that during the Great Famine of 1847 Protestant missionaries offered starving Catholics soup provided they abandoned their faith. It's a matter of record that Quakers fed the hungry, doubtful that those good people attached conditions. Giving Gaelic Bibles to the poor was also seen as aggressive prose-lytizing. Converts were derided as 'Soupers'. Such anxieties were understandable in a time when the Catholic majority was forced to contribute tithes in support of Protestant clergy.

At this conference too I first met a delightful professor who seemed to be friends with all the Irish poets. Maurice Elliott was to succeed Desmond Maxwell as Master of Winter's College. An Englishman who specialized in Anglo-Irish literature, Maurice was funny and articulate, becoming in later years York University's public orator. Acclaiming honorary doctors, he would speak clear, elegant English, leaving obsolete Latin to Old World universities.

In 1986, three years before the horror of Tiananmen Square, I went to China with Garry Marchant and two other Canadians, as guests of the Chinese government, Japan Airlines and Cultural Tours of Vancouver. At sixty-three, I was the senior member of the group and still a complete idiot, in the sense that I could neither read the signs nor understand a word of the language. I was treated with the respect given to age in China. Confucian values had persisted, though overlaid with socialist dogma. In Guangzhou the young woman in the greeting party insisted on carrying my camera-bag. Pretty Miss Mai later took us to a noisy dance hall. To my sorrow, I was not up to waltzing.

We visited southern cities, to assess them as winter destinations for Canadians. In Kunming we walked in gardens that resembled the designs on willow-pattern china. Vermilion bridges led to dragon-roofed pavilions in a lake. Ornamental bamboos were incised with characters that seemed to be poetry but were probably advertisements for Chinese beer. In one restaurant there was braised elephant trunk on the menu. The writer from Edmonton ordered it at once. After a while the waiter returned to ask if anyone else wanted this unusual dish? There were no takers. 'I'm sorry,' the man said. 'I'm afraid we can't kill our elephant for just one order.'

The joke had been planted. The waiter had been waiting months for this credulous visitor, his face squeezed into a thousand wrinkles with laughter. We had seen in the markets of Guangzhou so many creatures offered as food or medicine – owls, snakes, civets, servals, dogs – that the item did not seem improbable. It is illegal to kill elephants in China.

In Guilin we embarked in flat-bottomed boats to cruise down the Li, which runs into the Pearl river on its way to Hong Kong. I had seen the exotic landscapes in Chinese watercolours, tusks of craggy Karst formations rising hundreds of feet from shores feathery with phoenix bamboos. On the river, men in flat conical hats fished from rafts made of three large bamboo poles, with the aid of big pelicans. I was happy!

As I bicycled through the rich fields of Szechuan near

Chengdu, with low, half-timbered buildings like those of Tudor England, I met a man carrying a pig on the bar of his bicycle, the poor beast securely trussed in a way that allowed him to breathe but not move. Other countryfolk trotted along carrying buckets or panniers two at a time on shoulder yokes.

At that time people we met were open and communicative, boldly critical of their leaders. Mr Deng was moving too slowly for them. When the challenge came, he was quick enough to shed their blood.

To remind us that the south was warmer than the north, we were flown to Beijing and the wonders of the Forbidden City. We bussed to the Great Wall, where even the Edmontonian complained of the cold. But perhaps the strangest event on our visit to the capital was a trip to a munitions factory nearby, where we were taken to the firing range and given pistols to shoot at targets. The Chinese were downsizing their army and hoping to make big bucks from surplus munitions. I hate handguns, which are dangerous and inaccurate, but my colleagues loved firing their guns. Marchant became the bank robber with $2000 on his head. The *Readers Digest* man was James Bond. There was little in the way of range discipline. Luckily no one was shot.

That was China in a time of bright promise. Three years later hopes were blighted. The Chinese people were to be allowed riches but not freedom.

Our Chinese journey had seemed the trip of a lifetime, viewing an ancient and decaying culture in many ways the antithesis of all I had known. There were art-forms – like calligraphy or miniature gardening – that did not exist in Western experience. There were religions that were not intolerant or mutually exclusive. Overall, though, the polity was cruel, corrupt and oppressive. The people would be gathered to watch executions in a football stadium. Yet the Chinese imagination could also conceive exquisite images of compassion and loving-kindness in the face of a Buddha or a Boddisattva.

I continued my love affair with Mexico. Over the years the population, cheered on by the Popes, more than doubled, adding its crowding numbers to the sum of human misery. Here was another culture offering antithesis to the Western tradition. In the magnificent anthropological museum of Mexico City I saw a new heaven and a new earth, recalling a lost, cruel civilization that seemed to have frightened itself to death with the aid of sophisticated mathematics and astronomy. And everywhere in the country I saw the colourful arts of an ingenious and skilful people. Like others, I also saw the effects of corruption on an almost inconceivable scale. From the lowest policeman to the highest official, nearly everyone seemed mired in graft and extortion. Honest men and women had a hard struggle to rise above these official sewers.

In the travel books I read, authors were often entertained and aided by the ambassadors of their countries. This happened to me only once. I was given the brush-off by our Canadian ambassador to the US, even though we knew each other. Or maybe *because* we knew each other. But when I was writing a piece on 'Our Man in the Vatican' for *Weekend* magazine, our ambassador to the Holy See gave me a luncheon party with Cardinal Pignedoli and a pass to visit Pope Paul VI in Castel Gandolfo, but it was the British *chargé d'affaires* in Laos who was most warmly hospitable. Linda and I spent Christmas 1981 with him in Vientiane, where we also visited Prince Souvanna Phouma in his house-captivity. The prince gave me cigars which his doctor had forbidden him and treated Linda with old-world gallantry. He spoke excellent French. The other person I remember well was the Australian ambassador. He asked had I noticed anything special about Laos. I said I was surprised to see *white* water buffaloes – elsewhere they were black. 'You must remember,' said His Excellency with a sly look, 'that there was a considerable American presence here.'

The British *chargé,* soon to be ambassador, was so kind because he happened to be my brother. I was proud of Bernard's genial dignity. Mrs Thatcher was trying to cut costs, so Bernard, not without guile, had the high-power radio removed from his embassy. He was now more or less out of touch, therefore for once a true plenipotentiary. Later he had to close the embassy. The first British ambassador to Laos had been Lord Talbot de Malahide. So it happened that the first and the last were Irish.

Bernard had given a Christmas party for all the British in Vientiane – about sixteen of them. It was The Night the Hostess Caught Fire. My sister-in-law Brigid had set up a small Christmas tree with real candles. At one point the naked flames made me nervous. I blew them out. While I was accompanying carol singers on the piano in an adjoining room, Brigid lit them again. She was wearing some kind of shawl or veil. The party was in full swing when the hostess went up in flames. By the time we could get a blanket to smother the fire she had nasty burns. The only doctor available was from the Soviet embassy, but some kind of impasse between the diplomats made it impossible to call him. Among the guests, though, was a Canadian expert on the multiplication of pigs, a veterinarian. He applied first aid. Poor Brigid, although she made light of the burns at the time, later had to undergo plastic surgery to erase her scars.

Twenty

I have said little, if anything, about my work as an author. There isn't much of interest one can say. From the outside, writing is not an exciting topic. In films the writer is forever balling up paper and hurling it into the wastepaper basket. Even Shakespeare is depicted like this, though Ben Jonson reports that 'he never blotted line'. Today all you get to see is the figure sitting at the computer (I never loved typewriters) and his discouragement at the end of the day.

After Clarke Irwin went bankrupt just as they were bringing out *Pride and Fall*, I had no publisher. Some years on, Little, Brown took me up. My dear friend Beth Appeldoorn had persuaded Kim McArthur to reissue *Running to Paradise*. It did not set Lake Ontario on fire but it got me going again. Little, Brown of Canada published three more books of mine before the branch was shut down by the US conglomerate that owned it. Profits of 8 per cent were not enough. Kim started her own company.

The books were the aforementioned *Anatolian Suite*, which recorded travels in Turkey, *Ribbon of Highway*, describing bus trips along the Trans-Canada Highway, and *Smiles and Chukkers and Other Vanities*, about the habits of the Canadian rich. Little, Brown did not want to see my first book of poems, *The Eleventh Hour*, which was duly published by Mosaic Press. Don Marquis has said that publishing verse is like dropping a feather into the Grand Canyon, and waiting for the echo. My slim volume was by that standard well received, and praised in enigmatic terms.

In my first book of verse I used classical, biblical and Irish mythology. Now I wanted something with more resonance for contemporary ears. I chose the popular and richly ambiguous film *Casablanca* as the controlling myth of this second book. Again I used the eleven-syllable line, sometimes in Sapphic strophes, sometimes in rhyme. The film's ambiguities gave scope for invention; the story afforded a medium for thoughts and imaginings about World War II. I tried to find a mainstream publisher, but after a Toronto firm dithered over it for many months I tried another 'little press', Ekstasis of Victoria, B.C. Poets and other readers were complimentary, but the distributor – working for about forty little presses – went bankrupt. The little presses and distributor were subsidized by the Canada Council, so that they had little incentive to go out and sell books. *Casablanca* was a bust.

As an acknowledged poet I took part in 'readings'. These can be painful when the poet mumbles. Audiences titter politely at feeble jokes. It seems to me that a reading is a kind of show, to be approached in that manner, head up and belting it out. In Canada, a poet seems to be part of a subculture, with in-jokes and groupies. I wished I had published poetry while still young enough to enjoy it. I was lucky, though, to find myself among good and dedicated poets, often learned persons. They were generous and helpful.

In 2002 I was made writer-in-residence at the University of Toronto, with rooms in Massey College. I gave readings in all three campuses; the one in Massey College was well attended. The great merit of the appointment was a salary paid for one semester. I'd almost forgotten what it was like to receive a cheque at the end of the month.

In my early seventies I was in reasonable health. I took pills for high blood pressure and gout, and watched my diet for mild type-two diabetes. I suffered more from pills than diseases, which led me to formulate the ruling principle of modern therapy – that the cure for any disease is another disease.

And so in the summer of 1995 I landed in St Michael's Hospital emergency ward with a complete heart block, requiring a pacemaker.

Five days at most, I was told, but it was nearly six weeks before I escaped. The cure for heart block, in addition to the wonderful pacemaker, had turned out to be a deep-vein thrombosis in my right leg, haemorrhagic cystitis, and several episodes of severe bleeding. It took a lot of pain and a few months, and it was an anxious time for Linda. The good thing about a pacemaker is that it seems to keep one more or less normal in cardiac function.

The experience of hospital care confirmed a belief I had held for some time – that the best way to endure the ordeal was to avoid a private or semi-private room. Best to be with other patients in a ward, where there's always someone worse off than yourself, and always drama or something funny going on.

As soon as I became reasonably fit, I resumed travelling. I was lucky enough to cruise around the world in a ship; the voyage took four months, with a week out to celebrate the Millennium with Linda in Santiago de Chile. I set foot in Antarctica, viewed the tempestuous Horn and passed though the Straits of Magellan. Crossing the Pacific, I saw Easter Island, Pitcairn, and other ports I had never expected to see. Before returning to Piraeus, the port of Athens from which we'd started, I visited Petra, the famous 'rose-red city half as old as time'. Fellow-passengers were even older than me; two died of old age, God rest them; and the rest consumed one and a quarter tonnes of prunes. The Prune Ship itself, launched in 1944, was almost ready for the scrapyard.

I watched on television the famous disaster of 11 September 2001 while it was happening. Like all the world, I found the horror almost insupportable – so many deaths at a single blow. New Yorkers took it well, led by their tough-minded mayor. But elsewhere in the US this single act of terrorism resulted in moral defeat. The first to show panic was President Bush, who allowed himself to be whisked away by security men. Elsewhere throughout the great republic, citizens cowered at home. The stock market sagged, air travel fell away to a point where airlines went bankrupt. The president embarked on a course of ill-conceived military aggression, incurring massive deficits.

Just after the disaster, the US had enjoyed the goodwill and sympathy of the whole world. 'We're all Americans now,' the French president had said. The goodwill quickly vanished when American bombs began to fall in the Middle East. The US was a super-power in the economic and military sense, but as a nation it lacked the moral sinew for leadership.

My own livelihood had depended upon free air travel. That came to an end.

After *The Eleventh Hour* was published in 1997, I knew that poetry was my true vocation, unprofitable though it was. Like other forms of knowledge, this insight came too late in life to be rewarding in the fullest sense, but it did lead me in new directions, with new friendships. I had always been lucky enough to have scholarly friends, asking nothing better than to be with persons who know more than me. Now increasingly I enjoyed the friendship of academics who were poets, or rather of poets whose livelihood was scholarship.

One scholar especially dear to me was the late Desmond Conacher, husband of my lovely cousin Mary, and eminent authority on Euripides and other Greeks. Modest and immensely learned, he possessed a delicate sense of humour. His stories were like filigree or embroidery. He detested pomposity. His kindness was infinite.

After poet and professor Richard Greene, an Oxonian Newfoundlander and almost-Jesuit, reviewed my poetry in glowing terms, it was not surprising that he too became an intimate. For years Howard Engel, a close friend and man of letters, had been talking about Sheldon Zittner, who taught Shakespeare at Trinity College, Toronto. He too I met at last, a poet and wit of the first water, and a man with a conscience about language.

As writer-in-residence at Toronto I met other university celebrities. I confessed to Sheldon that I was glad I hadn't been smart enough to become an academic. I was thinking of the careerists and institutionalized personalities, not about the noble Grecians and poets. He said, 'You don't have to be smart. You just have to be *there*.'

One day in mid-2000, I answered the telephone, to hear a woman say, 'I have *wonderful* news for you ...' I was about to declare that I didn't want to buy insurance when she identified herself as an official from the provincial government's protocol section, reponsible for awards. Now I listened. I was to be invested with the Order of Ontario, a distinction conferred by the sovereign through her representative the lieutenant governor. About three hundred of the province's thirteen million citizens are so decorated. Hence, one winter evening in the Parliament Building, resplendent in evening dress with my medals from war and peace, I was festooned like a three-star chef with the badge and ribbon of the Order. Lieutenant Governor Hilary Weston, a beauty from Dublin, did the honours. Having been publicly disgraced in East Africa, I was now happy to be officially canonized as a provincial worthy, although I still suspect a mistake.

One more boastful anecdote and I am done.

Linda and I were visited by a friend of her brother Kirby, then living in Palm Beach, Florida, that watering place of the rich. The friend was Father Allen Duston, the Dominican friar who directs the Patrons of the Arts in the Vatican Museums. The patrons' donations are used to maintain and restore the priceless works of art in the papal collections. Father Allen proved a man of great energy and presence, who quickly established himself in our affections.

And so it happened that in March 2003, when Father Allen's family sponsored celebrations in the Vatican of his Silver Jubilee as a priest, Linda and I were included with the hundred or so friends and family who met there to toast him. On the first day we gathered in the lofty rooms of the Ronanini Palace on the via del Corso, now the premises of the Circolo della Scacchi, an exclusive Roman club for gentlemen. Linda and I moved around under the richly frescoed and sculpted Renaissance ceilings making new friends, some of them priests from our host's native California. Sipping wine while nibbling the odd canapé offered by white-gloved waiters, I decided that my poor old legs needed a rest from marble floors.

A cleric in black cassock and cape sat at one end of a sofa. I took the other end. The Californian priest was a chaplain to the Knights of Malta, resident in Fatima, Portugal, where he conducts retreats. Father Guilbert said, 'D'you mind if a beautiful woman sits between us?' I looked up at the lady. 'Not at all,' I said, laughing. 'She's my wife.'

We were off to a good start. Linda introduced another new friend, Dame Molly, the tiny widow of a Portuguese ambassador. Her title belongs in Portugal's Order of St Michael of the Winds.

Next day was Sunday. We followed a clutch of Dominicans, their magpie habits blowing in the wind, past the sentinels of the Swiss Guard in the blue and yellow uniforms designed by Michelangelo, around the flank of St Peter's to the Palace of the Governatorato, and through it to an airy baroque chapel. A choir of nine voices sang from the gallery at the west end.

Linda had been dunked Orthodox, myself Anglican, though neither of us were convinced. Yet we both felt at home. I only thought that the English of the *Book of Common Prayer* was on a higher plane than that of the new Roman Mass. The music was by Perosi, Palestrina and Fauré – I believed every note of the heavenly sequences. A message was read from Cardinal Szoka, Governor of the Vatican, who was ill. Father Allen was the celebrant, there was a short sermon on the theme of restoration (if only someone would restore my legs, I thought) and near the end our friend quoted a passage on happiness from Homer's *Odyssey*. Near to tears of joy, he exclaimed, 'Thank you, Lord!'

In the Palazzo delle Rovere – the Rovere were the family of Julius II, the warrior Pope who had commissioned Michelangelo to decorate the Sistine Chapel – the fare at luncheon made me understand the expression 'eating like an archbishop'. A cardinal was present, though I did not see him.

Monday was St Patrick's Day and Father Allen's anniversary. In the morning we took a walking tour in the vicinity with a curator of European paintings from Detroit. As we strolled from the Farnesina villa with its Renaissance murals to Santa Maria in Trastevere, I chatted with Sister Carmel Molloy who comes from my home county in Ireland. 'Not wearing green for Saint Patrick, Sister?'

'I don't do green. There's altogether too much of that in America.'

Later we spent an enchanted hour in the Sistine Chapel. I sat by the walls, first on one side, then the other, breathless under the glowing frescoes, especially those on the vault overhead and east end that carry Michelangelo's monumental vision of the human journey from Creation to Last Judgment. Seen now free of time's brown gravy in their pristine colours, the images are clear and forceful, like comic-book art. 'The language of the gods,' said Sir Joshua Reynolds. The painter is reinterpreting the Bible stories, his figures massive and muscular, his female nudes like lady wrestlers, and the 'Last Judgment' stark and vindictive. 'Maybe to keep the Popes honest,' a friar murmured. The image of Hell, as always in such visions, is far clearer than that of Heaven. But perhaps Hell is an essential part of Heaven – the righteous happy to see enemies suffering.

There was Mass in the Raphael room of the museums, in front of the painter's immense 'Transfiguration', Christ dancing in the clouds with Elijah and Moses above the human scene. This masterpiece by Michelangelo's great rival was flanked by two other newly cleaned paintings. Again, the music was celestial, two sopranos singing Vivaldi, Gounod, Franck, Mozart, the rite, conducted by our celebrant friend, stately and moving.

After a drink in an octagonal room dominated by a Caravaggio 'Deposition', we moved to a gallery of classical sculpture where tables were set for the black-tie jubilee dinner.

A genial archbishop said grace. I had the privilege of reciting for the company a poem I had written in our host's honour, surrendering to what Keats called 'negative capability', entering into the Catholic myth. As I cheerfully succumbed to the sin of pride, I thought that it wasn't every day a lapsed Irish Protestant got to declaim his own poem in the palace of the Popes of Rome.

Now that I am old and grey I have to report that I am not full of sleep or nodding by the fire. I am wakeful at night and in the small hours. These vigils are painful only if one uses them to fret about life's miseries or the approach of death.

My father had learned to recite Milton's *Lycidas* to beguile the hours. An exercise of my own is just difficult enough to be interesting. It's an attempt to strengthen memory.

In one of these mental excursions I leave the front door of Viewmount, cross the gravel sweep and stroll down the avenue to the gate. I try to evoke every shrub and tree along the way. On the left is the spreading copper beech that we children called the Ship Tree. On the right are laurel bushes, and here I'm already in trouble. I cannot be certain about the trees. I think they're limes, and at once I hear the murmuring of bees visiting the tiny green flowers. The bees vanish as I grow doubtful. A little farther on, to the left, is an open glade in which Father has planted three silver birches, so that their white stems catch the evening light slanting in from the west. From here to the gate the trees and shrubs keep changing, now tall beeches, now dwarfish yews and more laurels. Memory refuses to be precise. Laurel leaves, I recall, contain cyanide, and the little red berries of yews are also poisonous. The gate itself is a ponderous thing of cast iron.

Now I walk in the public road, which is macadamized but not tarred. Many years earlier it was still part of the private avenue. Sometimes at this point I recall the heavy steamroller moving back and forth over the broken limestone rubble. There's a smell of steam and hot oil, a hissing and puffing of the black machine with its tarnished brass fittings. The sulphurous smell of a lighted match comes off the crushed stones.

A similar traction-engine, without the big roller, brings the Victorian marvel of steam to the thrashing machine, which it drives with a long belt from its flywheel. This huge, shuddering contraption spits out yellow grain from a spout and gathers and binds the straw. Its sound is a high whine, punctuated by the *put*-put-*put*-put of the engine.

Later the farm-hands will sit down to a dinner of pig's cheek, cabbage and baked potatoes in their jackets, washed down with pints of black porter.

To the right is the lawn field with more trees, including a fine walnut in the distance. The leafy canopies have been browsed by cattle to a uniform level at the lower edge. The field on the left borders the farm of the Power family, a brood of wild, handsome men under the command of their big, stern-looking mother.

A hundred yards down the road, on the right, is the orchard, eight acres of aged apple trees.

While I walk, the fruit trees vanish. Not long after Viewmount was sold, the new owner sensibly cut them down as unprofitable. The orchard is screened by more beeches, and I hear the clatter of woodpigeons flying out.

Now, on each side of the road, granite gateposts mark the original entrance to the estate. To the left is a tiny, tumbledown cottage with a slate roof – the gate-lodge, where Mrs Neale lives in the sorrow of her widowhood. Like Dublin Jack Walsh, the gardener and factotum who inhabits another half-ruined estate cottage, she lives rent-free. Both are paid sixpence a year as caretakers – a measure designed to prevent their acquiring squatters' rights.

That is one of my exercises. It takes longer in practice than it does in print. Not seldom it dissolves into dreams.

Another game is more congenial. This one is a litany in which I silently recite the names of every person I love, or ever cared for, in my life.

With each name I try to bring the face to mind. Sometimes I am distressed because the face has become blurred or even lost. So I go through a list of family, and friends. In a long life friends become lost along the way, left behind in another country or another mode of life or – increasingly as the years speed by – by dying. For the sake of mental hygiene, I also make a conscious effort to forgive people who have done me dirt. I thought I had exorcised the memory of Tom Skinner, chief of my persecutors, until I caught myself looking him up in *Who's Who*. Why? Because I wanted to be sure he had not been knighted. And in fact he never rose above his CMG. He was missing from the last edition, gone to his reward.

Friends are more important than ever. Among them is Howard Engel, who writes mysteries featuring a Jewish detective in small-town Ontario. I got to know him many years ago when Howard produced my broadcasts at CBC. Despite his talents and erudition, he has suffered much misfortune. Two years ago he awoke one morning to find that he could not read, a catastrophe for a man-of-letters. He could, however, write. The first of two books written since his stroke appeared with an afterword by the famous neurologist Oliver Sachs. He remains as witty and genial as ever, though struggling with depression, the best of company when we lunch together almost every week.

The friend I see most often is Ted Roberts, whose life is absorbed by music and in caring for his sons, both gifted guitar players like himself. Tall and handsome, he loves to entertain, though at heart he is a deeply serious, warm-hearted man. Through Ted I've come to know other jazz musicians. What I admire is their ambition, not for money or fame, but for music itself, and for the esteem of other musicians encountered in the performance.

And there are the women friends – Nuala Fitzgerald, Aspasia Dassios, cousin Mary Conacher, and my sisters and daughters.

Married to Linda for the past twenty-four years, I acknowledge my great luck in having her as my closest friend. Her good nature and humour, her gifts of beauty, talent and self-confidence, have made life pleasant.

I tell my four children, ten grandchildren, and five great-grand-children (pending a recount) that they belong to a large international family: some are fair or dark Europeans, some black, some cousins oriental, some Icelandic, some Scots and English. Since that is who we are, we should look at the world in that way, each cherishing a distinct ethnic identity, yet all of us belonging together. This is no sentimental illusion but fact.

At my age, I have survived many cherished contemporaries. Daydreaming, I seem to be in a vast railway terminus, like an infinitely extended Victoria Station in London. Platform beyond platform recedes into darkness. Somewhere in the station a train leaves every two minutes, each with an old friend or relation on board. Along with the crowds on the platforms, all are heading to the same destination. And I'm wondering vaguely, though not too anxiously, which is mine.

Like the Spanish poet Machado, I'm ready; my briefcase is packed.